Anarchist Ideology and the Working-Class Movement in Spain, 1868–1898

Anarchist Ideology and the Working-Class Movement in Spain, 1868–1898

George Richard Esenwein

UNIVERSITY OF CALIFORNIA PRESS
Berkeley · *Los Angeles* · *Oxford*

University of California Press
Berkeley and Los Angeles, California

University of California Press, Ltd.
Oxford, England

Copyright © 1989 by The Regents of the University of California

Library of Congress Cataloging-in-Publication Data

Esenwein, George Richard.
    Anarchist ideology and the working-class movement in Spain,
1868–1898 / George Richard Esenwein.
        p.   cm.
    Bibliography: p.
    Includes index.
    ISBN 0-520-06398-8 (alk. paper)
    1. Anarchism—Spain—History—19th century. 2. Labor movement—
Spain—History—19th century. I. Title.
HZ925.E74 1989
320.5′7′0946—dc20   89-4889
                                                                        CIP

Printed in the United States of America

1 2 3 4 5 6 7 8 9

The paper used in this publication meets the minimum requirements of American
National Standard for Information Sciences—Permanence of Paper for Printed Library
Materials, ANSI Z39.48-1984 ∞

To the memory of Gussie Roland (1922–1973)
and
August Esenwein (1918–1987)

Contents

Acknowledgments

In the course of preparing the dissertation on which this book is based, I incurred a number of personal and intellectual debts. When I began this project some years ago, I was given expert guidance by James Joll and Joaquín Romero Maura. Besides being most helpful in securing financial aid for my studies and giving me intellectual stimulus, Professor Joll has been exceedingly patient with me, for which I am very grateful. Dr. Romero Maura kindly took time away from his full business schedule to impart to me some of the fundamentals of Spanish history.

While conducting research in Spain, I received valuable assistance from the following people: Antoni Jutglar, Josep Termes, and José María Jover Zamora. José Alvarez Junco and Carlos Rama read over my thesis outline and provided useful suggestions. For answering my many questions about the obscure lives of the Spanish anarchists I am grateful to J. A. Durán (Madrid), the late Renée Lamberet (Paris), and Vladimiro Muñoz (Montevideo).

In this country, I have benefited from the help of a number of individuals. For their encouragement and warm personal generosity shown over the years, I am especially grateful to Professor Paul Avrich and the late Burnett Bolloten, both of whom have been particularly inspiring to me. I want to thank the following people who also freely gave of their personal time to review all or part of the manuscript: Professor Tony Judt, Professor Paul Preston, Professor Peter Stansky. Dr. Gary Steenson deserves special thanks for having checked through the manuscript page by page, and for having made many useful suggestions.

Much of my research in Europe was financed by grants awarded by the Central Research Fund of the University of London. I am also very grateful to Dr. and Mrs. Wolff, Jane Hustwit, my family, and other friends who from time to time permitted me to continue my research by providing me funds.

The knowledgeable staffs of a number of libraries have greatly facilitated my research. At the International Institute of Social History in Amsterdam, I received assistance from Rudolf De Jong and Thea Duiyker. The late Maria Hunink and Arthur Lehning, also from the Institute, have been most generous in providing me with indispensable articles and books. I found the librarians at the Catalán Municipal library as well as the University of Barcelona to be quite helpful. So were the staff at the following libraries in England: British Museum (London); British Library of Economic and Political Science (LSE); University of London Library, Senate House; London Library; Bodelian Library (Oxford); and the Public Record Office (London). While working at the Stanford University and Hoover Institution libraries I have acquired a better understanding of the interdependent relationship between scholars and academic libraries. I should like to thank the staff at the Hoover Institution and Green Library for assisting me in many ways, but not least for their friendship.

The editorial staff at the University of California Press read the manuscript with exceptional care. I want to thank Scott Mahler, Shirley Warren, and Nancy Atkinson for having helped me avoid making too many careless mistakes. Any errors that remain are due to my own myopia.

Abbreviations

CNT — Confederación Nacional del Trabajo—predominantly anarchosyndicalist trade union founded in 1910.

FAI — Federación Anarquista Ibérica—vanguard revolutionary body that affiliated itself with the CNT during the Second Republic and Civil War (1931–1939).

FRC/Pacto — Federación de Resistencia al Capital/Pacto de Unión y Solidaridad—Catalán-based organization that superceded the FTRE.

FRE — Federación Regional Española—Spanish branch of First International established in 1870.

FSORE — Federación de Sociedades Obreras de la Región Española—national anarchist organization formed in 1900.

FTRE — Federación de Trabajadores de la Región Española (1881–1888)—anarchist organization that succeeded the FRE.

IWMA — International Working Men's Association, First International.

OARE — Organización Anarquista de la Región Española—anarchist organization established in 1888 that attempted to give unions (*sociedades de resistencia*) revolutionary orientation.

PSOE   Partido Socialista Obrero Español—political party of Spanish socialists, founded in Madrid in 1879.

TCV   Tres Clases de Vapor—reformist union of the textile industry in Catalonia that rose to prominence in the late nineteenth century.

UGT   Unión General de Trabajadores—trade union branch of the Spanish socialist movement, founded in Barcelona in 1888.

Introduction

As a movement long associated with revolution, violence, and rural rebellion, Spanish anarchism rarely fails to attract the attention of the student of European history. This interest has of course waxed and waned over the years but it has been fairly steadily sustained since the late 1960s, as witnessed by the steady output of scholarly works on different aspects of the history of the anarchist movement in Spain. Because of the overwhelming interest in the Spanish Civil War, it is scarcely surprising that most of the historiography on anarchism is focused on the years 1936–1939. With few exceptions, the earlier stages of its development have been poorly surveyed, particularly the late nineteenth century. While the existing historiography on nineteenth-century Spanish anarchism sheds light on the nature of the movement, there remains considerably more work to be done before we truly understand this complex historical phenomenon.[1]

For many years, Spanish anarchism was generally regarded as essentially a millenarian doctrine, a prepolitical ideology whose main strength lay in its emotional appeal to the masses. It was characterized as a type of secular religion which lacked a systematic framework of political and economic analysis necessary for developing a cogent and coherent revolutionary strategy. This "millenarian" view was popularized by a notary named Juan Díaz del Moral, whose scholarly study of the Anadalusian peasantry in the province of Córdoba, *Historia de las agitaciones campesinas andaluzas* (1928), won the respect and admiration of several generations of historians.

Gerald Brenan was the first non-Spaniard to echo the main themes of Díaz del Moral's findings, in his work entitled *The Spanish Labyrinth* (1943). Brenan's illuminating study of the social and political background of the Spanish Civil War went beyond his predecessor in placing anarchism in the general context of Spanish politics, and in distinguishing the phases of its historical development. In the end, though, his portrayal of the anarchists is no less romantic than the one first presented by Díaz del Moral. For Brenan, the popularity of anarchism among the Spanish proletariat (*obreros*) and peasantry (*campesinos*) can be explained in terms of its moral-religious appeal. Anarchism, in his eyes, spoke to the downtrodden classes in the language of a genuine religion. It promised them salvation from the poverty and suffering they endured at the hands of the ruling classes, and it pictured their redemption in terms of a millenarian conversion. Viewed in this way, Spanish anarchism appeared to be a fundamentally irrational or, at best, a naive political doctrine.

In *Primitive Rebels* (1959), the noted British historian Eric Hobsbawm utilized the millenarian view of Spanish anarchism in developing his widely influential "primitive rebel" thesis. Grounding his analysis in an economic framework, Hobsbawm posited a "stages" view of anarchism. According to this, anarchist doctrine represented a transitional phase in the development of Spanish working-class consciousness. It was characterized as an inchoate or "primitive" political theory, which, because it was tied to the rhythm of the economy, corresponded to the level of social-political development of a modernizing country.

Hobsbawm was particularly interested in exploring the major reasons why anarchism had for so long exercised such a powerful spell on the Spanish working classes. Briefly, he held that it was Spain's entrenched economic backwardness, especially in Andalusia, that accounted for the persistence of a so-called primitive theory such as Bakuninism. Hobsbawm explained that anarchism had taken root in a region that was known for its extreme poverty and that, from 1850 onwards, was also known for its chronic social revolutionism. For him, what had triggered the endemic social upheavals of rural Andalusia was the introduction of capitalistic legal and social relationships in the southern countryside. The disentailment of church lands in the early part of the nineteenth century, when vast tracts of ecclesiastical property passed into the hands of the aristocracy and prosperous middle classes, was a key element in this process. As a result of disentailment, long-standing economic and social ties were severed between the Church and the lower classes. This forever changed the matrix of social stability in the region. Before, the Church had usually acted as a protector of and provider for the poor; it now stood aloof from them, forcing them into a state of economic and political uncertainty. Given these conditions, Hobsbawm concluded, anarchism seemed to be tailor-made for the Spanish *bracero*, or landless agricultural worker, most of all, he believed, because it "reflected the spontaneous aspirations of backward peasants more sensitively and accurately in modern times" than any other ideological movement.[2]

That the millenarian model has long served as an analytical tool for historians studying Spanish anarchism is understandable. The cyclical regularity of rural rebellion in the nineteenth and twentieth centuries, the apostolic fervor with which the workers in the towns and the countryside embraced the revolutionary doctrine, and the chiliastic vision many adherents held of a new world order were salient characteristics of Spanish anarchism that were satisfactorily accounted for by the millenarian model. In fact, this model has proved itself most convincing when applied to the landless agricultural laborers of the south, where anarchism largely existed in remote villages and small towns. Given that the *braceros* in the *latifundia* (large estates) were overwhelmingly illiterate and chronically unemployed, they seemed prone to the kind of irrational behavior that is consistent with millenarianism. After all, this is the region where the *Mano Negra* affair (1882–1883), the Jerez rising (1892), and many other celebrated episodes in anarchist history had occurred.

In recent years, the validity of the millenarian explanation has been increasingly thrown into doubt by a growing number of historians.[3] This trend is exemplified by the social historian Temma Kaplan. In *Anarchists of Andalusia* (1977), Kaplan broke decisively with the millenarian historical tradition when she sought to explain anarchism as a rationally based political movement. Marshaling an impressive array of evidence she gleaned from municipal and national archives, Kaplan convincingly demonstrated that the millenarian model is too mechanistic to explain the complex pattern of Andalusian anarchist activity of the late nineteenth century. Many of the rural anarchists in the south, she argued, were not guided by a quasi-religious understanding of the nature of social oppression. On the contrary, Kaplan proved, they had a clear idea of who their enemies were, namely, the absentee landlords and wine-producing bourgeoisie, who together formed the ruling class of the region. Furthermore, she pointed out that, for all their revolutionary élan, the anarchists developed a rational strategy of revolution, channeling their energies into organizing a trade union movement that could be used as a vehicle for social and economic change.

On another level, the millenarian school of historians can be faulted not for having inaccurately described a form of anarchist behavior in Spain but for having generalized from such behavior.[4] All too frequently the millenarian viewpoint has been used as a blanket explanation for all types of anarchist activity. Even events that occurred at different times and in radically different circumstances—such as the Jerez rising (1892) and the Casas Viejas incident (1933)—have been classified by many writers, including the ones referred to above, as classic examples of millenarian behavior. This is partly because the millenarian school has been content to give a largely impressionistic picture of the anarchists' deeds. Yet, by lumping together disparate phenomena, these writers have collectively produced a historical synthesis of the anarchist movement that is both unsatisfactory and incomplete. Among other things, they have failed not only to differentiate between the urban and rural aspects of the movement but also to account for the sustained popularity of anarchism among a diverse group of adherents that included middle-class intellectuals, landless agricultural laborers, artisans, and industrial workers.

While the present study pointedly challenges the millenarian explanation, it does not attempt to refute all the claims made by this school of thinking. Nor does it offer any broad generalizations about Spanish anarchism, such as a comprehensive explanation as to why the libertarian movement was such a significant political force in Spain. Rather, the argument of this work is that the more closely we examine the texture of anarchist history the more difficult it is to sustain major portions of the millenarian thesis. I have confined my inquiry to one crucial aspect of anarchism: the ideological dimension. Against the general political background of the period, I have examined the role ideology played in shaping the course of anarchist development during the last quarter of the nineteenth century. The period selected for review is significant for several reasons, not least because these years are, in the words of Gerald Brenan, "the most obscure and ill-defined in the history of Spanish anarchism."[5] Although written nearly half a century ago, this statement still generally holds true.

That these crucial chapters of Spanish anarchism have been overlooked is understandable. With only sketchy historical narratives serving as reference points, it is an exceedingly difficult terrain to survey. To make the task even more daunting there is a dearth of reliable historical evidence. Accurate statistics recording the conditions of the working classes—strike activity, for example—are almost nonexistent. Much of the history of anarchism in this period is contained in the radical press and in the limited personal papers of some of the participants. Partly out of fear of prosecution and partly because they were in principle opposed to it, anarchists rarely kept records of their activity in the form of either diaries or published material. The precious few extant collections of newspapers, journals, and assorted ephemerae of the era are incomplete. Other potentially useful sources of historical evidence, such as autobiographies, are also extremely rare and confined to a few participants. Spanish police files and public records are another potential source of information. But, in the main, these are notoriously difficult to gain access to, and even when it is possible to do so they are so poorly organized that they are of little use to the historian. In addition, as the historian James Joll has stated with regard to the French anarchist movement, police files present certain difficulties as a source of historical evidence. The police in both France and Spain not only tended to exaggerate the size and significance of anarchist activity but also relied heavily on paid informants—many of whom were known criminals—as a means of gathering information. Partly because of these inherent obstacles to the study of anarchism, I chose to focus on the ideological dimension of the movement, something which proved to be feasible as there is a sufficient body of anarchist publications on which to base such a study. I believe that taking this approach also lends itself to a general history of Spanish anarchism insofar as this is an aspect of the movement that transcended regional boundaries.[6]

The history of Spanish anarchism formally begins with the advent of the September Revolution of 1868. With the overthrow of Queen Isabella II, Spain was plunged into a period of intense social turmoil that was to last until the restoration of Bourbon rule in 1875. At a time when the military, republicans, and other groupings were vying for political ascendancy, representatives of the Bakuninist wing of the International movement crossed the Spanish borders, bringing with them the tactics and strategy needed to launch a revolutionary movement. Significantly, the International not only was introduced to Spain by anarchists but remained under their control throughout its existence. As a result, the two became synonymous throughout the period under consideration.

The first section of the book investigates two aspects of the early development of anarchist ideology: its relationship to the trade union movement and its relationship to Federal Republicanism. Although workers' associations had been in existence since 1840, it was not until the 1860s—when anarchism was introduced—that a substantive working-class movement began to emerge. For several reasons anarchism was eminently suited to Spanish political conditions. First of all, its fiery brand of revolutionism appealed to a proletariat that was already becoming increasingly radicalized by the insurgent activities of the revolutionary wing of the Federal movement. Indeed, the ideological affinities shared between anarchism and Federalism were an important reason why anarchism found a receptive audience among the Spanish workers. Although in differing degrees, both doctrines were antistatist, and both were profoundly moralistic, inveighing against the evils of capitalism and aspiring to bring about the spiritual regeneration of the people.

On another level, anarchism supplied the Spanish working classes with a language of class identity. It is essential to note in this connection that, in the mid—nineteenth century, Spain was a classic case of uneven economic development: capitalism flourished in some areas—such as Catalonia—but was yet to emerge in vast regions of the south, where the *latifundista* land tenure system acted as a brake on economic progress. For this reason, the "working class" comprised a rather broad group of people, ranging from artisans in urban centers to the agricultural laborer in the villages of the south. Because Bakuninism spoke in generalities, it appealed equally to the interests of the industrial worker and to those of the nonunionized *bracero*. Above all, it provided the workers with a vocabulary that enabled them to define themselves and the relationship they held with other social classes. The anarchist representatives of the International brought with them a political idiom that pictured the social and economic world in polar opposites. Some of the consequences that flowed from accepting this new language were immediately apparent. Unlike Marxism or other branches of socialism, anarchism precluded the possibility of the workers' forming political alliances with the middle classes. Instead, it underscored the importance of direct action tactics, using terms like *huelga general* (general strike) and *propaganda por el hecho* (propaganda by the deed) to suggest ways that the workers could achieve both short- and long-term goals.

The periodic social eruptions of the early 1870s gave rise to a succession of progressively weaker governments. The Paris Commune of 1871 and the cantonalist risings of the summer of 1873 were the two events that finally divorced the International movement from republicanism and to a lesser extent from Marxism, which had also been introduced to Spain by this time. The Federals proved to be incapable of consolidating their rule over the first Spanish Federal Republic established in 1873, and, in the end, they were driven from power by the military. The resulting right-wing backlash brought about governmental stability at the expense of the extreme left. The anarchists bore the full brunt of this repression, being forced underground for nearly seven years.

The chapter covering these years is particularly concerned with the impact of long-term repression on the International movement. Most of the reformist working-class associations that had been affiliated with the Spanish Regional Federation (FRE) broke away, preferring instead to form alliances in the political arena. Thanks largely to the continued existence of the Alliance—the secret body modeled on the Russian anarchist Michael Bakunin's international brotherhood, the Fraternité Internationale—the anarchist movement was able to survive these harsh years. The introduction of new tactics at this time, notably "propaganda by the deed," split anarchists over the question of whether or not they should pursue a revolutionary maximalist line.

The Restoration Settlement (1875–1923) created by Antonio Cánovas del Castillo brought to Spain a political stability it had not had before. Cánovas's achievement, however, did not impress the majority of workers, who were effectively excluded from the power-sharing scheme he had carefully devised. Furthermore, the political atmosphere during the last quarter of the nineteenth century was tainted by corruption. Throughout the latifundist districts of the south and the northwest, political life was dominated by an unmitigated form of *caciquismo*, that is, a system for controlling the elections through *caciques*, or political bosses. Each of the dynastic parties employed this form of electoral manipulation in order to secure for itself the votes necessary to stay in power. Elsewhere, bribery, graft, and other kinds of unsavory practices seduced politicians at both the municipal and national levels.

The fact that workers were effectively disfranchised throughout the period under review helps to explain the enduring relevance of anarchism in Spain. For a system that persistently denied the workers access to the political process inevitably reinforced the antipolitical trajectory of those who had fallen under the influence of anarchism.

When the right to associate was restored to the working classes in 1881, the International reemerged onto the political stage as a legally recognized body, Federación de Trabajadores de la Región Española (FTRE). Although the anarchists were now under the direction of a syndicalist-minded leadership, they were still deeply committed to antipoliticalism and revolutionism. Above all, the syndicalists sought to push to the background the insurrectionary elements of the movement, hoping to restore the International's footing in the trade union movement. At first their policies were remarkably successful: in just two short years the FTRE mushroomed from a mere 3,000 (in 1881) to around 60,000 members (in 1883). One of the common features of anarchist history of this period was government repression. The authorities' relentless persecution of Internationalists following the *Mano Negra* scandal of 1882–1883 not only interrupted the spectacular growth of the FTRE but served ultimately to destroy the syndicalist base of anarchism.

Another main theme developed in this study is concerned with the theoretical content of anarchism. Anarchism was never a homogeneous ideological movement, and it will be shown that significantly different and competing tendencies flourished alongside and even overlapped one another. By focusing on the transition of anarchist ideology, I also hope to gain a new perspective on the role intellectuals played in the anarchist movement. In particular, my work in this area challenges the long-standing assumption that Spanish anarchism—in contrast to republicanism and Marxism—failed to attract and sustain a following among intellectuals. The theoretic contributions made by such writers as Juan Serrano y Oteiza, Ricardo Mella, and Fernando Tarrida del Mármol lay to rest such groundless assumptions.[7]

Anarchism, as it was first conceived in Spain, was a mixture of Proudhonian federalism and Bakuninist collectivism. Of the two anti-statist tendencies, however, Bakuninism predominated until the mid-1880s. At this time, Bakuninism was forcefully challenged by anarchist communism, another strand of anarchist thinking which was a product of the theorizing of several eminent international anarchists, notably Elisée Reclus, Errico Malatesta, and Peter Kropotkin. Anarchist communism offered an alternative style of thinking, emphasizing direct action tactics that did not rely on formal labor organizations. The introduction of this ideology created profound problems for the anarchist movement, generating a whirlwind of heated discussions that did not completely die down until the close of the nineteenth century. Perhaps the most serious consequence of this debate was that it brought about a reorientation in the anarchists' strategy and tactics, significantly altering their relationship with the trade unions.

A little-known chapter of anarchist history is its connection to working-class associational life, which is briefly reviewed in chapter 7. The decline of the anarchists' nationally based organization, FTRE, coincided with the growth of libertarian influence in working-class social organizations. In both rural and urban settings, neighborhood clubs, bars, and other social centers became the focal points of anarchist activity. In this way, anarchism played a pivotal role in the socialization and politicalization of the worker. This proved to be vitally important in perpetuating the life of the doctrine, for it was through social forms that anarchist values and beliefs were passed from one generation to another. A thriving anarchist cultural life was manifested in a variety of ways but most notably in the proliferation of libertarian newspapers, sociological journals, pamphlets, and books.

One of the by-products of the collectivist/communist debate was the crystallization of an anarchist theoretical perspective known as *anarquismo sin adjetivos* (anarchism without adjectives), Spain's only real contribution to anarchist theory. The formulation of anarchism without adjectives also represented a high point in the development of anarchist thinking in Spain. The level of theoretical sophistication attained by thinkers like Tarrida del Mármol and Ricardo Mella is the subject of chapter 8.

The anarchist movement developed alongside, but rarely intersected with, the activities of other trade union groups. The Marxian socialists, whose party (PSOE) and trade union counterpart (UGT) remained small and comparatively insignificant until the turn of the century, insulated themselves from both the ultrarevolutionaries and the mainstream of the reformist labor organizations. I have therefore chosen to mention the socialists only in passing, as when I discuss the convergence of their activities with those of the anarchists during the eight-hour campaign and the May Day celebrations.[8]

Violence, which was endemic to the working-class movement in Spain before the arrival of the International, grew especially acute under the influence of a revolutionary doctrine like anarchism. Recurring throughout the thesis is a discussion of the various strategies the anarchists turned to in their efforts to bring about social revolution. Apart from the general strike tactic, the anarchists increasingly relied on violent methods like propaganda by the deed, a tactic that had far-reaching implications. More than anything else, this commitment to violence determined the pattern of anarchist development. Throughout the late 1880s and 1890s the anarchists were locked in a vicious circle of activity: violent acts committed in the name of revolution would be met by stout reprisals from the government, which were themselves answered by further acts of violence. This syndrome peaked with the Jerez rising of 1892 and was not finally broken until the notorious Montjuich repression of 1896–1897.

It took several years for the anarchists to recover from the Montjuich persecutions. The terrorists were forced into clandestinity and, in the meantime, anarchist intellectual and associational life languished. My study ends before the anarchists formally adopted revolutionary syndicalist ideas at the turn of the century, most of which were imported from Italy and France. From that point on, they began forging more permanent links with the trade unions. This was especially true following the establishment of the Confederación Nacional del Trabajo in 1910, when the history of anarchism entered a new stage of development.

CHAPTER I

The Origins of the First International in Spain

As dawn was breaking on 17 September 1868, General Juan Prim boarded the frigate "Zaragosa," where he proclaimed the end of Queen Isabella's regime with the rousing phrase "¡Viva la Soberanía Nacional!" (Long Live the Sovereign Nation!).[1] Prim's cry signaled the beginning of *La Gloriosa,* or the September Revolution, which plunged Spain into a period of intense political and social unrest until yet another *pronunciamiento* announced the restoration of the Bourbon dynasty in the winter of 1874–1875. Although the coup d'état had been brought about by a coalition of discontented generals and civilian politicians, the time appeared ripe for increased activity throughout the political spectrum. Liberal Unionists, Progressives, Federal Republicans, and the representatives of burgeoning working-class organizations were all animated by the turn of events. The Federals themselves seized on the possibilities of revolution with more enthusiasm than any other group, and throughout the Continent, prominent Federal exiles were anxious to return home in order to set in motion their plans to install a federal system of government.[2] Beyond the Spanish frontiers, leaders of the international labor movement were also training a watchful eye on political developments in the Iberian arena. Just as the September Revolution was beginning to unfold, the Second Congress of the League of Peace and Freedom convened in Berne, Switzerland.[3] News of the event electrified the audience, prompting one well-known delegate to deliver a stirring speech on the theme of revolution. The orator was the Russian agitator Michael Bakunin, an imposing figure in European radical cir-

cles who was at the point of forming his own revolutionary organization, the Alliance of Social Democracy. Apparently Bakunin thought
that the Spanish revolution might provide the spark needed to ignite a
universal insurrection.[4] As we shall see, he would waste little time in
exploring this much-hoped-for possibility.

SPANISH WORKERS AND RADICALISM:
THE BACKGROUND

The revolutionary tide about which Bakunin speculated did not
sweep through the Continent. Yet, within Spain, the volatile political
atmosphere engendered the rapid dissemination of radical ideas, especially among organized labor groups. The workers in Catalonia, the
center of Spain's textile industry, were quick to react to the ever-
changing circumstances. By October 1868, when the right to associate
was restored, they set about dissolving most of their old organizations,
and, in their place, created new federations or societies. The coordinating body of this system was called the Dirección Central de las
Sociedades Obreras de Barcelona, which functioned both as an organizing force for labor groups and as the headquarters for the working-class
organ, *La Federación* (Barcelona).[5]

At this early stage, however, the proclivities of the workers were far
from revolutionary given that they evinced both a strong attachment to
republican ideas and a commitment to a political alliance with middle-
class parties. Workers first publicly declared their republican sentiments
in December 1868 at the founding congress of the Dirección Central,
where the delegates unanimously agreed to work toward the establishment of a Federal Republican government.[6]

As regards organization, the majority of workers coming from areas
with a long tradition of associationism favored cooperative economic
forms. Their familiarity with cooperative ideas dated from the early
decades of the nineteenth century. The person most responsible for
promoting cooperatives at that time was Fernando Garrido. A veteran
of the Democrat party, Garrido had for many years been connected
with progressive causes. He regarded himself as a socialist, and during
the 1840s—when a number of Spanish intellectuals flirted with utopian
theories of Étienne Cabet and Charles Fourier—Garrido served as editor of the Fourierist paper *La Atracción* (1846). Later he developed
personal relationships with several prominent international socialists,
including Michael Bakunin, who apparently convinced Garrido to en-

roll in his Fraternité Internationale.[7] Deeply impressed by his own experiences with the Rochdale Cooperative Society in England, Garrido came to believe that the emancipation of the workers would come through their free association in producers' and consumers' cooperatives. For a brief time during the 1860s cooperativism became popular among working-class associations in Seville and in Catalonia, but the movement had little impact elsewhere. Despite the fact that cooperativists sought to work through the legal channels of society, their organizations were viewed with suspicion by the government. As a result, they were frequently targets of repression. It was not until the September Revolution, when they were legalized, that cooperatives began to enjoy a relatively secure existence.

While it is not surprising that many cooperatives were formed after the fall of Isabella, it is important to note that the workers' attitude toward them was rapidly evolving. This was partly because of the changed political and economic circumstances in Spain, and partly because of recent developments in the international labor movement, whose repercussions were felt throughout the Continent. For example, the 1860s saw a dramatic rise in strike activity among the European trade unions. Because it was generally perceived as a proponent of such direct action tactics, the International Working Men's Association (IWMA, popularly known as the International) especially benefited from this sharp rise in labor unrest, for its membership was soon swelled by the influx of more militant workers.[8] Against this background, the delegates at the IWMA congresses held in Lausanne (1867), Brussels (1868), and Basle (1869) attempted to define the attitude to be taken up by the International toward the question of direct action.

At these congresses it became increasingly apparent that the tendency of the international working-class movement was away from unrevolutionary methods, as represented by the cooperative movement, and toward a policy of confrontation between capital and labor. Thus, at the Lausanne Congress the majority of representatives voiced their unwillingness to work within the boundaries of the capitalist system, demanding instead the collectivization of banks and the means of transport.[9] Some delegates promoted the creation of organizations that could give both economic and moral support to the workers' struggle. To what extent, if any, cooperatives could fulfill these objectives was a hotly debated topic. The militant factions were highly critical of cooperatives, arguing that consumer cooperatives in particular tended to breed a nonrevolutionary consciousness. They further maintained that cooperatives were not suitable vehicles for promoting working-class demands because such societies benefited only those who belonged to them, thereby ignoring the plight of the vast majority of workers.

When the debate over cooperatives arose at the Brussels Congress, compromise finally seemed possible. The Belgian delegate and ardent syndicalist César de Paepe suggested that, rather than abandoning cooperatives altogether, they should be regarded as the basis of the decentralized system of the future. At the same time, it was generally agreed that the immediate demands of the workers could best be met by establishing societies of resistance. The resolution the congress adopted on strikes declared "that from the point of view of the organization of the strike there is need, in the professions that still lack societies of resistance, for the creation of these institutions."[10]

Meanwhile the intrusion of the International in Spain represented a real threat to the dominant position that the cooperativists held among the workers. As we shall see, the rapid dissemination of imported radical ideas divided the leaders of the labor movement into opposing camps. On the one side stood the cooperativists and reformists, who professed their faith in legal methods to advance the workers' cause. They were opposed by the antipolitical and apolitical syndicalists, who, because they were influenced by Internationalist ideas, sought to give the working classes a revolutionary orientation.

THE INTERNATIONAL IN SPAIN: THE EMERGENCE OF ANARCHISM

Since its creation in 1864, the General Council of the IWMA expressed an interest in establishing formal ties with Spain. Yet several years elapsed before any progress in this direction was made. In fact, apart from a few working-class circles in Barcelona and Madrid, the Spanish public remained unaware of the existence of the International for some years after it came into being. No direct relations with the International were established until 1867, when the Social-Republican League from Barcelona delivered an address to the Lausanne Congress. The following year another Spaniard, Antonio Marsal Anglora (using the nom de guerre "Sarro Magallán"), reported on the underground activities of the labor organizations in Catalonia and Valencia to the delegates at the Brussels Congress.[11]

It was the Bakuninist wing of the International movement that was the first to establish concrete relations with the Spanish working classes.

As mentioned, Bakunin himself had turned his attention to political developments there while he was still associated with the League of Peace and Freedom. After he broke with the League in September 1868, he founded the Alliance of Social Democracy (the successor to the Fraternité).[12] The function of this new group can briefly be outlined as follows. Bakunin believed that the formation of a secret body of devoted radicals within the International was absolutely necessary for it to maintain a revolutionary orientation. In Bakunin's eyes, the Alliance was to be used as an instrument for transforming the International—and all the popular masses outside it—into a power that could effectively destroy the capitalist system.[13] It is well known that his plans to direct such a society within the framework of the International was to become the chief element of the divisive arguments with Marx and his supporters. When the Alliance formally applied for affiliation with the IWMA in late 1868, the Marxist-dominated General Council summarily rejected its application on the grounds that a second international body would likely prove to be a disruptive influence, fostering division and discord within the IWMA. The Council's decision forced Bakunin publicly to declare the dissolution of the organization, although, as we shall see, the Alliance was not actually disbanded at this time.

The rapidly deteriorating political situation in Spain prompted Bakunin to dispatch several of his most trusted associates to investigate the extent of discontent there. His close friend and fellow anarchist Elisée Reclus declined the invitation. However, Elisée's brother, Elie, agreed to make the journey along with the French Bakuninists Alfred Naquet and Aristide Rey. The group arrived in Barcelona during the last days of October 1868.[14]

According to Bakunin's personal instructions, Reclus and his traveling companions were to initiate the process of establishing contacts with Spanish labor leaders and thereby pave the way for the later arrival of Giuseppe Fanelli, a former member of Bakunin's Fraternité who was to act as the principal emissary. As an ex-Mazzinian and veteran of the revolutionary movement in Italy, Fanelli appeared to be well appointed for the task of spreading propaganda.[15] Yet for all his revolutionary credentials, Fanelli faced several obstacles at the outset of his mission. To begin with he was given very little money to finance such an ambitious expedition. In fact, Fanelli found himself chronically short of funds during his three-month sojourn and was forced to rely on the generosity of the Spaniards to make ends meet.

Fanelli was also somewhat handicapped by the fact that he spoke no

Spanish. In Spain, where nearly two-thirds of the population were illiterate, there were relatively few people fluent in Italian and French, the two languages in which Fanelli could freely converse. Yet, as we shall see, the language barrier proved to be a relatively minor impediment to Fanelli's propagandizing efforts.

Most important, though, was the fact that Fanelli left for Spain under the mistaken belief that he was to sow the seeds of anarchism as a representative both of the Alliance of Social Democracy and the IWMA. This was because, when he set off on his mission, the General Council had not yet officially announced its decision to reject the Alliance's bid for membership. Apparently unable to maintain contact with his comrades in Geneva while he was in Spain, Fanelli did not learn of the General Council's decision until he returned to Switzerland.[16] He therefore gave the statutes of the Alliance along with those of the IWMA to the first sections of the International he organized in Spain.

Not long after Reclus's party arrived in Barcelona, Fanelli met up with them. There he was introduced to several prominent Federal leaders, including José María Orense and Bakunin's old acquaintance Fernando Garrido. Fanelli made a whirlwind trip through Tarragona, Tortosa, and Valencia before leaving for Madrid. He arrived in the Spanish capital on 4 November.

In Madrid Fanelli contacted José Rubaudonadeu, a lithographer and prominent republican who was well connected in working-class political circles. Rubaudonadeu warmly received the Italian visitor, and even generously provided his studio as the setting for the first meeting of the Spanish branch of the International, held on 24 January 1869. At this, Fanelli addressed a group of around twenty men, most of whom were artisans (printers and masons) and middle-class professionals associated with the Madrid working-class club Fomento de las Artes. Apart from the engraver Tomás González Morago, who was fluent in French, no one else in the intimate circle could communicate freely with the speaker. But Fanelli's inability to speak Spanish did not prevent him from conveying his message of revolution. Perhaps, as one impressionable eyewitness has written, this was possible because Fanelli was particularly skilled at making his points visually with expressive gestures. As a public speaker, Fanelli possessed all the personal attributes required to mesmerize an audience. The printer Anselmo Lorenzo has left the following vivid recollection of Fanelli's fateful speech:

Fanelli had black expressive eyes that took on the appearance of kindly compassion according to the sentiments dominating him. His voice had a metallic tone and was susceptible to all the inflections appropriate to what he was saying, passing rapidly from accents of anger and menace against tyrants and exploiters to take on those of suffering, regret and consolation, whenever he spoke of the pains of the exploited.[17]

Fanelli's dramatic efforts produced the desired effect: everyone in attendance enthusiastically proclaimed his allegiance to the International.

The Madrid nucleus of Internationalists rapidly developed into a full-fledged section of the IWMA in Spain. Within a year, the branch had attracted some 2,000 members, and was strong enough to begin publishing its own periodical, *La Solidaridad*.

Following his success in Madrid, Fanelli returned to Barcelona, where he found another receptive audience for his ideas. This was hardly surprising, for, compared to Madrid, Barcelona had a longer tradition of organized labor activity and workers there seemed to be politically advanced.[18] Fanelli's task was further facilitated by the fact that he encountered Republican students, doctors, lawyers, and artists who could speak and understand French.[19] Within two weeks he was able to organize a Catalonian section of the IWMA. The nucleus itself was composed of about two dozen members, who had a background similar to that of their counterparts in Madrid. The artist José Luis Pellicer was selected as president, and his nephew, Rafael Farga, became the first secretary. Other notable members of this group included Trinidad Soriano, an engineering student; José García Viñas, a medical student from Malaga; and Gaspar Sentiñón, an eminent doctor who later became a close associate of Michael Bakunin.

THE FOUNDATION OF THE SPANISH REGIONAL FEDERATION

In September 1869, the Centro Federal de las Sociedades Obreras (formerly the Dirección Central) sent Gaspar Sentiñon and Rafael Farga Pellicer as delegates to the Fourth Congress of the IWMA in Basle. Before he departed, Rafael Farga warned Bakunin that socialism in Catalonia was not yet well developed. He thus recommended that considerable care be taken in preparing the program of socialist propaganda in order to "avoid future divisions" within the labor movement.[20]

At the Basle Congress, the Spanish delegates gained an awareness of the developing rifts in the International. Their sympathies with Bakuninist ideas were quickly put to a test when heated debates over the question of the future tactics of the IWMA were waged. In the wake of the discussions, it was evident that Farga and Sentiñon were faithful adherents to the Bakuninist program, which was decidedly anticentralist and antipolitical.

After the congress, the two Spaniards traveled to Geneva, where they enrolled in Bakunin's Alliance. Rafael Farga and Sentiñon then returned to Spain with a clearer understanding of the objectives they thought they should pursue. In practice this meant doing what Fanelli had not done, namely, formally establish a Spanish branch of the Alliance that could be used for coordinating the ideas and directing the action of the IWMA in Spain.

In the meantime, Federal ideas continued to exert considerable influence over the workers, who were still absorbed by the political struggles of La Gloriosa. Nevertheless, after the Basle Congress it was growing ever more apparent that the moderate forces were steadily losing their influence over labor organizations. The various organs of the IWMA clearly reflected this gradual shifting of ideological positions. The first issues of La Federación, for example, characterized sociedades de resistencia (societies of resistance) as being too disruptive, while enthusiastically endorsing workers' cooperatives.[21] Two months after the Basle Congress, however, La Federación significantly qualified its position on cooperatives. Thereafter, the paper prompted a view more consistent with the policies of the International. Cooperatives were now criticized on the ground that they were too exclusive, while societies of resistance were looked on favorably.[22]

By January 1870, the IWMA branches in Barcelona and Madrid began taking steps to complete the unification of the workers' movement. In its early days, the IWMA in Spain was not formally linked by a national organization: worker federations were grouped on a regional level through the organizations like the Centro Federal based in Barcelona. The different branches now sought to create a nationally based organization. The pro-Madrid section decided that, since Barcelona had by far the largest working-class population, a national conference should be held there. Between 19 and 26 June 1870, a congress was convened at which the Federación Regional Española (FRE), the Spanish branch of the IWMA, came into existence.

In an atmosphere of comaraderie and enthusiasm, close to one hundred delegates representing some 150 workers' societies from the provinces assembled at the Teatro Circo. While the high spirits of the delegates promoted a free exchange of ideas, once the proceedings got underway, the theoretical differences among the delegates surfaced. The factions fell roughly into three principal categories: (1) reformist cooperativists, (2) radical cooperativists, and (3) apolitical and anti-political delegates, most of whom were sympathetic to the revolutionary collectivist ideas of Bakunin. The first group comprised the representatives of the indigenous cooperative movement. As noted earlier, this group deplored the use of illegal tactics in the attempt to improve worker conditions. Influenced by César de Paepe and other radical cooperativists in the IWMA, the second group of cooperativists differed from the reformists insofar as they advocated a policy of collectivization and emphasized the need for a revolutionary orientation of the labor movement. Their dictum on traditional cooperatives was highly critical: "[C]ooperatives and their branches of production and consumption cannot be regarded as a direct and absolute means of bringing about the emancipation of the working classes."[23] Thanks largely to the coalition formed by the radical cooperativists and Bakuninists, the idea of using cooperatives as a vehicle for social reform was rejected by the congress.

It was evident that Bakuninist doctrine had shaped the opinions of the apolitical and antipolitical groups at the congress. Earlier that year, a key tract of Bakunin's had been serialized in *La Federación*, which powerfully evoked the dynamism of Bakunin's revolutionary collectivism:

> Do you see that, in order to become a power, you [the proletariat] must unite—*not with the bourgeoisie, which would be a folly and a crime, since all the bourgeoisie, so far as they belong to their class, are our deadly enemies!* . . . The liberation of the Proletariat must be the work of the Proletariat itself. . . . But the working class is still very ignorant. It lacks completely every theory. There is only one way out, therefore, namely—*Proletarian liberation through action.* And what will this action be that will bring the masses to Socialism? It is the economic struggle of the Proletariat against the governing class carried out in solidarity.[24]

The extent to which the two factions had assimilated Bakunin's message can be gauged by the stance they took on certain issues. For example, the apolitical delegates proposed that the IWMA in Spain should renounce all methods of political reform. They further argued that the working class's participation in the government of the bourgeoisie would result in the paralysis of the revolutionary action of the proletariat.[25] Though many of their views were unmistakably of a Bakuninist flavor, the apolitical faction had yet to absorb the basic tenets of this doctrine. Not only did their program fail to allude to the "class struggle," which is central to Bakunin's theory, but it did not promote a revolutionary agenda for the working classes.[26]

The antipolitical faction was, however, exclusively Bakuninist, thanks largely to the efforts of Farga Pellicer and Gaspar Sentiñón. The discussions in the antipolitical camp revolved around the question of collectivization. The Bakuninists pressed for the collectivization of all property and the means of production, and then went on to describe their plan of a future society, one which would consist of a federation of free agricultural and industrial labor organizations. Unlike most of the apolitical members, the radical antipoliticists adhered to a policy of total abstention from politics. In their judgment, it was not enough to have the IWMA abstain from middle-class politics, for they thought it was also futile for the individual (that is, anyone not affiliated with a labor group) to participate in the sphere of politics. As one of their delegates put it:

> I support the dictum that states that, as a body, the International should remain aloof from politics, and I am saying and recommending to you that as individuals each one of its members should follow suit; after all, of what use is it for us to make something tonight which we will destroy the next day.[27]

The diversity of opinion expressed by the delegates at the congress indicated that the FRE was not yet fully committed to anarchist principles. Thus, for example, when the resolution on the IWMA's attitude toward politics was debated, the majority of delegates did not think that reform methods should be abandoned in favor of direct action tactics. In the end, the congress decided that, while the FRE should not involve itself in the political arena, individual members of the Spanish Federation did not have to abstain from politics.

The Bakuninists may have failed to push through their resolutions on antipoliticalism; but perhaps more important, they did manage to impose their ideas regarding the organization of the FRE. And, apart from some minor modifications, this scheme was to serve as the basic framework of the organization for the next few years. The basic unit of the trade union structure was the craft union (*oficio*). The craft unions of different trades in an area were grouped into a local federation; and the local federations of the various regions in Spain were united by the Spanish Federal Committee. As a way of reinforcing the interconnections among the unions, alongside the trade union body just described, a parallel system of unions was to be erected. According to this, all unions of a particular craft were to be linked through a national federation of that craft, forming a widely based network of craft unions. This second system of unions, however, was never developed.

The organizational pattern laid down by the Bakuninists was to serve several purposes. For example, the local federation, by bringing together the different craft unions of an area, was meant to function as a fulcrum with which the workers could bring economic pressures to bear against their employers. Above all, the Bakuninists made certain that the trade union structure of the FRE conformed to their anarchist principles: there were no paid trade union officials or bureaucratic hierarchies, and power flowed from the bottom upward. In practice, this meant that each craft union was not bound to any decision made at the regional or national levels; thus the FRE had an extremely flexible base. This feature was to prove itself indispensable in a variety of ways, but not least because it allowed the FRE to expand or contract according to the prevailing circumstances.

The foundation of the FRE in 1870 marked the true beginning of the International movement in Spain, and it was clear from the Barcelona Congress that this movement was to be largely propelled and controlled by Bakuninist elements.

CHAPTER II

The Struggle for an Ideology: Federalism versus Bakuninism

It was a peculiarity of the September Revolution that as the Federal Republicans were making their debut on the political stage, the working classes were also just emerging as an independent force. During the early days of La Gloriosa, however, the disparate natures of the two movements were not immediately manifested. One reason for this was that, up to 1868, a tradition of cooperation existed between the Federals and the workers. They were united in their opposition to the old regime, and the republicans themselves presupposed that the political interests of the radical middle class—which the republicans represented—were identical with those of the working masses. Early signs of such solidarity were evinced during the municipal elections in December 1868, when the workers backed the Federal Republican candidates.[1] But the period 1869–1874 was a critical one in the development of the relationship between the Federals and the workers. At this time the workers began to formulate a political agenda that was peculiar to their own class, and as a result, it became increasingly apparent that their partnership with the Federals could not be taken for granted.

Perhaps the agent most responsible for altering the course of the labor movement during this period was the International.[2] There can be no doubt that the advent of the International in Spain and the subsequent dissemination of Bakuninist ideas significantly diminished the influence that Federal ideas had hitherto exercised over the working classes. The many obstacles the Federals faced in implementing their programs, combined with a political system thoroughly tainted by corruption, made the antipolitical doctrine of Bakuninism an attractive alternative for those striving for economic and social change. But it would appear as though the early success of the International was not simply a product of the Bakuninists' persuasive revolutionary rhetoric. Rather, in a broader sense, the ideological content of Bakuninism offered the working classes something that was lacking in federalism: a cogent system of ideas that could be used for directing the collective activities of workers' organizations.[3]

While the ascendancy of the International owed much to the shortcomings of Federalist theory, it is also important to bear in mind that the International arrived during a period of general economic and political instability. Attempts by successive provisional governments to restore order generally worked against the interests of the working class. This was especially evident following the Paris Commune in 1871, when the government decided to outlaw the International, and after the uprising at Alcoy two years later, when the activities of labor groups as a whole were repressed. It was within the context of growing state repression that Bakuninist ideas were particularly significant to the workers, and, as a result, federalism lost its commanding position in the labor movement.

WORKERS AND POLITICIANS: THE FEDERALIST PROGRAM

At the height of political confusion in October 1868, José María Orense, Emilio Castelar, and other leading Federals had successfully popularized their ideas by means of an efficient propaganda program.[4] The chief tactic that the Federal publicists employed in their campaign was to exploit their newly acquired press freedom. By November, they were circulating their ideas in several newspapers: *El Federalist,* directed by a leader of the Barcelona Federals, Valentín Almirall, appeared in October; and *La Alianza de los Pueblos* came out in the following month.[5] The general trend toward expanded publication of periodicals was incongruous in a country where only thirty percent of the population of some sixteen million were literate.[6] The fact is that the reading audience of republican publications was largely confined to middle- and lower-middle-class professionals, mainly lawyers, doctors, journalists, and teachers. Among the working classes, where illiteracy ran the highest, Federal publications reached only a small number of readers.[7]

The low rate of literacy among the workers posed a major problem for the Federals who were attempting to instill in them a political awareness. Earlier efforts to surmount this obstacle had taken place during the 1860s, when it had been possible to educate a limited number of workers in associations like the Ateneo Catalán or the Fomento de las Artes. *Ateneos* in particular played a pivotal role in the socialization and politicalization of the worker. Although they had originated in Spain as bourgeois institutions, *ateneos* had become by the mid–nineteenth century focal points of working-class activity. They served not only as recreational centers, where one could go to play chess and billiards in the evenings or on weekends, but also as learning centers. For it was usually in the *ateneo* that the worker could go to learn to read or make use of a modest library.[8] When the right of association returned after 1868, the Federals promptly made use of these types of institutions in their propaganda program. In addition to their work in the *ateneos,* they created clubs—social forms introduced by the Federal movement—which could serve both as educational facilities and as centers for indoctrination.

The immediate impact of these propaganda techniques was to endow the workers with a republican political perspective. In the early days of the September Revolution, the workers had rallied to the Federal cause primarily because it fed their desire for the creation of a decentralized and secularized republican state. But, as the prospects for such a political revolution began to diminish, it became increasingly harder for the Federals to sustain working class support.

The sources of the workers' ideological commitment to federalism help to explain why this was so. The fact is that the workers were never exposed to a homogenous doctrine, but rather were introduced to an assortment of Federal ideas that meant different things to workers in the different regions.[9] For this reason, one group of workers' expectations of federalism sometimes varied considerably from another's.

In the desperately poor rural areas of the south, where the political atmosphere was highly volatile, federal ideas had acquired revolutionary connotations. During the turbulent days of La Gloriosa the workers' perspective of federalism had been shaped by extremists, like Fermín Salvochea, who emphasized the need for a complete social revolution. Another Federal radical, the Sevillano deputy F. Rubio, defended the seizure of old common lands because he believed that this was a "revolutionary antecedent to what must inevitably come from the *Cortes* [Spanish Parliament]."[10] Because the *reparto de bienes* (redistribution of property) was a particularly explosive issue among the landless laborers, it is not surprising that they regarded federalism in a socialist sense.[11]

Elsewhere, as in the industrialized region of Catalonia, Federal ideas acquired a different emphasis. In Barcelona, republicanism developed in relatively stable circumstances. Because there was a well-established tradition of cooperation between the middle and working classes, the Federals discovered that workers' demands could be canalized into political—as against revolutionary—activities. Also in contrast to the south, workers in Barcelona maintained some degree of control over their own political activities by virtue of their well-organized network of associations. Most important, however, they were not subject to the maneuvers of the political bosses of the *cacique* system as their counterparts were in the south. Where this iniquitous institution existed, politics was completely dominated by the *caciques,* who exercised considerable influence over the local elections through an elaborate patronage system as well as through the practice of electoral intimidation, popularly known as the Partido de la Porra (Party of the Cudgel).[12]

Workers in Barcelona were also inclined toward federalism because of their regionalist aspirations. In fact, since the overthrow of Isabella there had been a resurgence of regionalist feelings throughout Catalonia.[13] This made a political alliance with the Federals even more attractive, considering that their proposals to form a decentralized state and thereby allow for more regional autonomy appeared to complement the interests of this group of workers. On another level, the economic problems peculiar to that area drew the numerous textile workers into a closer relationship with the Federals. In particular, the representatives of the textile cooperatives argued that a policy of protectionism was needed in order to prevent a fall in the price of cotton, which would, in turn, inevitably bring about a reduction in wages. In view of this, the Federals were careful to assure the Catalan workers that federalism necessarily implied a policy of protectionism.[14] At least until the arrival of the International, many of the textile workers assumed that their economic interests were identical to those of the Federals.[15]

Throughout 1869 a series of revolts shook the provinces. The highly disruptive anticonscription (*anti-quinta*) campaign[16] culminated in the spring, and the unsuccessful pactist uprisings were sparked off in October. These events brought to the surface the general confusion that existed about the overall aims and political implications of federalism. For this reason, the Federals were no longer in a position to concentrate their efforts on proselytizing the workers, for they were now

forced to confront the problems plaguing their own movement. The
first indications of sharpening differences among the Federals began
with the signing of the Tortosa pact in May—which marked the shifting of the focus of the movement from the activities of the parliamentary party to those of the Federals in the provinces.[17] This development
was, in effect, merely a symptom of the growing impatience among
Federals known as *Intransigentes* regarding the use of parliamentary
methods. They stressed that, by itself, reformism could not bring about
the transition to a republic, and therefore it was incumbent upon them
to complete the social revolution by forming pacts among the various
provinces. By the end of August 1869 it was apparent that a general
movement toward pactist federalism had been set in motion, and that
the question of reform versus revolution was coming to a head.

Several leading republican figures, most notably the literary journalist and theoretician Francisco Pi y Margall, recognized the damaging
effects that an uncoordinated strategy could have on the movement. Pi,
who was regarded as the chief architect of federal theory and who later
served briefly as prime minister under the republic (1873), attempted to
harmonize the discordant elements by delineating the boundaries of
federal principles. Following the *anti-quinta* demonstrations in Jerez,
for example, the opposition attempted to divide republican ranks by
suggesting that all Federals were socialists. Although deputies such as
Rubio had supported the *reparto* of common lands there were others,
including Juan Paul y Angulo and Moreno Rodríguez, who vehemently
rejected the socialist charge.[18] The issue raised challenged the Federals
to take a position on the socialist question. Pi responded by declaring,
"One can be a republican and accept or reject the theories of socialism";
and he went on to say that state intervention was only warranted whenever other means for dealing with social evils had failed.[19] By arguing in
this way, Pi had shown that federalism could not be narrowly defined as
a socialist doctrine but rather should be regarded in a wider sense as one
that embraced a variety of concepts concerned with social reform.

Later, when the question of reform versus revolution arose during
the pactist crisis, Pi was confronted with a much more thorny problem.
He then needed to outline a strategy for social revolution which would
unite the disparate tendencies within the Federal movement. On a
purely theoretical plane, Pi's views on this subject could be summarized
in the expression *abajo-arriba* (under and above). Briefly defined, the
terms refer to the creation of a federal state from the restructuring of the
economic and social base of society.[20] Concerning this point, it should

be remembered that once Pi was in power he thought this process of change should be brought about by means of a controlled program of propaganda (change from below) as well as through legal opposition in the constituent Cortes (change from above). More than anything else, Pi was loath to use violence as a means of bringing about change. His aim, then, was not to instigate a spontaneous revolution but to organize a political framework based on federal principles within which the gradual reconstruction of society could evolve.[21] In the wake of the pactist revolts, Pi's proposals thus appeared to be a compromise between the revolutionary and reformist wings of the movement, particularly since they embodied the idea of contract or provincial pact without abandoning his own idea of revolution by propaganda and legal opposition.[22]

As far as the majority of the working classes were concerned, however, Pi's as well as other Federals' efforts to iron out the contradictions in their ideology had come too late. By the end of 1872, a general air of disillusionment with politics had settled over most workers, turning many of them away from Federal ranks. The workers who had pressed for a social revolution immediately following the overthrow of Isabella II and who had gone to the barricades with the Federals during the *antiquinta* uprisings soon discovered that their efforts to bring about permanent political changes were to no avail. Not only did General Prim default on his pledge to abolish conscription but the government did not hesitate to use force to put down attempts at insurrection. That the Federals failed to make good on most of their campaign promises is understandable. For, as we have seen, between 1868 and 1870 the movement's nagging internal divisions prevented them from functioning as an effective political force. The widening breach between the "revolutionary" and "legalist" wings of the Federal party served further to sap their political strength. Even the inflammatory speeches and writings of radicals such as Paul y Angulo failed to convince the majority of the working masses that the Federals could successfully spearhead a social revolution. And, after the provisional government installed a new monarchy at the end of 1870, the prospects of a Federal Republic seemed more remote than ever.[23]

THE BAKUNINIST CHALLENGE

Parallel to the Federals, the Internationalists were conducting their own intensive program to popularize their views. Since the arrival of Bakunin's agents in October 1868, prominent Federals like Fernando

Garrido and José María Orense had demonstrated their willingness to cooperate with the Internationalists by welcoming them to participate in the activities of republican social organizations. By penetrating these associations, the Bakuninists found a convenient forum for putting across their ideas and gaining adherents. At the outset, the educational pursuits of the respective groups complemented one another, for the ideas of the Internationalists, although almost exclusively Bakuninist in character, were presented in conjunction with the Federals' lectures on Proudhonism and Auguste Comte's positivism.[24] The apparent harmony between their respective educational programs during this early period was attributable in part to the fact that the Internationalists, like the utopian socialists and "Old Democrats" who preceded them, regarded the education of the worker as central to their propaganda program. This belief was particularly strong among the Bakuninists, who stressed that the *enseñanza integral*—the intellectual as well as practical enlightenment of the worker—was essential for the proper development of "le travailleur qui comprend et qui sait."[25] Indeed, this Bakuninist notion regarding the education of the worker formed an indispensable part of the revolutionary ideology that was being dispensed in the various sections of the FRE.

Before 1870, the extent to which Internationalists were winning over workers in *ateneos* and other associations was not easily discernible. Yet it was becoming increasingly evident that the Federals' monopoly as educators of the working classes could no longer be taken for granted. In fact, by this time Federal influence within the labor movement was declining in direct proportion to the ever-increasing role Internationalists were assuming in the affairs of the workers. In addition to their activities in *ateneos,* Internationalists managed to enlarge the scope of their influence in a variety of ways: "meetings" were held in the streets of the towns, in the patios of cafés, and in rooms of neighborhood bars (pubs); manifestos and posters were plastered on streetcorners; and even the lyrics of popular traditional songs and poems were altered in order to convey the message of revolution.

But perhaps the most effective method of systematically disseminating their ideas was through the publication of newspapers and pamphlets (*folletos*). Like the Federals, the Internationalists readily seized the opportunity to publish extensively in an environment where relaxed censorship laws and inexpensive paper allowed for an unprecedented increase in the number of periodicals available in Spain.[26] The anarchist press was clearly an integral part of their propaganda program: it was thanks principally to the wide circulation of anarchist journals, newspapers, and political tracts that revolutionary ideas spread from town to town. Even in areas where illiteracy was commonplace, papers were read aloud by those who were literate. Another interesting fact about anarchist publications was that, on the whole, they were well written and intellectually diverse. Often attracting readers and writers from outside the revolutionary movement, the anarchist press published articles not only on political themes but also on philosophy, scientific achievements, recent technological advancements, and current trends in European literature.

Once the Internationalists began publishing their own periodicals, they were better able to maintain their independence from the Federals and other political groups. Among other things, using the press to disseminate their ideas meant that it was possible to codify Internationalist principles. It is significant that, prior to 1871, a majority of the editors and contributors to the Internationalist press were either Bakuninist or sympathetic to this doctrine. This was especially evident in working-class centers: in Madrid *La Solidaridad,* which appeared in January 1870, was directed by Anselmo Lorenzo, Francisco Mora, and Tomás Morago (all members of the Madrid section of the IWMA); in Barcelona *La Federación* was controlled by Bakunin's close associates Rafael Farga Pellicer and Gaspar Sentiñón; and in Palma de Mallorca the Bakuninist position was promoted by Francisco Tomás in *El Obrero.*[27]

As noted earlier, the defaults of the Federals gave rise to renewed demands for a radical approach in the campaign for social and economic changes, especially from the more militant sections of the working classes. Because it emphasized the urgent need for direct action, Bakuninism offered an attractive ideological alternative for those who were still bent on social revolution. The dynamic radicalism of Bakuninism was clearly reflected, for example, in the distinctive vocabulary used in the various Internationalist periodicals at this time. Terms like "la huelga" (strike)—which were used with greater frequency from 1869 onward—were almost certainly instrumental in widening the dimensions of the workers' concepts of social action. An example of this was the notion "La huelga," which suggested a form of direct action that could be used to exploit the collective strength of labor groups. This was a significant tactical advance over mounting barricades.[28]

Other terms, like "la burguesía" (Spanish for bourgeoisie) and "burgués" had similar implications. They were an important element of the Internationalist vocabulary, not least because they encouraged the workers to define their demands in society in relation to other social classes.[29] We find in *El Ariete Socialista Internacional,* for example, that "burgués" was introduced to the Spanish workers' periodicals in order to "classify those persons who live from the work of others, or whose work is generally nonproductive, as being excessively remunerated."[30] The bourgeoisie, according to this definition, represented a distinctive class of people whose interests diametrically opposed those of the working classes. We know that, at least by the early 1870s, class terminology of this kind was already making an impact on the workers. In a letter to Friedrich Engels, Paul Lafargue recorded the following impressions of the International movement in Catalonia:

> As you rightly say, there is genuine class fanaticism here. One has to hear the Catalonians say "burgués" to form an idea of the fanaticism. It is this sentiment that gives us our strength, for in such provinces as Aragon and La Mancha, where clans are barely defined, we exist only by virtue of this feeling of hatred.[31]

Although Lafargue had not anticipated it, this kind of animosity actually reinforced Bakuninist influence among the working classes. As class tensions intensified in the following months, Bakunin's anti-political doctrine became increasingly attractive to the workers. The rivalry between the Bakuninists on the one hand and the Federals on the other was soon brought into sharper relief owing to circumstances that had their origins outside of Spain. In March 1871, the Paris Commune was established. This event, perhaps more than any other of the decade, sent shockwaves throughout Europe, but they were to reverberate the loudest within the Spanish context.

THE PARIS COMMUNE AND ITS REPERCUSSIONS IN SPAIN

In Spain the events of the Paris Commune created a sensation of enormous proportions, not only among the conservative bourgeoisie— who were alarmed by its revolutionary implications with regard to Spain—but also among the Federals and the Internationalists. At first the Federals applauded the efforts of the communards, believing that they had set an example of how the Federalist principle of decentralization could be realized. Their enthusiasm, however, was not shared by the majority of the government in Madrid, for whom the events of Paris were most disturbing. Fueled by sensationalist press reports, which,

among other things, described the Paris Commune as a "reign of terror
imposed by the communists," the government immediately took measures to eliminate any threat from the left: the right to associate was
suspended and public meetings were suppressed.[32] In the Cortes, the
minister of the interior, Práxedes Sagasta, led right-wing factions in an
attack on pro-Internationalists like Pi y Margall and B. Lostau. Re-
sponding to this diatribe, Lostau, who was himself a member of the
International, charged the government with having violated the constitution in its campaign of repression. According to the conservative
elements, the International was, now that it was crushed in France,
endeavoring in Spain to stir up discontent among the working classes.
To support their allegations, they presented as fact the rumor that
several hundred French Internationalists had fled across the French-
Spanish border and were now occupied with the task of inciting the
workers to rebellion.[33]

Thanks to the Paris Commune, the Spanish Internationalists almost
overnight acquired an inflated reputation as a force for revolutionary
change in Spain. Thus, while the emotionally charged debates against
the communards in the Cortes were ostensibly aimed at expelling all
foreign Internationalists, they were also providing the government with
sufficient grounds for suppressing the activities of the FRE itself. It was
the fear of the latter that spurred the Federal Council of the FRE to
action. Anticipating stern reprisals from the government, the Federal
Council disbanded. Enrique Borrel and Ángel Mora remained in Madrid, but Francisco Mora, Tomás González Morago, and Anselmo Lorenzo were dispatched to Portugal with the official documents of the
Federation. In this way, the ruling sections of the FRE escaped persecution, thereby sparing the International from feeling the full force of the
government crackdown.

The government's near-hysterical reaction to the Paris Commune
was not wholly without foundation. While the International was too
weak to mount any rebellion on the scale of the Commune, it was
clearly in a position to benefit from the climate of revolutionary excite-
ment engendered by that event. Not surprisingly, the number of strikes
throughout Spain rose dramatically in the months immediately following the Commune, and it seems that these attracted new members to the
FRE. It was also true that Internationalists seized the opportunity to
promote their own revolutionary propaganda. By glorifying the Commune in their press, the Internationalists drove home the point to their
enemies that they recognized the inevitability of class war. In a particu-

larly inflammatory manifesto that was circulated on the streets of Madrid during June 1871, the bourgeoisie were unequivocally threatened:

> In a word: we accept the events of Paris, by which we refer to the Commune, in all of its aspects, without qualifications or exceptions of any kind; these events have demonstrated to us that if one day we [Internationalists] are dragged into the class struggle, if we have been burned, if we have been assassinated, then we shall be obliged to reduce these three extremes to one: We shall blow up the cities and with them you too.[34]

As for the threat posed by foreign Internationalists operating in Spain, it is true that several important Internationalists had crossed the border with the intent of continuing the revolutionary movement that had been set in motion by the Commune. According to one well-informed source, some prominent organizers of the Commune were prepared to ship arms to Spain with the intention of fomenting revolution.[35] The widely held belief that French Internationalists were behind strike activity also appears to have had some basis. British consulate reports of the period, for example, give detailed accounts of politically motivated strikes in which French socialists were allegedly responsible for recruiting the workers to the Internationalist cause and even supplying funds for the strikes themselves.

Of all the refugees coming from France, the most notable were the Frenchman Paul Brousse and the Cuban émigré Paul Lafargue. Brousse, who was at the time a distinguished figure in the Bakuninist wing of the International, settled in Barcelona, where he immediately set about establishing a cell of revolutionary activity, Comité de Propagande Socialiste Révolutionnaire de la France Méridional, and then publishing the radical journal *La Solidarité Révolutionnaire*. Although his primary aim seems to have been to sustain the revolutionary work in France that had begun with the Commune, he was also caught up in the affairs of the FRE. As we shall see, the close relations he cultivated with Alliancists like José García Viñas were to have an important bearing on the theoretical development of the Spanish anarchist movement during the period of the FRE's repression, 1874–1881.

The arrival of Paul Lafargue, Karl Marx's son-in-law, was also to have far-reaching effects on the fate of the FRE. As Lafargue's role in the Spanish International will be discussed later, suffice it to say that his presence in Spain at this juncture was significant for the Federals insofar as it represented a faint hope for the creation of an alliance between their party and the International. As a Marxist, Lafargue was interested in disabusing the workers of their Bakuninist-inspired antipolitical beliefs and directing them instead toward political action—a change of outlook that the Federals were also keen to see come about. But, as both Lafargue and the Federals were soon to learn, the workers' commitment to Bakuninism was deeply rooted, and consequently their hopes for a reversal in the political orientation of the workers were never realized.

On another level, the experience of the Paris Commune gave renewed stimulus to the Internationalists' feelings of antimilitarism and antipatriotism. Even before the Commune, the Madrid sections of the FRE were exhorting workers to abandon their nationalistic beliefs. Chauvinism, they argued, formed part of the ideology of the old, barbaric order.[36] In keeping with these sentiments, the socialists of Madrid held an elaborate banquet on Dos de Mayo of 1871—normally a patriotic national holiday with Francophobic overtones—that demonstrated their solidarity with the communards and recognized French-Spanish unity in the struggle against their common enemy, the bourgeoisie.

The defiance that the Internationalists showed in the face of government persecution was, in a sense, illustrative of the profound impact the Paris Commune had on the Internationalist movement in Spain. Above all, it provided a powerful impulse for the growth of the FRE. The most significant development in this respect was the identification of the International with strike action. Unlike the Federals, who were clearly reluctant to recommend strikes to the workers as a means of improving their economic position, the Internationalists were increasingly urging the use of the strike as a weapon. With respect to the working classes, this further emphasized the ideological differences that existed between the Federals and the International.

The ever-widening cleavage between the Federals and the International was also reinforced by their differing responses to the Commune itself. As we have seen, the collapse of the Commune and the subsequent repression of the communards elicited violent revolutionary rhetoric from Internationalists. Their emphasis on class war and the need for the workers to abandon their political ties with the middle classes contrasted sharply with the policies being promoted by the Federals, which were primarily aimed at persuading the workers to take an active part in politics. Underpinning the Federals' approach to the working classes was their belief that it was possible for the different classes to live in harmony with one another. As far as they were concerned, what was needed for this to come about was the granting of political and civil liberties to all, including groups like the International. But for the Internationalists, who were seeking to overthrow the existing economic and social order, this call to political participation was nothing more than another palliative being offered by the bourgeoisie.

More than any other event of the period, the Paris Commune hastened the dissolution of the tenuous bonds between the Federals and the workers under International control. The final rupture, however, did not come until the summer of 1873, when the First Republic was established and Spain was thrust into a state of intense social conflict.

CHAPTER III

The International and the Collapse of the Republic, 1871–1873

We have seen that, after having established roots in Spain, the International won a strong following among the working classes. Branches had become so numerous that by June 1870 they formed a Spanish Regional Federation and were fully recognized as sections of the IWMA.[1] Yet the peculiar way in which the International was introduced in Spain more or less determined the pattern of its early development. Guiseppe Fanelli helped to set up the first provisional groups of the IWMA there, even though he was acting as a representative of Bakunin's banned organization, the Alliance of Social Democracy. Apart from distributing the statutes of the IWMA, Fanelli left behind an assortment of Bakuninist literature—including the statutes of the Alliance—all of which were regarded by the first converts as the principal textbooks for constructing the revolutionary movement. Eventually this gave rise to a rather paradoxical situation in which the Spanish Federation and its members officially belonged to the International in spite of the fact that the organization itself was being directed by adherents of the supposedly defunct Alliance. But since the Spaniards regarded themselves as representatives of the IWMA, the labels "International" and "Internationalists" persisted throughout the 1870s and 1880s, although, after 1872, they more accurately referred to the Bakuninist wing of the international working-class movement.[2]

THE ORGANIZATION OF THE
INTERNATIONAL: THE ALLIANCE

In chapter 1 above we saw how the structural framework of the FRE conformed to Bakuninist theory. During the initial stages of the International's development in Spain, this scheme operated successfully for several reasons. Fanelli had succeeded in recruiting a substantial number of adherents to the Alliance, including such outstanding activists as Gaspar Sentiñón, Farga Pellicer, and García Viñas, all of whom were capable of effectively controlling the Federal Council.[3] In addition, as noted earlier, these men not only edited and published the chief organs of Internationalist propaganda, but they also supervised the *enseñanza integral* of workers' groups. By the time the International movement was forced underground in 1874, the initiates of the Alliance had proved themselves to be indispensable in forging its ideological and organizational framework.

Since the overall organization of the FRE was fairly flexible, especially at the base, where local and trade sections were virtually free either to unite with or remain separate from the federation, it is important to consider the components of this malleable organization that gave it coherence and direction.[4] At the heart of the FRE stood the central directive body known as the Federal Council (called the Federal Commission after 1872). This consisted of a committee of twenty-one members, who were divided into three commissions of seven individuals each: the first (*primera*) performed administrative duties, the next one (*segunda*) handled correspondence, while the third (*tercera*) and perhaps the most important commission oversaw the propagation of "Internationalist" ideology.[5]

The relationship between the Federal Council and the organization's rank and file was a curious one. The infrastructure of the FRE clearly did not allow for or encourage broad participation in policy decisions, although the workers exercised some power through the sections of local federations. Each section elected delegates who represented them at local and regional conferences. At workers' congresses, for example, these delegates voted on policy decisions and elected members to the Federal Council. And, on a local level, sections were responsible for conducting workers' affairs—such as the coordination of strike activities.

It can be inferred from Bakunin's scattered writings on the subject that members of the Alliance were supposed to control the central apparatus of the FRE in order to safeguard the development of the social revolution. Perhaps the clearest expression we have of his conception of how the Alliance was supposed to operate is in some rough drafts of a letter he wrote to Tomás Morago (a.k.a. Paulo) in May 1872. In these we find that Bakunin considered loyalty and discipline as the essential elements required to cement the framework of an effective revolutionary body. Discipline, he explained, would only be maintained if a simple rule was religiously obeyed: each group or section of groups should not admit anyone without the unanimous approval of its members. The foremost criterion by which a prospective candidate should be judged was also intimated:

> Thus, we have imposed the law of never receiving in our *sanctum, sanctorum,* in our intimate and fraternal collective, anyone ambitious or vain; as compatible as their ideas and tendencies would be with ours, as intelligent and knowledgeable they might be, and as great as their help would be with our relations and influence in the world, we should reject them. We prefer not to receive them among us, certain as we are that their ambition and vanity would eventually produce—sooner or later—the seeds of division and disorganisation.[6]

Above all, Bakunin thought that a member of the Alliance should be able to renounce his initiative to act alone, and should always be prepared to subordinate his own actions to the collective will of the group as a sign of his genuine belief in the Alliance's cause. However, Bakunin never spelled out exactly how discipline within the hierarchy would be maintained, and therefore it was vulnerable to forms of autocratic control—either by an individual or a clique.[7]

Although it is possible to establish a definite connection between Bakunin's Alliance and the International in Spain, much of the evidence substantiating their links is fragmentary, and therefore the overall picture of the history of their relationship lacks consistency. Some details of the period 1869–1872 are contained in documents from the Alliance of Social Democracy in Geneva and in extant letters from Bakunin to prominent members of his group, particularly his correspondence with the physician Gaspar Sentiñón and the engraver Tomás González Morago. These data not only provide lists of "official" members but also give us an idea as to their social background. For example, we know that the Spanish members of the Geneva section were mostly artisans and middle-class professionals.[8] From 1872 onward, the story of the Alliance becomes increasingly clouded. There are several reasons for this, but above all, it is due to the fact that the society's active involvement in the Spanish branch of the International was shrouded in secrecy.

THE MARXIST CHALLENGE TO THE ALLIANCE

By the end of 1870, the Bakuninists had established themselves as a powerful and influential force in the Spanish labor movement. Yet the rise of Marxist and reformist influences after 1872 caused Bakunin more and more to fret about the operations of the Alliance in Spain, which was now one of the last citadels of the society. In fact, for a brief time, a handful of Marxists posed a threat to the Alliance when they began agitating for its disbandment.

Up to early 1870s Marxism was unfamiliar to the Spanish working classes. The first Marxist grouping in Spain was not organized until Paul Lafargue arrived in 1871, posing as a refugee from the Paris Commune. Born in Cuba of French Creole parents, Lafargue spoke English, French, and Spanish fluently. It was primarily because of his linguistic abilities rather than his knowledge of Spanish political affairs that Lafargue had been sent by Friedrich Engels to do whatever he could to dislodge the Bakuninists from their commanding position within the FRE. Engels, who was at the time the correspondence secretary in the General Council and thus responsible for overseeing the International sections in Spain, Italy, and Portugal, was especially interested in using Lafargue as a conduit both for directing the activities of the Marxists in Spain and for gathering information about the general political situation there and about the inner workings of the Alliance in particular. To this end Lafargue served Engels well. As their correspondence reveals, Lafargue provided him with copious details of political events as they were unfolding. Within the FRE, Lafargue succeeded in attracting a loyal following among the printers of Madrid, whose most notable members included Pablo Iglesias, José Mesa, and, for a short while, Anselmo Lorenzo. Lafargue was particularly skillful at exploiting to his advantage the factional strife that already existed within the Federal Council, and he was even able to draw some key Alliancists, like Francisco Mora, into the Marxist camp. Working closely with Lorenzo and Mesa, Lafargue began using the Madrid Internationalist paper *La Emancipación* for promoting the Marxist line.

Until Lafargue's arrival, the Spaniards had been vaguely aware of but largely untouched by the Marxist-Bakuninist polemic that was irrevocably splitting the IWMA into opposing camps. Anselmo Lorenzo, who had met both Karl Marx and Friedrich Engels when he represented the FRE at the London Congress of 1871, was probably the first member of the Alliance to become fully aware of the implications of this brewing conflict. Yet he was so perplexed and disturbed by this ominous development that when he returned to Spain, he informed only a few people of what he had discovered in London. Thus, it was largely thanks to Lafargue's intervention that the workers of the FRE were introduced to the standard Marxist tracts and, more important, exposed for the first time to the theoretical issues around which the Marxist-Bakuninist controversy revolved.

Despite these impressive first efforts, the Marxists made little progress toward developing a mass following. This was due partly to the emphasis they placed on political action and partly to their inveterate opposition to Bakuninism, which inevitably estranged them from the mainstream of the FRE. From the very beginning, disputes flared up between the Bakuninist ruling factions of the FRE and the Marxists. At the Zaragoza Congress convened in April 1872, some steps were taken to patch up their differences. Under pressure from Lafargue and his cohort, the Bakuninists agreed to dissolve the Alliance, thus diffusing Lafargue's charge that the Spanish branch of the International was controlled by an illegal, secret body. But this mood of reconciliation was easily dissipated, for by the next month the Marxists were again locked in conflict with their rivals over the question of the operations of the Alliance in Spain. Now using *La Emancipación* as their principal weapon against the Bakuninists, the Marxists began vehemently denouncing the alleged intrigues of Bakunin's secret body, claiming, among other things, that Bakunin was using the Alliance as a vehicle for his plans to destroy Marxist influence in the IWMA. By the end of June, the increasingly bitter dispute between the Marxists and Bakuninists had reached the boiling point: Lafargue and his "*La Emancipación* group" were expelled from the Madrid section of the FRE. Not surprisingly, the Marxists swiftly responded by establishing in July their own section called the Nueva Federación Madrileña (New Madrid Federation), which was based on Marxist principles. From then on, the political trajectory of the Marxists was to take them along a separate path from the anarchists.[9]

The Marxist-Bakuninist conflict that dominated the affairs of the FRE during the summer of 1872 foreshadowed the much greater contest between these groups that was shortly to take place at the Hague Congress convened in September of that year. Although it is not my concern here either to investigate the nature or describe the denouement of this fateful debate, it is important for our purposes to consider how the resolution of the question of the Alliance affected the Spanish Federation.

By exposing the secret operations of the Alliance in Spain, Lafargue and his followers raised very serious doubts about the credibility of the Federal Council, especially as it was well known that it was dominated by Alliancists. At the Hague Congress, Lafargue—who was the only Marxist delegate from Spain—boldly asserted that he had been illegally ejected from the Madrid section on orders of Bakunin himself. Lafargue was, naturally, promoting the view that Marx, Engels, and their followers were hoping would win acceptance at the congress. That is to say, they sought to prove that the Alliance, which was supposedly dissolved in 1869, was still in existence and that it threatened to disrupt the proper functioning of the International. If this were true, then it followed that the other Spanish delegates—as well as anyone else who belonged to that illegitimate body—should not be admitted as official representatives of the IWMA.

The other Spanish delegates—Tomás Morago, Charles Alerini (a Frenchman who belonged to Brousse's Solidarité Révolutionnaire group in Barcelona), Farga Pellicer, and Nicolás Marselau—were visibly incensed by this charge, and Morago in particular took the floor to denounce Lafargue as a traitor. According to one eyewitness who was sympathetic to the Marxists, when Lafargue began citing "proof" of his case against the Alliance the Bakuninists reacted hysterically, "rushing wildly about, shrieking and howling interruptions."[10]

However distracted they might have appeared to be, the Spanish delegates were nonetheless alive to the fact that they were the object of political intrigues that were being orchestrated at the congress by Lafargue and the Marxists. Nicolás Marselau announced his suspicion as to why the General Council was hesitating to grant them recognition:

> The Alliance consists of devoted friends of the party, true soldiers of the revolution. I do not mind if we are expelled. This question is decided in advance. . . . Just say frankly that we are to be expelled and we shall leave and let you have the money that belongs to you. The Alliance was dissolved at Saragossa after it had done its work of propaganda and was no longer necessary. Previously it was necessary because we had no right of assembly in Spain.[11]

As the congress progressed it became increasingly evident that the Spaniards were not the primary targets on the Marxist agenda. Most of the delegates realized that the Marxists were really aiming to expel Bakunin and his leading associates of the Jura Federation in Switzerland. In the end, the Marxists were unable to prove conclusively their allegation that the Alliance was still at work. After sifting through the testimonies of both sides, "[t]he Committee of Inquiry into the Alliance" concluded that, although the Alliance had been established with rules entirely opposed to the IWMA, there was "insufficient proof of its continued existence."[12] This did not inhibit the committee from making the rather contradictory recommendation that Bakunin and his chief lieutenants, James Guillaume and Adhémar Schwitzguébel, be ousted from the International on the ground that they were active members of the Alliance. This motion was carried in the final voting at the congress, although, curiously, Schwitzguébel was not included on the list of those expelled.

At the Hague Congress, none of the Spanish delegates ever denied that he had once belonged to the Alliance. What was difficult for them to prove was whether or not they were concealing the fact of its continued existence. Although Marselau insisted that the various branches of the Alliance in Spain had been abolished at Zaragoza, this order had not been fully implemented. The fact is that all of the Spanish delegates at The Hague belonged to a select group of individuals who had not abided by the Federal Council's decision to do away with the Alliance. Perhaps in response to the Marxists' determined attempts to secure a toehold in the Federal Council, this intimate circle of Alliancists decided to use the public dissolution of the Alliance as a smoke screen for their plans to continue conducting the day-to-day operations of the FRE through their "inner" Alliance. This move was consistent with the views Bakunin expressed at the time. Writing to Morago in May 1872, he spoke of the advantages of erecting a newly constructed Alliance:

> [T]he dissolution [of the Alliance] that has taken place in some centers of Spain can be regarded in a certain way as something positive, since this allows for the reconstitution of the Alliance among us upon new foundations which would be much more serious than before.[13]

About this time, Lafargue became aware of the fact that Morago, Alerini, and Viñas had indeed reconstituted the Alliance, and he told Engels in a letter that, though he had no material proof of this, no one in Spain would ever dare to deny its existence. As it happened, Lafargue was unable to produce any concrete evidence of this "inner" society at the Hague Congress.

Given that Marselau, Morago, and the others had been brazenly hypocritical about their affiliation with the Alliance in Spain, it would seem the Marxists had sufficient cause to raise the question of its existence. Although they were right about this, it would be wrong to conclude that their entire case against the Bakuninists had been proved. For though the Alliance did exist in Spain, the society did not bear any resemblance to the nefarious organization that the Marxists depicted at The Hague. Instead of functioning as one of several conspiratorial organizations dedicated to realizing Bakunin's plans to set up a revolutionary dictatorship within the International, the Alliance, at least in Spain, was something altogether different.

While it was true that Bakunin's direct intervention during the early days of the International's development in Spain had assured the predominance of his influence in the various federations and sections of the FRE, it cannot be said that he manipulated or otherwise used the Spanish Alliance as a tool for his own subversive designs. The Spaniards eagerly received Bakunin's advice and instructions on how to go about organizing a revolutionary workers' movement, and to this end they adopted the model of his secret Alliance. At the time of *La Gloriosa* this development was understandable, not only because a sub rosa organization appeared eminently practicable in a country experiencing chronic political convulsions but also because such a *carbonario* type of society was familiar to the Spaniards, who had a long tradition of using secret societies as vehicles for furthering political causes.[14]

There is no doubt that Bakunin wanted his intimates in Spain to serve as an enlightened "general staff" of the revolutionary forces, whose task it was to act as intermediaries between the revolutionary idea and the instincts of the working classes. To achieve this, he believed it was crucial to maintain a close-knit brotherhood of radicals who operated in secrecy, not because they intended to impose their own dictatorship over the people or, for that matter, the International but because Bakunin and his followers thought that this was the only effective means of bringing about a successful general revolution within the context of a highly repressive society.[15] As we have already seen, one of the vital functions of the "brotherhood" was to preserve the ideological purity of the revolutionary movement, and this necessarily involved combating Marxism or any other doctrine that the Bakuninists deemed pernicious to the working-class movement they envisaged. This explains, for example, why Morago brought out the highly polemical *El*

Condenado once the Marxists began using *La Emancipación* to undermine Bakuninist influence in Spain. Bakunin and his adherents were no
more willing than the Marxists to give way to the challenges of their
ideological rivals. This, of course, did not mean that the Alliance was
prepared to destroy the International in order to counter Marxist influence in Spain or elsewhere—something of which they were falsely accused by the Marxists. In his *Statism and Anarchism* (1873), Bakunin
made it clear that he did not see the International and the Alliance as
being mutually exclusive:

> Sous la direction collective de l'Internationale et del l'Alliance des révolu-
> tionnaires socialistes, il rassemble et organise ses forces et s'apprête a fonder,
> sur les ruines de l'Etat et du monde bourgeois en décomposition, la société de
> l'homme-travailleur émancipe.[16]

If it was at all possible, Bakunin wanted instead to reduce the
Marxist-controlled London Council to a bureau for correspondence
and statistics, in order to give complete autonomy to the various sections and federations belonging to the International. In this way, the
Alliance would have been able to continue operating as an independent
body within the International movement. Whether or not this would
have provided Bakunin with the long-awaited opportunity to use his
internationally based Alliance to exercise an "invisible" collective dictatorship over the forces of revolution in Europe cannot be said with any
certainty. From what we know about the Alliance in Spain, the largest
such branch of the society, we can safely say that Bakunin was never in
a position to exercise such a dictatorship. As we shall see, the Spanish
Alliance survived Bakunin, who died in 1876, yet with few exceptions it
continued to function in much the same way as it had done during
Bakunin's lifetime.[17]

Meanwhile, in the aftermath of the congresses at The Hague and
Saint-Imier, the Alliance was attempting to tighten its control over the
Federal Council. This was becoming increasingly difficult to achieve for
several reasons. At the Saragossa Congress the secretive nature of the
Alliance had enabled it to diffuse the criticisms of its adversaries; but in
the months that followed the Alliance faced much more formidable
obstacles in its campaign to transform the FRE into a power capable of
destroying the ruling classes.

A former member of the Alliance, Anselmo Lorenzo, has suggested
one reason why the society had failed to convert the working masses

into an "invincible power." He thought it was because the Alliance had "forged an organization that was like a perfect mechanism, which did not approximate to the mentality nor the customs of the Spanish workers in general."[18] According to this view, the complex principles embodied in the Alliance program could not be transformed into action in a country where there had been virtually no experience of massive organized struggle of the working classes. However, the greatest single obstacle to the success of the Alliance and the International movement was the government. Beginning in 1871, the provisional government resolved to treat the threat of the International as a problem of public order. By November, the organization had been banned by the Cortes, and consequently a pattern had begun which was to characterize the history of the International movement: periods of repression by the authorities alternated with periods of toleration. Although brief spells of government persecution did not seriously handicap its development, sustained suppression produced dramatic effects. This was especially true after 1874, when the FRE was forced underground for seven years. Within three years the number of local federations affiliated with the International dropped precipitously, from approximately 320 to 73.[19] The decimation of the FRE undoubtedly affected the ability of the Alliance to perform its role in the revolutionary process. While the society itself needed very few members—serving, as Bakunin phrased it, as "a sort of revolutionary general staff" in the army of the "Revolution"— the real power of the Alliance turned on the numerical strength of workers at its command.[20]

Following the Zaragoza Congress, the Alliance in Spain became increasingly isolated from branches in the rest of Europe. Inspiration from them was not forthcoming inasmuch as by this time Bakunin had more or less retired as an active revolutionist, and, apart from a handful of despondent adherents in Geneva, the society had no other objective existence. Nevertheless, in contrast to other countries, in Spain this fact alone did not seriously threaten the survival of the Alliance. Even the bitter dispute between the Marxists and Bakuninists there had not succeeded in seriously disrupting its covert operations. For at the Córdoba Congress in January 1873, the basic body of doctrine of the Spanish International organization, anarchism, remained sacrosanct, and, perhaps more significant, its governing sections stayed in the hands of Alliancists or ex-Alliance members. At this time, however, the activities of the Alliance and the International movement were interrupted by other forces. For they now suffered the consequences of an intense government campaign to restore order in Spain.

THE INTERNATIONAL'S RESPONSE TO CANTONALISM

From the September Revolution in 1868 onward, Spain had been plagued with internal disorders of one form or another. In the northern provinces of Aragón, Navarre, and Catalonia, the Carlist movement was rapidly gaining momentum. In 1870 the Carlists declared war on the Spanish government, a conflict that was to last for another six years. By 1873 the Federal Republican movement had also come to a head. In February, Amadeo of Savoy, the Italian aristocrat who had been elected king on 16 November 1870, resigned from the throne and fled the country. The Federals immediately seized the opportunity and proclaimed the establishment of a republic. But the new form of government only made matters worse; for it appeared to give impetus to the Carlist struggle and the various separatist movements in the provinces (such as Catalonia). The government's inability to check these rapidly deteriorating political conditions gave rise to numerous regional, or cantonal, rebellions, which were to last throughout the year.

By 1872 the International in Spain had grown powerful enough to assert itself as an independent political force. Yet it is clear that the leaders of the FRE entertained only a slender hope of spearheading a successful social revolution. This is partly borne out by the policy the International adopted at the Córdoba Congress in December 1872. At this, the Federal Commission, by refusing to spell out any program of action, failed to assume the responsibility of leadership in the event of massive social disturbances. Then, following the proclamation of the Republic on 11 February 1873, the Federal Commission reiterated its laissez faire policy, which effectively gave to the local federations a free hand in determining their own role during a social revolt.[21] As we shall now see, the Federal Commission's reluctance to define the role the International should play in a revolutionary situation, and the continuing threat of repression during the summer of 1873, revealed just how far the Internationalists were from realizing their goal of social revolution.

Ever since 1872, the International had been proscribed in Spain. Yet it was not until the cantonalist revolts during the summer of 1873 that central and regional authorities resolved to repress systematically the

FRE, thus forcing the organization to remain underground. The first severe blow dealt in this campaign was at Alcoy—a small town between Alicante and Valencia that was known for its textile and paper industries. By 1873 Alcoy had also become a center for the International's activities. A growing number of the town's sizable working class was joining the organization, and in addition, it was now the seat of the Federal Commission of the FRE. After a year of agitating for a reduction of the work day and an increase in workers' wages, Internationalists had convinced the majority of the factory workers that collective action against their employers was necessary in order to secure their demands. The ever-mounting tension between the two groups culminated in July when the paper workers, who were under the direction of the Federal Commission, called a strike of solidarity among the workers of different professions.

On 8 July, the Federal Commission hastily convoked an assembly at which the principal reason for calling a general strike was announced: "The sad and miserable situation in which the workers of Alcoy find themselves and their just desire to improve their own living conditions."[22] And, despite some dissension, most of the five or six thousand workers in attendance were in favor of the motion.

Within hours after the strike began, attempts were made to extend it to the neighboring towns of Enguera, Anna, and Xativa. Next, a deputation of strikers asked the republican mayor, Agustín Albors, to arbitrate in their negotiations with the factory owners. Alarmed by the overwhelming number of workers out on strike, Albors sent to Alicante for troops and then told the workers that he refused to recognize their form of protest. According to Internationalist sources he issued a proclamation that "insulted and slandered the workers and sided with the manufacturers, thus destroying the rights and the freedom of the strikers and challenging them to fight."

The following morning, a large crowd of angry demonstrators gathered round the town hall. As the mood of the agitators grew more and more restless, the municipal guards assumed strategic positions among the buildings surrounding the town plaza. Then, after Albors gave the signal, the guards began shooting into the crowd, killing one worker and wounding several others.

The temerity with which Albors set about dealing with the hostile strikers sparked off a melee, which spread quickly throughout the town. The riot continued for the next twenty hours, during which buildings were burned and about twenty people were killed, including the mayor himself. On 10 July, the workers emerged victorious, and, for a brief time, the Internationalist Junta controlled Alcoy.

That the uprising had not been carefully planned by the IWMA was reflected in the fact that, after having seized power, the Federal Commission did not seem to have a clear idea as to what it should do next. It is not surprising that rumors of retaliation from an approaching army dampened its resolve to continue ruling any longer. Fearing the worst, members of the Committee resigned and then fled to Madrid, leaving the now-leaderless Junta to collapse of its own accord.[23]

The events at Alcoy created an enormous stir not only in Spain but in other countries as well. Various leading newspapers, such as *The Times* (London), *Le Soir* (Paris), and *El Imparcial* (Madrid), circulated sensational tales, describing in graphic detail atrocities supposedly committed by the Internationalists. According to some of these, priests and monks had been publicly hanged, women violated, and, in a final act of defiance, the heads of victims cut off and paraded on pikes through the streets. Just how accurate these reports were is impossible to say. For their part, the Internationalists denied that they played any role in the excesses of the revolt. Most of the details of the Alcoy insurrection were not based on incontrovertible evidence, and in this respect these reports resembled the apocryphal stories that had issued from the Paris Commune in 1871. In both cases, the press had generated a climate of hysteria about the International by reporting exaggerated accounts of the events.

The immediate upshot of the Alcoy insurrection was that it gave the International a widespread reputation as a formidable threat to public order. In fact, though, it was hardly the menace that the bourgeois press made it out to be. In determining the part the International played in the cantonalist movement between 1873 and 1874, it must be borne in mind that although the International had acquired notoriety as a result of its insurrectional activities, the organization itself had in fact played a minor role in the cantonalist disturbances. Of all the risings that took place during the summer of 1873, the International was responsible for only two significant rebellions: the risings at Alcoy and at San Lucár de Barrameda. Thus, compared to the insurgent wing of the Federal movement, the Internationalists' newly acquired reputation as an independent revolutionary force was merely a fiction. The failure of the International to instigate a successful uprising in Barcelona illustrates just how impotent it was to direct a general social revolution.

Ever since 1871, Barcelona had been a significant base of operations for the International. This was especially apparent following the Paris Commune, when French anarchists like Brousse and Alerini took up residence there, and again after the proclamation of the Republic in February 1873. Throughout this time the International energetically promoted a wide-ranging revolutionary propaganda program that included infiltrating the militia and exploiting the antimilitaristic feelings that were already running high in the region. Their proselytizing efforts peaked in the summer of 1873, when a group of Barcelona Internationalists decided that the time was ripe for the workers to revolt. At the beginning of June, several Internationalists, including García Viñas and the French agitators, Alerini and Brousse, hoped to set a rebellion in motion by calling a general strike:

> Workers! We are calling a general strike to show the profound abhorrence we feel on seeing the government using the army to fight our brother workers, while neglecting the struggle against the Carlists.[24]

But, from the outset, it was evident that the workers were largely indifferent to the Internationalists' pleas for revolutionary strikes. Upon finding themselves without any support from the masses they were supposedly leading, the strike committee quickly disbanded. The news of the Alcoy rising a month later, coupled with a Carlist victory at Alpers in Catalonia, could not provoke the Barcelona Internationalists to take further action. In view of this, perhaps Friedrich Engels was correct to conclude that "Barcelona was the only town whose participation [in the cantonalist movement] could have provided firm support for the working-class element."[25] Thus, the failure of the Internationalists in Barcelona effectively meant that there could be no general revolutionary movement in Spain.

THE FALL OF THE REPUBLIC

To understand the ultimate ramifications of the failed cantonalist revolts we must examine briefly the sequence of events that led to the demise of the Republic. One of the most dramatic consequences of the events of Alcoy was that it served as an impetus for the Intransigents' successful rising at Cartagena. The coup itself dealt a severe blow to the already shaky administration of Pi y Margall, whose intractable belief in a policy of conciliation isolated him from both the right and left wings of the government. Unable to respond effectively to the crisis created by the Cartagenan coup, Pi was forced on 18 July to resign as president. His immediate successor, Nicolás Salmerón, immediately set about the business of restoring public order, leaving little doubt in the minds of political observers that the political pendulum had indeed begun to swing to the right. Facing a rising tide of regional discontent, Salmerón did not hesitate to call in the army to subdue the insurgents. By mid-September nearly all the cantons either had collapsed or had been crushed by military force, including those at Castellos, Almemsa, San Lucár de Barrameda, and Salamanca. Only the canton established at Cartagena, a Federal citadel and last refuge for the cantonalist leaders, could not be easily subjugated by the army. It held out for nearly four months before finally succumbing to General Manuel Pavía's troops.

Salmerón's repressive policies soon alienated him from the left in the Cortes, but his fear of excessive militarism—that is, giving the army too much power—lost him the support of the right. He was replaced in September by Emilio Castelar, who was not afraid to use the full might of the army to restore public order.[26] The drift further to the right was reflected in Castelar's policies: the Cortes was prorogued, constitutional rights were suspended, and the army was once again in ascendency. By December, Castelar's actions, like those of his predecessors, had so divided the Republicans that it was notorious that his government would have to resign. This left the door open for the army, which, thanks to Castelar, was now in a position to step in and assume power. On 3 January 1874 the captain general of Madrid, General Pavía, and his troops forcibly dissolved the Cortes, sounding the death knell of the Republic. Except for the Carlist problem in the north, the army was now in virtual control of the government. The fate of the International was sealed, for now nothing prevented the army from eliminating all traces of the FRE. Only in Barcelona, perhaps the last holdout of International activity, was there any sign of resistance. A general lockout was declared by the International on 7 January, and barricades were even erected at some suburban factories. By the ninth, however, this revolutionary impulse evaporated when the captain general of Barcelona ordered the military governor to dissolve the International.[27]

The most pressing question facing the FRE was whether it should interpret the new situation as yet another brief spell of repression like that of 1872, or whether they should regard it as a permanent state of affairs until the revolutionary movement finally triumphed. At first, some groups adopted a militant posture. For example, in a report to the Federal Commission, the International representative from Paterna de la Ribera reported the defiant attitude that his federation had adopted in face of government repression:

> The Internationalists of this locality are also ruthlessly persecuted by the authorities of the Federal Republic, and so cowardly are these vagrants of the dictator Castelar that it takes a group of fifty-five of them to break into the home of one worker. This serves to fortify the revolutionary socialist spirit of the workers of Paterna, the majority of whom are still disillusioned with the politics of the bourgeoisie.[28]

Also initially undaunted by the government's resolve to break the back of the International movement was the Federal Commission, which even laid plans to hold an antiauthoritarian congress in Barcelona in 1875. This kind of inflated optimism, however, soon gave way to a hard realism. In June 1874, the Federal Commission hastily contrived to salvage what it could of the FRE by reorganizing it along the lines of loosely federated districts (corresponding to nine general regions, or *comarcales,* in Spain), and this decision was far more revealing of the true position the Internationalists held at this juncture. Facing the threat of possible extinction—for the army fully intended to stamp out for good the revolutionary cells—the Internationalists had little choice as to what they were to do next. Thus, despite the fortitude shown by federations like those in Paterna de la Ribera and many others, the Internationalists could not escape the bleak reality of the situation: they were now forced to turn to a life of clandestinity.

CHAPTER IV

The Spanish Federation in the Period of Repression, 1874–1881

Up to the time of Pavía's *pronunciamiento,* when the FRE was forced underground, the principal weapons of the International had been the strike and the act of revolt. While both tactics had provided impetus for the growth of the International movement in Spain, they were to prove themselves completely unrealistic during the period of repression between 1874 and 1881. Throughout this time, the FRE sustained its commitment to the doctrine of anarchism. But because the praxis of anarchism demanded a revolutionary agenda, the most vexing problem facing the leaders of the FRE was to determine which tactics should be employed in the daily struggle now that the movement was obliged to operate in a circumscribed environment.

In the early days of the International, direct action in the form of strikes was the preferred means of pursuing the FRE's revolutionary strategy. Indeed, between 1871 and 1873, a sharp increase in the number of strikes in Spain seemed to suggest that the workers were responsive to the International's call for economic warfare. Between 1870 and 1873, for instance, an estimated 20,000 workers had participated in some 216 strikes, with the greatest percentage of these occuring in the summer of 1872.[1]

For its part, the Federal Commission of the FRE encouraged the federations to confine their action to "scientific strikes." Unlike reformist or other types of strikes, these were supposed to be calculated in a "scientific manner." Drawing upon statistics and other information garnered by the local federations, the Federal Commission was expected to determine with "an infallible mathematical certainty" the most propitious moment to call a strike. Most important, it was commonly believed within the FRE that, by possessing a knowledge of statistics, it was possible to control the fate of the revolution:

> The federal regional Council holds in its hands, with these Statistics the movement. . . . The Statistics thus accomplished and published for the wellbeing of individuals and for the fulfillment of all duties, is the social Liquidation, put in practice from the very first day; it is the revolution (made) accomplished by merely trying to carry it out.[2]

For all the faith they invested in "scientific" strikes, the Internationalists rarely staged any of these during the early 1870s. Not only were statistics difficult to obtain, but, as we have already seen, the FRE lacked the strength and influence required to employ such a sophisticated tactic. The fact is that the strike pattern of the workers did not move in the direction urged by the Internationalists. Instead, most strikes of the early 1870s were basically of two types: dignity strikes, in which the workers' relations with their employers (e.g., the way they were treated) were at issue, and *huelgas parciales,* that is, strikes solely aimed at improving working conditions. Thus, while it is true that the International was to some degree responsible for radicalizing organized labor as well as promoting strikes, the evidence suggests that most of the strikes in these years were probably inspired by economic opportunism rather than the revolutionary rhetoric of the International.

This was in no small way due to the fact that the concept of the strike lacked precision. At the time, a variety of expressions were being used to characterize strikes. Even the FRE itself subscribed to different views regarding the tactical objectives of strikes. On one hand, the Federal Commission defined them as the worker's "principal weapon of defense" against capitalist exploitation:

> We accept struggle whenever we are provoked, and, if today we choose not to provoke strikes, remaining in a defensive position, at the same time we will not permit sections to accept reduced wages, nor increased hours without increased wages, nor blacklisting because of membership in the International.[3]

On the other hand, some Internationalists also regarded the strike as an offensive weapon, and because of this, they refrained from advocating strikes that they thought were not conducive to the revolutionary process. The Internationalists' attitude toward the strike tactic inevitably shifted in the light of the changing political and social circumstances, and thus different conceptions of the strike developed at this time.

The mood of insurrectionism that flowed from the political turmoil of the early 1870s was, despite the severity of government repression, hard to dispel. In a sense, its persistence showed how much the Internationalists overestimated their own strength as well as the revolutionary potential of the masses. As the prospects for an imminent social revolution diminished, the leaders of the FRE saw the need to revise their revolutionary strategy and tactics. To be most effective, for example, strikes and similar forms of economic action required a functioning trade union apparatus, something which obviously could not exist as long as the FRE organization remained suppressed. For many Spanish Internationalists, the emergence of the tactic known as "propaganda by the deed" during the late 1870s was the answer to their dilemma. Above all, it was a form of direct action that did not rely on trade union activity, and that seemed in the circumstances to be the only realistic means of pursuing the revolutionary aims of the movement.

Both the introduction of "propaganda by the deed" and the strike question had an important bearing on the development of anarchist strategy and tactics during the seven years of repression (1874–1881). To understand why this was so, it is necessary to turn to a discussion of how these concepts were then evolving both within and outside of the Spanish arena.

THE FIRST INTERNATIONAL AND THE STRIKE QUESTION

We noted earlier that, during the late 1860s, there was a marked increase in strike activity in a number of European countries. Although the International was directly responsible for very few of these, it is true that the organization encouraged the growth of strikes not only through its propaganda but also through the financial aid it provided to striking workers. And, insofar as strikes seemed to attract new recruits to the organization, the IWMA benefited from the intensified labor unrest of the period. Against this background, it was natural that the strike question became increasingly important.

Throughout this time the concept of the strike itself was continuously undergoing modifications. The formation of the First International in 1864 made it possible for the first time for the trade unions of different countries to consider using strikes in a variety of ways, not least being the staging of "general strikes" on a massive scale. Nonetheless, what precisely the "general strike" entailed on a practical level and what it was meant to achieve in the working-class movement was subject to different interpretations.

Early attempts to give coherence to the idea of the strike tactic only served to provoke controversy. This happened at the Third Congress of the International, held in Brussels in September 1868, where the question of strikes was vigorously debated. As noted earlier, around this time the strategy of direct action was beginning to challenge traditional forms of working-class activity, such as cooperativism. Yet there were still many delegates, like the French mutualists, who refused to incorporate strikes into their working-class program. This group objected to strikes partly because they believed them to be disruptive for the workers but above all because they adhered to the view that society's ills could be cured through class reconciliation as opposed to class conflict.[4] Trade unionists like the Belgian César de Paepe, however, argued that the strike tactic was the only effective weapon that could be utilized against the increasingly powerful industries of capitalism. De Paepe, who was the leading spokesman for the syndicalist wing, also introduced a resolution calling for the general strike to be used as a means of opposing war, thus adding a political dimension to the concept. Even though this motion passed, the broader question regarding strikes and particularly the general strike was not fully resolved:

> Strikes are not a means to the complete emancipation of the working-classes, but are frequently a necessity in the actual situation of the struggle between capital and labour. . . . The unions of all trades and countries must combine. In each local federation of trade societies a fund destined to support strikes ought to be established.[5]

These differing perspectives reflected some of the fundamental ideological cleavages that existed within the International. For the Marxists, who interpreted society in terms of class conflict, strikes were significant manifestations of the social and economic warfare indigenous to capitalist society. On a practical level, they advocated using strikes as vehicles for obtaining workers' rights and demands in the daily struggle. But, significantly, they drew a clear distinction between the "economic" and "political" aspects of strikes. Marx differentiated between these in the following way:

> [A]n attempt in a particular factory or in a particular trade to force shorter working hours on individual capitalists through strikes, etc., is a purely economic movement; on the other hand, a movement to compel the enactment of an eight-hour law, etc., is a political movement. And in this way, out

of the workers' separate economic movements there grows everywhere a *political* movement, that is, a movement of the *class,* aiming to effect its interest in a general form.[6]

It therefore followed that, as important as strikes were in the revolutionary struggle, they were not, as far as the Marxists were concerned, to be employed as the principal means of emancipating the working classes. Instead, they maintained that the only way the proletariat could ultimately overthrow the ruling classes would be by conquering political power.

The anarchists' attitude toward strikes was more complicated than this, not least because the libertarian wing of the International movement was divided into prostrike and antistrike factions. Until 1868, the strongest and most vociferous opposition to the Marxists in the First International had come from the *mutuellistes,* better known as the Proudhonists. When their influence began waning, the Bakuninists (or "collectivists") replaced them as the principal rivals of the Marxists. At this time, the debate on strikes was again revived, but the conflict now revolved around different issues. While it was true that the Proudhonists and Bakuninists shared fundamental ideological beliefs, such as their antistatism and aversion to politics, there were important differences in their respective outlooks. In contrast to their predecessors, for instance, the Bakuninists endorsed the concept of class struggle, and consequently, they concurred with the Marxian view that strikes were powerful weapons in the workers' economic war against the bourgeoisie. Where the Bakuninists departed from the Marxists was in their belief that, without resorting to politics, the workers could use strikes alone to create the preconditions for a general revolution.[7] Bakunin himself viewed individual strikes as the building blocks of what he called the general or insurrectionary strike:

> Strikes awaken in the masses all the social-revolutionary instincts. . . . Every strike is more valuable in that it broadens and deepens to an ever greater extent the gulf now separating the bourgeois class from the masses of the people. . . . When strikes begin to grow in scope and intensity, spreading from one place to another, it means that events are ripening for a general strike, and a general strike coming off at the present time, now that the proletariat is deeply permeated with the ideas of emancipation, can only lead to a great cataclysm, which will regenerate society.[8]

This passage illustrates that Bakunin attached far more importance to strike action than his ideological foes were prepared to do. In fact, the chasm separating the Bakuninists from the Marxists on this point could not be bridged. The former abjured all forms of political action, and therefore maintained that it was essential for the proletariat to ignore all local and national politics so that the labor agitation of every country could be imbued with an exclusively economic character.[9]

After they formally broke with the Marxists at the Hague Congress of 1872 and the seat of the IWMA was transferred to New York, the Bakuninists joined forces with other anti-Marxist elements in order to salvage the remnants of the International movement in Europe. Shortly after the Hague Congress, these groups met in Switzerland and formed what came to be known as the "Antiauthoritarian" International, which continued to hold congresses until 1877. Interestingly, the debate on strikes resumed at these meetings, albeit for different reasons. At the Geneva Congress of the Antiauthoritarian International held in September 1873, the general strike was suggested as a nonpolitical tactic to be used in overthrowing capitalism. Yet from nearly every quarter there was growing pessimism regarding the efficacy of strikes of all types. Only the pure syndicalists and individuals like the Spanish representative, Rafael Farga Pellicer, remained optimistic about the potential of the general strike. (Farga's enthusiasm was doubtless colored by the state of tumult in his country, for he predicted that in Spain the time was drawing near when the working men in the large towns would rise en masse to bring about the triumph of anarchy.)[10]

It was over the issue of strikes that the antiauthoritarians began splitting up into distinct factions. In one camp were the "syndicalists," comprising both anarchists and pure syndicalists, who followed the founders of the IWMA in believing that the key to the emancipation of the proletariat lay in the development of trade unions. Furthermore, strikes were viewed as an important indicator of working-class strength and solidarity. For them, the growth of labor federations went hand in hand with the general strike tactic. Once the unions were strong enough to wield their own economic power, the belief was that a general strike could be called to bring about the collapse of the capitalist system.

Opposing this faction was an ultrarevolutionary group composed exclusively of anarchists. Beginning in 1876, they increasingly challenged the dominance of the syndicalist elements in the Antiauthoritarian International. The radicalism of this tendency was undoubtedly fed by the rapidly changing economic climate of the latter part of the 1870s. The rise of unemployment throughout Europe at this time, the inroads made by the Marxists and reformist socialists into workers' groups, and the inevitable persecution of radical labor organizations—especially following the Paris Commune—had profoundly affected the position anarchism held within the European labor movement. In view of this, the anarchist militants argued that syndicalist action alone was a grossly inadequate means of workers' resistance when compared to the forces opposing it.

From a practical standpoint, then, the militants were seeking ways of broadening their field of revolutionary activity. Under the leadership of the syndicalists, this had been confined to the economic struggle, or, as the socialist maxim had it, the conflict between capital and labor. Two of the leading figures of the militant tendency, the Frenchman Paul Brousse and the Spaniard José García Viñas, were particularly hostile toward the strike tactic. They argued that as strikes were the chief weapons of reformist groups, they tended to foster the development of a "trade union" attitude among the rank and file. As a result, workers mostly struck for economic demands, where pay, hours of work, and working conditions were at issue, and not the crucial question of an out-and-out revolution. They warned that, without the proper revolutionary indoctrination, the workers' movement was in danger of waxing complacent (i.e., antirevolutionary). At the Berne Congress of 1876 Viñas, using the nom de guerre "Antonio Sánchez," explained his faction's position on reformist strikes:

> Notwithstanding the oppression of the dictatorship, the Spanish workers have carried through several important strikes. . . . The coopers' strike and the dyers' strike cost the unions more than 50,000 duros (about 10,000 pounds); if this sum had been devoted to the development of revolutionary organisation, great and fruitful results might have been secured. The Barcelona stonemasons were able to get their working day reduced to seven hours. Still, the down-tools spirit is loosing ground in proportion as the revolutionary spirit gains headway.[11]

The point Viñas was driving at here was that, instead of exhausting the revolutionary élan of the workers on strike activity, the vanguard elements preferred to channel the proletariats' energies into acts of revolt. In order to accomplish this, it was necessary to give primacy to revolutionary propaganda, for this was the catalyst that was to animate the insurrectionary movement. Their argument closely followed Bakunin's prescription for revolution. According to this, alongside the economic struggle there was to take place an active campaign of propaganda:

> The International will continue to propagandize its principles, because these principles, being the purest expression of the collective interests of the workers of the whole world, are the soul and living, dynamic power of our

association. It will spread its propaganda without regard for the suscepti-
bilities of the bourgeoisie, so that every worker, emerging from the intellectual and moral torpor in which he has been kept, will understand his situation and know what he wants and what to do, and under what conditions he
can obtain his rights as a man.[12]

Even though this faction was highly critical of strike activity, it
would be misleading to suggest that they denied the usefulness of some
strikes, especially those which fomented social unrest. Yet they never
quite visualized how revolutionary acts could be successfully combined
with strike action. In fact, this synthesis was only achieved at the turn of
the century with the advent of revolutionary syndicalism.

The differences between the syndicalist group on the one side and the
militant one on the other were never wholly resolved. In any case, their
dispute was eventually overshadowed by the introduction of "propaganda by the deed," a tactic that was to have more far-reaching implications for the international anarchist movement than strikes.

THE DEBATE ON STRIKES: THE SPANISH CONTEXT

In the wake of the cantonalist risings that erupted during the summer
of 1873, the idea of staging both economic strikes and the revolutionary
general strike was increasingly coming under attack by Viñas and other
key figures of the FRE. The events of Alcoy, for instance, had illustrated
graphically that even an insurrectionary strike could easily get out of
hand and turn into an uncontrollable rebellion. Perhaps in view of this,
Tomás Morago wrote an article in the International paper *El Condenado* in which he cautioned that the general strike needed "a long
period of preparation and of propaganda that would have to precede it,
the latter being the fundamental task of the movement at hand."[13]

Indeed, in Spain it was becoming more and more difficult to stage
almost any type of strike, let alone the general strike. The FRE not only
lacked a sufficiently strong national or regional network linking the
different unions that could provide the economic support (in the form of
strike funds) needed during a long-term strike but was also encumbered
with a bureaucracy that made it extremely difficult to implement such a
tactic. Anselmo Lorenzo, who served as a member of the Federal Commission at this time, has described the labyrinthine system of regulations
and procedures that the Federal Commission imposed on the respective

sections of the International, making it virtually impossible for a strike movement to occur. Among other things, each *oficio* (craft union) was obliged to submit a list of its strike objectives to the local commission. Then, even if it was approved on this level, the strike could not be called until it was also sanctioned by the regional and national commissions— a process that might take up to eight weeks or more to complete.[14] Given these restrictive conditions, any attempt to enlarge the scope of a planned strike movement had little chance of succeeding.

It has been suggested that the Federal Commission insisted on pursuing such a strict policy toward strikes at this time simply because it wanted to prevent them from occurring at all. After all, the Federal Commission, which was doubtless aware of its limited ability to exercise control over strikes, knew that if it encouraged this form of action the workers might be inclined to employ the strike weapon indiscriminately.[15] This would not only prematurely exhaust their revolutionary strength but also provoke the authorities further to suppress the FRE.

At the Fourth Congress of the FRE—held secretly in Madrid in June 1874—the question of whether or not strikes should remain in the workers' revolutionary arsenal remained open. Nevertheless, the final resolutions approved at the meeting reflected the growing influence of the antistrike faction:

> The Congress, without rejecting completely the general strike tactic as a pacific method of ultimately changing society, advises the workers to undertake an open and decidedly revolutionary path, conserving all their revolutionary strengths in order to prepare and organize for the great International Social Revolution that must overthrow the current iniquitous system, planting in its ruins the principles of Equality and Justice by means of our own strengths. . . . The Congress resolves: That, insofar as it is possible, the number of partial strikes [*huelgas parciales*] should be reduced in number . . . that these are limited only to instances in which this method or tactic is necessary.[16]

REPRESSION AND THE EMERGENCE OF "PROPAGANDA BY THE DEED"

The origins of the expression "propaganda by the deed" are rather obscure. The concept was first seriously considered as a possible tactic to be adopted by the anarchists as early as 1876. In the course of the next few years the idea was frequently discussed by anarchists everywhere but particularly by the cadre of anarchist thinkers associated with the Jura Federation in Switzerland. During the late 1860s and early

1870s, the Jura became the geographical center of the Bakuninist wing of the International. This fact, combined with the relatively relaxed attitude of the Swiss government toward the presence of foreign political agitators, made the Jura an ideal place for anarchists and other political exiles to congregate. According to the Russian anarchist Peter Kropotkin, who after Bakunin's death in 1876 emerged as the leading international anarchist personality of his day, the Jura Federation counted among its adherents such anarchist luminaries as James Guillaume, Adhémar Schwitzguébel, Elisée Reclus, Carlo Cafiero, Errico Malatesta, and Severino Albarracín. The Austrian historian Max Nettlau has suggested that this circle was an informal continuation of Bakunin's Alliance:

> Prior to their trip to Belgium and La Chaux-de-Fonds (Jura), the members of the International Alliance and Kropotkin had agreed to reorganize their "revolutionary intimacy," the old brotherhood of 1864. Kropotkin was appointed its correspondence secretary, and it was agreed that each country would enjoy autonomy as to tactics, and that members would correspond regularly with each other; and that the secretary send letters that passed from one member to the other with each adding his opinion.[17]

"Our main activity," wrote Kropotkin in his memoirs, "was in working out the practical and theoretic aspects of anarchist socialism, and in this direction the federation has undoubtedly accomplished something that will last."[18] From 1876 onward, the theoretical question that occupied a great deal of the federation's time was that connected with the concept of "propaganda by the deed":

> We knew that a tedious propaganda and a long succession of struggles, of individual and collective revolts against the now prevailing forms of property-holding, of individual sacrifice, of partial attempts at reconstruction and partial revolutions, would have to be lived through, before the current ideas upon private ownership would be modified. . . . Long years of propaganda and a long succession of partial acts of revolt against authority, as well as a complete revision of the teachings now derived from history . . .[19]

At the Berne Congress of 1876, the issue of propaganda by the deed was brought up by a group of militants who felt that it was necessary to adopt such measures in order to breathe life into a rapidly degenerating revolutionary movement. There Errico Malatesta and Carlo Cafiero announced the policy their federation was adopting:

> The Italian Federation believes that the insurrectionary deed, destined to affirm socialist principles by acts, is the most effective means of propaganda

and the only one which, without corrupting and deceiving the mass, penetrates to the deepest social stratum and attracts the living forces of humanity in the struggle that upholds the International.[20]

The new tactic that the militants were advocating was primarily aimed at forging links between anarchist groups and workers' organizations. Up to now, anarchism had failed to make headway among the industrial working classes of Europe. And, except in Spain and Italy, where anarchism appealed to a cross section of industrial and agricultural laborers, its influence was confined to artisans engaged in small, locally based industries—such as the watchmakers of the Jura. The proponents of propaganda by the deed believed that if anarchism were to establish a secure footing among the working classes, the doctrine would have to be introduced by utilizing a variety of methods, including shocking the workers from their supposed "aesthesized" condition.[21]

Propaganda by the deed made its first real impact on the anti-authoritarian movement following several widely popularized episodes involving noted anarchist figures. One such event, the Benevento affair of April 1877, was actually the first planned attempt at anarchist insurrection on a large scale. In brief, this plan, as conceived by Malatesta, Cafiero, and their Russian comrade, Sergei Kravchinskii (a.k.a. Stepniak), was aimed at provoking the masses to rebel against the authorities through a series of guerrilla-like operations. The conspirators selected the Matese mountain range—a particularly rugged group of mountains which provided an ideal place for insurgent activity—for their campaign. At first their "planned" revolts achieved the desired results. In the hamlet of Lentino the insurrectionists succeeded not only in sacking the local public record office containing deeds of property holdings and the like but also in inciting the villagers to make common cause with their mission. Subsequent attempts to enlarge the rebellion, however, were soon thwarted by government troops. The authorities eventually rounded up most of the conspirators involved in the insurrectionary plot, and all of them were arrested.[22]

Despite the fact that the Benevento affair had ended disastrously for the anarchists, it served as an impetus for the acceptance of the tactic. In the following months several articles on the subject appeared in the Jura *Bulletin,* and it was soon apparent that propaganda by the deed was well on its way to becoming a part of anarchist orthodoxy. Paul Brousse, the head of the French émigré group of anarchists who had sought refuge in Barcelona following the demise of the Paris Commune and who later edited the Berne libertarian paper *Arbeiterzeitung* between 1876–1877, was especially enthusiastic about the new tactic, and he soon became the leading exponent of propaganda by the deed in the Jura. Brousse's views on the subject went beyond those held by the Italians Malatesta, Cafiero, and Emilio Covelli, who envisaged propaganda by the deed simply as an act of popular revolt. Although Brousse shared with his Italian comrades the belief that propaganda by the deed was linked conceptually to the Bakuninist notion that rebellious instincts were latent in everyone and that they needed only to be "awakened" through examples of revolutionary acts such as violent deeds against authority, he also felt that the tactic should entail more than just demonstrating to the people how to go about staging large-scale social revolts. He thought that revolutionary deeds should cover a wide spectrum of activities, ranging from attacking one's oppressor to inculcating workers with anarchist values. Most important, this interpretation suggested that propaganda by the deed could be employed not only by small bands of conspirators but by individuals as well.

Beginning in 1878 a series of terrorist acts, or *attentats,* took place which, although not inspired by the tactic of propaganda by the deed, were nonetheless identified as such in the public mind. Within a three-year period, Vera Zasulich wounded General Trepov, the infamous chief of police of St. Petersburg, Russia; Max Hoedel and then Karl Nobiling attempted to assassinate Kaiser Wilhelm I; Juan Oliva y Moncasi fired several shots at Alfonso XII; and Giovanni Passanante tried to kill King Umberto of Italy.[23] Whatever their true origins may have been, these acts inevitably aroused public sentiment against the anarchists and gave rise to the widespread belief that anarchists were plotting their disruptive tactics on an international scale. Within the anarchist movement itself, the tactic of regicide stirred debate, especially among theoreticians like Brousse who were attempting the rather difficult task of analysing the practice of propaganda by the deed before it had fully crystallized. Radical journals, like *L'Avant-Garde* (Berne, La Chaux-de-Fonds) viewed these acts approvingly, but not because they failed to distinguish between simple acts of terrorism and propaganda by the deed. Hoedel's attempt, for instance, was not classified as an act of propaganda but rather as a isolated or "particular" incident. For Brousse, the theme of "collective" action was necessary in order for an act to be of any propaganda value.[24] Furthermore, Brousse went on to argue that in order for an act to be regarded as propaganda by the deed, it ought to satisfy other criteria; for example, the deed itself had to be inspired by anarchist beliefs (e.g., as in the Benevento affair), and it had also to serve a practical purpose with regard to the overall aims of the revolutionary movement.

Quite apart from the efforts of intellectuals to clarify the concept of propaganda by the deed, there remained the question of whether or not the anarchist movement as a whole was ready to adopt this ill-defined form of practice. Within the Jura Federation this was by no means a foregone conclusion. Those anarchists, like Guillaume, who were inclined toward a cautious approach were clearly at odds with Brousse, Morago, Viñas, the Italians, and other militants on this question. It was not until the summer of 1881, at an international meeting in London called by anarchists and social revolutionaries, that "propaganda by the deed" was formally adopted as a tactic. But even then the debate on the subject was not over. In fact, in the course of the next two decades of the anarchist movement, no other subject caused as much dissension as this topic. This was particularly true following the emergence of anarchist communism, a variation of Bakuninist collectivism which did not rely on trade union support.

By the mid-1880s, the concept had evolved into something quite different from its original meaning. This was primarily due to the persistence of misconceptions about the tactic in the public press, but it was in no small way also due to the fact that, after 1881, the majority of anarchists refused to delineate the boundaries of such an equivocal term. During the 1880s and 1890s propaganda by the deed stood for almost any form of direct action, including bombings, robbery, and political assassination. Indeed, there were some anarchists at the turn of the century—like the infamous Frenchman Ravachol—who actively cultivated the myth of the anarchist assassin. As we shall see, this created profound problems for anarchists everywhere, for with the line separating this tactic from terrorism blurred, it was hardly surprising that the public came to regard most anarchists as common criminals.

"PROPAGANDA BY THE DEED" AND TERRORISM IN SPAIN, 1876–1878

The international connections that a handful of Spanish anarchists maintained at this time proved to be vitally important for linking the FRE to the outside world. Thanks to these personal bonds, the concept of "propaganda by the deed" was introduced to Spain by 1877. For several years, the schoolteacher Severino Albarracín was a member of the intimate circle of émigré anarchist intellectuals in the Jura Federation. It seems that after the Alcoy uprising, he sought refuge in Switzerland, settling in the mountain community of La Chaux-de-Fonds. There he worked closely with Kropotkin, Jean-Louis Pindy, and other well-known militants active in spreading anarchist propaganda. Albarracín was on particularly friendly terms with Kropotkin, who planned in the summer of 1877 to accompany his Spanish comrade back to Spain to take part in the much-anticipated insurrectionary struggles. Although Kropotkin postponed visiting Spain until 1878, Albarracín returned home, only to die of a stroke a few months later. Another significant link with the international anarchist movement was established by García Viñas. In his capacity as a FRE delegate to the various international congresses, Viñas worked closely with Paul Brousse and the militant wing of the Jura.[25] Precisely to what extent these associations influenced their own perspectives and, in turn, the ideas of the FRE is difficult to determine. What we do know is that the Spaniards were involved in the theoretical debates that shaped the policies of the AntiAuthoritarian International. At its Ninth Congress—which was, as it turned out, the final one—held in September 1877, Viñas and Morago joined Brousse, Andrea Costa, and others in promoting the adoption of propaganda by the deed:

> La ligne de conduite prise en Espagne est la propagande par le fait et la séparation de toutes les organisations bourgeoises. La proposition fut fait pour connaître l'opinion des fédérations sur cette forme d'action et savoir si, en cas d'action, les fédérations espagnoles auraient l'appui des autres federations; pour affirmer aussi que la Fédération espagnole est prête de son côté à soutener tout mouvement dans les autres pays. Les délégués jurassien et français, qui avaient reçu le mandat de passer à l'ordre du jour sur cette question, acceptent la discussion après ces explications.[26]

In the early days of its development, however, the concept of propaganda by the deed made little impact on the Spanish federations. Even though the activities of the AntiAuthoritarian International were faithfully reported at the various regional (*comarcal*) conferences held during the mid-1870s—as witnessed by the fact that the FRE without fail adopted the line of conduct that was being promoted at these congresses—it is not likely that the debates on the meaning of propaganda by deed had yet filtered down to the local federations. Furthermore, because it was introduced into a context where revolutionary agitation was already commonplace, propaganda by the deed did not appear to be a particularly distinctive form of action.[27]

As with the anarchist federations in France and Italy at this time, the militancy of the Spanish anarchists sprang from the brutal treatment Internationalists received at the hands of the authorities. Since Pavía's *pronunciamiento* in January 1874, the government had relentlessly persecuted anyone who was even vaguely associated with the International. In the circumstances there was very little that the FRE could do in response to these reprisals. Only by circulating inflammatory manifestos and, whenever possible, clandestine periodicals, was it possible for the FRE to retaliate against its oppressors and thereby keep alive the spirit of revolt. Shortly after Pavía's *pronunciamiento*, for example, the beleagured Federal Commission issued a circular that spoke of the numerous arrests and persecutions and announced the FRE's resolve to take revenge against the authorities. In March 1877, the clandestine *El Orden* published a series of emotionally charged articles that recounted horrifying stories about the alleged maltreatment of political prisoners. One such story claimed that over sixty-six men had fallen victim to the repression. The prisoners, who were mostly republicans and Internationalists who had participated in the Cádiz cantonal rising, had been put into sacks with bales tied to their feet before they were hurled alive into the sea. Hundreds of others, according to this account, had been deported to the Marianas (South Pacific) and the Philippines.[28] By reporting these conditions, the Internationalist press was obviously trying to whip up the workers' hatred for the government. For the next several years, the same kind of violent language was found in underground journals like *Las Represalias* and *El Municipio Libre*.

During the latter part of the 1870s, there were several futile attempts by individuals to revive the revolutionary workers' movement. The most widely publicized of these occurred in October 1878, when Juan Oliva y Moncasi, a twenty-three-year-old Catalán cooper and member of the FRE, fired several shots at King Alfonso XII.[29] Moncasi was quickly arraigned and then tried in an atmosphere of public hysteria. According to a London *Times* article, the defense claimed that the prosecutor's indictment of over 380 pages required over twelve hours to read. That Moncasi did not receive a fair trial is borne out by the disinterested observations of James Russell Lowell, then American ambassador to Spain. Lowell believed that the circumstances surrounding Moncasi's attempted assassination strongly suggested that Moncasi himself may not have been guilty of the crime:

> No pistol was found upon him (though there were caps and cartridges in his pocket), nor has any since been traced. He is said to have fired twice, but only one ball has been found, and this had apparently rebounded after

striking the house opposite. At first it was reported that a soldier had been slightly wounded; then the ball had passed through the sleeve of his coat, and now even this seems doubtful. . . . He denied having accomplices, though the disappearance of his pistol seems to imply it. It is a curious illustration of the artificial state of politics here, that, although the King would naturally be glad to pardon the criminal, it is said that he will be unable to do so lest the whole affair should seem a tragic comedy arranged beforehand between the ministry and actors as a test of popular sentiment.[30]

The fact that the goverment never proved conclusively that Moncasi had fired the pistol did not deter the court from finding him guilty. He was convicted of attempted regicide—a crime that carried the death penalty—and then executed.

Both during and after the trial it was apparent that the government was intentionally using the incident as a pretext for taking more repressive measures against the International and its member organizations. As late as December, the government was still trying to turn public sentiment against the International by circulating unsubstantiated conspiracy theories. La Época commented on 4 December:

> Switzerland must not be surprised if nations menaced by the acts of demented individuals [a reference to the fact that Moncasi was at one stage in the trial accused by the prosecution of having been a mental patient], should complain that a secure refuge is accorded in the mountains of Switzerland to cosmopolitan conspirators who there devise schemes of assassination.[31]

Moncasi's crime was not actually connected with the International movement in Switzerland or in Spain, for, if he was guilty, he had acted without the approval of any official body of the organization. Rather, his was merely an isolated deed, a symbolic gesture committed in the name of the International movement. Because it was aimed at a prominent "enemy" of the working class, his bold act was endorsed by the International, but only after the fact.

Another form of response to government persecutions was taken by the FRE sections in the latifundist districts of the south. The wave of repression which swept through that region of Spain, and which resulted in the crushing of many agricultural organizations, did not extinguish the workers' faith in anarchism. On the contrary, the increased brutality of the authorities, coupled with the growing misery of the landless laborers, probably drove a large number of workers into the anarchist camp. By 1877 there were unequivocal signs that at least some Andalusian sections of the FRE were making ready to strike back at their adversaries. At a conference of the Eastern Andalusian district, for example, the federations unanimously approved resolutions calling for the adoption of the tactic of propaganda by the deed and reprisals against the bourgeoisie.[32]

About this time, several incidents occurred that can be taken not only as a manifestation of the growing militancy among the FRE affiliates centred in the Andalusian provinces but also as strongly suggestive of the way in which propaganda by the deed was being interpreted by the more radical sections.

Beginning in January 1879, several arrests were made in the Jerez region, with the government claiming that it was successfully breaking up Internationalist cells. In July, several cases of arson were reported in the Provinces of Jerez and Arcos which again provoked a swift response from the authorities. Evidence used to substantiate the government's allegations that the hand of the International was behind these crimes was usually presented in official publications like *Correspondencia de España* (Madrid). In the houses of those arrested the authorities supposedly found documents linking the Internationalists to a variety of criminal actions. On 7 August, for example, seven members were detained in Jerez and were later charged with having conspired with others in killing sheep and setting fire to standing crops.

There can be little doubt that some of the incidents of incendiarism and other forms of reprisals taken by the workers in the Jerez region at this time were instigated by the International. International branches both in Spain and elsewhere were keen on promoting this view, and they did not hesitate to publicize these episodes as examples of the rampant class war in the south. The anarchist journal *Le Révolté* (Geneva), for example, frequently presented these "crimes" in this light: "[L]a petite guerre continue dans . . . la province de Xérès, les paysans continuent à incendier les maisons et les champs de leurs propriétaires, en s'acharnant surtout contre les plus rapaces; les incendies se font sur un plan bien organisé."[33] Nevertheless it would be wrong to conclude from this that all of the reprisals aimed against the landowners were attributable to the propagandizing efforts of the International. Violence of this kind was not new to Andalusia; it was in fact a traditional form of protest among the casual and landless laborers of the region. That is to say, crop burning, the destruction of vineyards, and similar deeds had been employed by the Andalusian peasants—as well as by the peasantry of Europe generally—years before the arrival of the International. Although there is no way of knowing the precise number, some of the violent protests at this time were probably not connected to International activity but rather were occasioned by economic crisis and committed out of sheer desperation and anger. Such acts, then, are better understood as expressions of a sense of helplessness by the dispossessed workers of the region than as examples of propaganda by the deed.

Whatever role the FRE actually played in inciting these incidents of violence, the government was able to use them as grounds for intensifying its campaign to smash workers' organizations that were sympathetic in the International. As a result, the FRE was forced to reexamine its strategy and tactics. The unconnected acts of violence pointed to the fact that the FRE was impotent to exercise any control over the tactics that were being employed by individuals or even sections belonging to the organization. Unable to hold anything other than clandestine conferences from time to time, which, in any case, were poorly attended, the Federal Commission was powerless to enforce its views on the respective federations. Moreover, the growing restiveness amongst the workers in both the agricultural and industrial regions tended to weaken Internationalist strength and influence. In Andalusia, local federations carried out "wildcat" strikes against employers, and in Catalonia more and more workers were simply abandoning the FRE because it had proved itself helpless against the organized repression of the state.

Before 1874, the FRE had drawn much of its numerical strength from organized workers in Catalonia. Yet, because it could no longer provide the kind of leverage in the daily struggle that was required to meet the demands of the worker, the FRE rapidly lost its syndicalist base. An example of this trend was the formation of breakaway trade union groups that formerly supported the anarchist-dominated FRE but now refused to operate underground. In 1876, the Centro Federativo de Sociedades Obreras de Barcelona was reconstituted as a body that held a decidely reformist outlook. The militants of the FRE considered this as an act of treason against the working classes, for they believed that the revival of such a federation in the prevailing circumstances fomented splits within the ranks of the proletariat and thereby only served the interests of the bourgeoisie.

An even greater threat to the FRE was posed by the well-organized and powerful textile union, Tres Clases de Vapor (Three Classes of Boilermakers), one of the few labor organizations that never fell under the influence of anarchism. By 1877, the TCV was actively seeking ways of expanding the nonrevolutionary workers' movement in Catalonia. At the general Workers' Congress held in Barcelona in August 1877, several leading members of Tres Clases, notably José Pamías, began to argue that instead of conducting class warfare underground, the workers ought to pursue a more realistic strategy of action. They urged the working classes to commit themselves to a program of political action. And, finally, within the Catalonian section of the FRE an antirevolutionary tendency emerged that promoted the idea that individual members of the FRE should participate in local elections.

THE DISSOLUTION OF THE ALLIANCE

It will be remembered that ever since the Alliance had been established in Spain, it had played a key role in determining the course of the International movement. Although it was generally thought to have disappeared following the Zaragoza Congress of 1872, we have seen how an inner circle of Alliancists had resurrected the secret body, allowing it to function throughout this time. During the first year of the repression, only a select group of individuals were aware of its existence. Anselmo Lorenzo recorded in his memoirs that, although he was a leading member of the Federal Commission, he was kept in the dark about the Alliance's activities until 1875. At the height of the government's campaign against the International, Lorenzo fled to France, where he found asylum until the summer of 1875. He was then able to make his way to Barcelona. Once there he revived his contacts with the Federal Commission and discussed with them ways of regenerating the FRE. To his astonishment, Lorenzo was informed by García Viñas, a pivotal figure in the secret organization, that the Alliance had endured the many hardships imposed on it and that as a result the International in Spain had survived.

Because it relied on very few members for its operations, the Alliance appeared to be particularly well suited to the harsh set of circumstances brought on by repression. Not surprisingly, then, during the early period of the FRE's clandestinity the Alliance was indispensable not only for keeping the International movement alive but also for giving it some measure of continuity. In fact, given the state of dissolution which existed among the various federations, the Alliance was for a while the only functioning component of the FRE. This inevitably gave to the cadre of militants comprising it a greater role in directing the affairs of the organization. At the 1875 conference held in Barcelona, for instance, it was decided that the Federal Commission, which was dominated by Alliancists, would be solely responsible for nearly every aspect of the FRE's activities. Besides maintaining statistics—which were used for evaluating the conditions necessary for "scientific strikes"—and the correspondence with the respective federations, the Federal Commission was empowered to take the initiative in determining what form of organization would be most conducive to revolutionary action.[34]

In the early days of its existence, the Alliance had a unity of purpose. Then, with the collapse of the Republic, the Alliance was forced to confront a new situation. As the prospects for revolution rapidly faded and the membership of the FRE precipitously declined, the Alliancists turned in on themselves, incessantly quarreling over the tactical and theoretical objectives of the International movement. As a result of this dissension, the Alliance eventually ceased functioning as it was intended to operate.

During the seven-year repression, certain tendencies emerged within the FRE which utimately determined the fate of the Alliance. Although there were points at which these respective tendencies overlapped one another, they fell roughly into three categories. The first can be described as "insurrectionary." When Bakuninism had been introduced to Spain during the tumultuous days of La Gloriosa, insurrectionism had been the touchstone of anarchist doctrine. Throughout the seventies several of Bakunin's apostles, notably Severino Albarracín and José García Viñas, remained committed to this understanding. They thought that the primary task of the workers' movement was to make the social revolution per se, leaving the issue of mass trade unionism and popular support for anarchism to the day when everyone had been liberated from the yoke of government. Guided by Bakunin's teachings on revolution, they held an apocalyptic view of social change. This is, they believed that revolution would come about at the point when the social and economic conditions were ripe for change and the revolutionary consciousness of the people had reached maturity. Most important, they subscribed to Bakunin's view that it was necessary for an elite corps of revolutionaries to bring about a convergence of these conditions. While this vision might have seemed appropriate during the stormy days of La Gloriosa, it became increasingly harder to sustain during the late 1870s.

Another tendency, which we shall call "terroristic," was composed of a diverse group of elements. In the main it included the militant sections of the Andalusian federations as well as small cells of ultra-radicals in Catalonia and Madrid. The chief spokesman of this position within the Alliance was the Bakuninist Tomás González Morago. More than any other group within the FRE, the terrorists were inspired by the nihilistic acts of violence that were being committed by foreign revolutionists and that were then capturing the public's attention.

At first glance, it would appear as though there were few differences separating this group from the insurrectionists, for these factions shared the belief that revolutionary violence was a necessary feature of the workers' struggle. For this reason, both groups welcomed the introduction of propaganda by the deed. Where the terroristic group differed most significantly from the insurrectionists was in the way in which its members interpreted propaganda by the deed. While García Viñas and other insurrectionists followed the Italians in regarding propaganda by the deed as acts of social revolt, Morago and the terrorists saw the tactic simply as a means of conducting class war in the manner of the nihilists in Russia. The terrorists, who did not share either the vanguard elitism of the insurrectionists or their optimism that a large-scale insurrection was imminent, believed that if the FRE was not in a position to carry through a general revolution, it was necessary for its constituents to combat their enemies by whatever means possible. This included both group and individual acts of violence, irrespective of whether these were coordinated by the Federal Commission or by a select body of revolutionaries, such as the Alliance.

Opposing both of these tendencies was the syndicalist wing of the FRE. Centered in Barcelona, this faction was headed by Rafael Farga Pellicer, José Llunas y Pujols, and Francisco Tomás. As leaders of the FRE, the syndicalists conceived their task in regard to the working classes to be twofold. First, in order to resuscitate the revolutionary workers' movement it was necessary to organize both industrial and agricultural workers into unions, and then to link them by means of a national federation of unions such as the FRE. While their emphasis on organization may have appeared to some as a rejection of their anarchist heritage, the syndicalists regarded themselves as anarchist, and, indeed, they thought their commitment to unionism was in keeping with the spirit of Bakuninism. Like Bakunin, they regarded trade unions as "the living germs of the new social order" which were to replace the institutions of the bourgeois world.[35] Second, in view of the growth of the Tres Clases de Vapor and other reformist unions that set themselves in competition with the FRE, the syndicalists believed that it was of crucial importance that the FRE operate openly. This led the syndicalists to adopt a policy of "legalism"; that is, they preferred that the FRE obtain legal recognition rather than maintain its underground status. In arguing for such a policy, the syndicalists stood in diametric opposition to the militant factions, which were convinced that the war against the ruling classes had to be conducted clandestinely.

But differences over tactical objectives were not the only reason why the Alliancists were at odds with one another. For frequent personality clashes also played a key role in splitting up the group. The anarchist historian Diego Abad de Santillán has pointed out that because the Alliancists were forced for a period of several years to work at close quarters and under especially harsh circumstances, it was inevitable that personality differences would surface among them. Personality was a determining factor in the fate of the Spanish International at this time not least because the FRE's operations relied heavily on the ability of the Alliancists to act in harmony.

The person most responsible for sustaining the Alliance during the repression was José García Viñas. He has been portrayed rather unsympathetically by historians as well as by those who personally knew him: Anselmo Lorenzo described him as the dictator of the Alliance, and, in the opinion of the historian Temma Kaplan, Viñas was "compulsive and rigid."[36] Viñas, however, appears to have been a more complex character than his critics would have us believe. We have already seen how Viñas's collaboration with international anarchists like Brousse contributed to the formulation of the tactic of propaganda by the deed. He also formed a lifelong bond with Peter Kropotkin. When Kropotkin visited Spain during the summer of 1878, he stayed with Viñas, and, according to the anarchist Soledad Gustavo—who knew both men— Kropotkin "conserved until his death a fine memory of his Spanish doctor friend."

It is true, however, that in Spain Viñas had few close associates. One notable exception was his friendship with Juan Serrano y Oteiza. The two worked jointly on the important organ of the Union of Manufacturers (Unión de Manufacturas de España), *La Revista Social* (Madrid, 1872–1881), of which Viñas was the director until 1880. Yet the fact remains that, for all his qualities as a theorist and organizer, Viñas never attracted a following within the FRE; perhaps because, as his detractors have suggested, he was temperamentally ill-suited to be a leader. In any case, as he was a pivotal figure in the Alliance, his unpopularity no doubt had some bearing on the outcome of the conflict between the militant and moderate factions.

Still another personality in the Alliance whose political career was characterized by polemics was the engraver Tomás González Morago. During the early days of the International in Spain, Morago had been

Bakunin's foremost apostle and principal contact, maintaining a copious correspondence with him regarding the activities of the secret Alliance. Following the events of the Paris Commune in 1871, when the International was suppressed and the Federal Council was forced to flee Madrid, Morago, Anselmo Lorenzo, and Francisco Mora were entrusted to transfer the papers of the FRE to Portugal. There they established sections of the International in Lisbon and Oporto. During their brief sojourn, personality differences arose between Morago and Mora, differences that anticipated the polemic that would soon split the FRE into warring camps: the Marxists, led by Mora and José Mesa, and the Bakuninists of the Alliance. Immediately after the Federal Council regrouped in Spain, Morago acquired a reputation as an uncompromising critic of the Marxist current within the FRE. Despite his antagonism toward the Marxists, Morago earned, albeit in a begrudging way, the respect of his adversaries. Paul Lafargue, who got to know Morago fairly well, had this to say about him:

> Myself, I believe that Morago is slightly deranged, but, nevertheless, a man with most lucid intelligence in his calmer moments. . . . Morago is the moving spirit of the Alliance in Spain; he is the one who directs everything. He is a rather second-rate man with, however, a considerable talent for oratory and he is feverishly active when he is personally involved.[37]

By the late 1870s, Morago appears to have become unpopular even within the anarchist camp. Not long after the repression began, his frequent and bitter personal feuds with Viñas, as well as his stubborn insistence on promoting terrorist tactics, caused him to lose standing within the Alliance itself. The fact that most of his comrades felt that his enthusiasm for violence bordered on obsession suggests that Morago came close to personifying the popular image of an anarchist: someone with a furtive personality whose almost pathological hatred for the bourgeoisie drove him to commit heinous crimes such as bombings, stabbings, and political assassinations. From 1878 on, Morago ceased playing a leading role in the FRE. A few years later he was expelled from his workers' section in Madrid for immoral conduct (allegedly for having forged checks).

Before leaving this subject, it is worth noting that the personality conflicts referred to here seem to have been reinforced by two factors. One was the presence of strong regionalist feelings within the FRE. Anselmo Lorenzo, who, unlike either Viñas or Morago, enjoyed a certain amount of popularity within the FRE, recorded in his memoirs that for all the solidarity to be found within the International movement, regionalist feelings still affected the relationships that existed between individuals and the respective federations:

> [I]f among the bourgeois youth there existed this plague [regionalist feelings], the proletariat was not entirely free of it either. For proof of this there are facts I can adduce which demonstrate that in some instances my Catalan anarchist friends made it clear to me that they had not forgotten that I had been born on the other side of the Ebro.[38]

It is probably no coincidence that the theoretical and tactical orientation of the FRE's membership was largely defined by regional boundaries. Nearly all of the syndicalist factions, for instance, were predominant in areas like Valencia and Catalonia, where there was a well-established tradition of trade unionism, while the majority of "insurrectionists" and "terrorists" came from Madrid, the latifundist districts of the south, and other parts of Spain where working-class associations were less developed.

A second factor contributing to the personality disputes was a form of class tension which had probably always existed within the International. Years after he had retired from the movement, Viñas explained to Max Nettlau that one of the major reasons why he had felt compelled to leave the FRE was that he lacked "callouses on his hands." He was referring to a sentiment commonly held among the working classes known as *ouvrièrisme*. It was a feeling predicated on the belief that since the FRE was grounded in the working-class movement it ought to be composed entirely of proletarians.

Of course, the idea of *ouvrièrisme* was not peculiar to Spain. At the Geneva Congress of 1866, the Proudhonists had tried in vain to impose this view on the membership of the First International. Although their efforts were partly aimed at barring from the organization such formidable middle-class opponents of the Proudhonists as Karl Marx—for, if passed, the resolution would have forced his resignation from the General Council—they also revealed a deep-seated contempt that some workers had for the middle classes. Later, Bakunin, who like so many other luminaries of the International had come from either the aristocracy or the middle classes, also expressed his reservations about what he called bourgeois socialists: "[T]he workers will receive guardedly at best the propaganda of intellectuals who come from a totally different and hostile social background."[39]

Ouvrièrisme was also a source of friction within the AntiAuthoritarian

International. No longer confronted by the Marxists, the Proudhonists were challenged by a group of middle-class anarchists, including such prominent figures as the former philosophy teacher James Guillaume and the medical student García Viñas. They defended the role of déclassé intellectuals on the ground that it would serve no purpose to exclude those bourgeois individuals who, like themselves, were prepared to devote their lives to the workers' cause. In the end, their view prevailed, and thereafter the question was only of marginal importance in the affairs of the International.

In Spain the question of *ouvrièrisme* was, from time to time, to play a minor but nonetheless significant role in the working-class movement. Although facts fail us in determining the depth to which this feeling ran through the FRE during the period of repression, we do know that it was one of the factors that contributed to the disintegration of the Alliance, which ultimately divided the "society" into syndicalist and insurrectionist factions. Within the FRE, the most outstanding representative of *ouvrièrisme* was the bricklayer Francisco Tomás. Born in Mallorca in 1850, Tomás joined the FRE soon after it was established.[40] On the strength of his outstanding qualities as an organizer and spokesman for the rank and file, Tomás rapidly rose to prominence in the FRE. After founding a section of the IWMA in Palma de Mallorca, he began publishing the pro-Bakuninist *El Obrero*. Tomás was one of the very few members of the Federal Commission who was of working-class origin. His distrust of the middle classes was reflected in the stance he took on many issues, for in his role as a representative of the proletariat he did not hesitate to define problems along class lines. Following the disastrous cantonalist risings, for example, Tomás was quick to condemn the middle-class politicians, accusing them of having dragged the working classes into their adventurist schemes. Writing to the Italian Federation on 18 August 1873, he explained:

> Some of our Italian brothers maintain the belief that the cantonalist movement, being that of the intrasigent federal republicans, was an International movement, whereas it was a political movement that was made by the politicians and without any previous exchange of communication with the Internationalists.[41]

Anarchists like Tomás obviously harbored a certain amount of resentment toward the déclassé participants in the workers' movement; and even though it is not empirically demonstrable, it may well have been that Internationalists of this tendency stiffened their opposition to concepts like "propaganda by the deed" if they were perceived as having been inspired by bourgeois intellectuals.

After 1880, when there was a perceptible relaxing of government persecution, the militant tendencies became increasingly isolated from the mainstream of the movement, primarily because they refused to abandon their belief that the FRE should remain underground. At the same time, the syndicalists argued that this liberal trend should be seized on as a propitious moment for the FRE to step up its public organizing efforts. Anticipating the government's move to grant to the unions the right to associate, this group of "legalists" sought to play down the revolutionary rhetoric of the FRE so that it would be possible to organize the workers without fear of persecution. The principal mouthpiece of the legalist position after 1880 was *La Revista Social,* which was from then until 1884 edited by the notary Juan Serrano y Otieza. Serrano later defended legalism on the ground that during the time the FRE was forced into clandestinity, its popular base had virtually been destroyed, with nearly ninety percent of its membership gone in less than four years.[42]

By promoting a policy of "legalism," this group of Internationalists were not suggesting that the FRE should abandon its commitment to direct action or revolutionism. Nevertheless, the syndicalists' emphasis on trade unionism did strongly suggest that they opposed propaganda by the deed or any other tactic that might possibly jeopardize the legal status of the FRE.

Meanwhile, the Alliance was in its last stages of decomposition, having been destroyed by years of internecine struggles. Viñas decided to abandon the workers' struggle in 1881, partly for personal reasons—he wanted to pursue a medical career in Melilla—and partly because he realized that his views were out of touch with the rank and file of the FRE. Writing to the anarchist historian Max Nettlau years later, Viñas mentioned the primary reason why he felt compelled to resign his position:

> [W]hat persuaded me was the fact that the organization [FRE] was going to operate publicly and legally, a decision that I believed threatened to undermine the aims of our revolutionary activity.[43]

The Alliance lost yet another key figure when Anselmo Lorenzo fell victim to the power struggle within the FRE. Like Viñas, Lorenzo was strongly opposed to the idea of the FRE leaving its clandestine existence. He was therefore perceived as a threat by the clique of syndicalists who

were now in ascendancy. In 1880, just when the debate between the
rival militant and syndicalist tendencies was about to boil over, he was
reelected to the Federal Commission. Although he received a majority of
votes, Lorenzo was accused of having falsified the election results. Lorenzo was, in effect, being forcibly ejected from the FRE because his
faction had lost the battle for control of the Federal Commission. Disillusioned by the experience, Lorenzo decided, at least for the time
being, to give way to the forces opposing him. His premature retirement
was to last until 1884, when he resumed his role as a prominent activist
in the anarchist movement.

This form of attrition exacted a heavy toll on the Alliance. For by the
end of 1880, the society had all but disappeared.

CHAPTER V

Anarchism and the Restoration: The Growth and Decline of the FTRE

As we have seen from chapter 3, the government formed as a result of Pavía's coup d'état in 1874 left Spain for a brief spell in the hands of the military. The overthrow of the Republic meant that the politicians would have to turn elsewhere for a new government. For many the solution was to restore the monarchy, but it was generally recognized that this could not be achieved by bringing back the unpopular Isabella II. Their dilemma was resolved at the end of 1874, when General Martínez Campos announced the return of the dynasty and proclaimed Isabella's son, Alfonso XII, the king of Spain. Unlike his predecessor's, Alfonso's reign (1875–1885) was not marked by controversy and court intrigue, yet his tenure of rule was cut short by his untimely death in 1885.

One of the king's first acts was to authorize the Conservative Antonio Cánovas del Castillo to oversee the political process of the Restoration. Cánovas was in many ways an ideal candidate to be entrusted with such an undertaking. Besides being an astute politician, he also enjoyed a certain amount of prestige and popularity in Spanish society. A government was immediately constituted, with Cánovas making sure that he kept a tight rein on developments. In order to ensure that Spain would not lapse into the state of chaos from which it had just emerged, he suspended the Cortes, banned public meetings, and suppressed the right to associate. Above all, Cánovas's abhorrence of social revolution led him to adopt a strict formula for reconstituting rule in Spain. The end product was what came to be known as the Cánovite system of govern-

ment, which was to dominate Spanish politics until the turn of the
century. The system of which Cánovas was the chief architect can be
briefly summarized in the following way. With a constitution guarantee-
ing the legitimacy of the monarchy, Cánovas believed that Spain could
be successfully ruled by two opposition parties. On the one side stood
the Conservative politicians who were under his own personal leadership. They were opposed by a coalition of progressive elements constituted at first as the Fusionist Liberal party.[1]

Although this was ostensibly an attempt to anglicize the Spanish
government, it should be borne in mind that the political blueprint that
Cánovas envisaged was altogether different from the English parliamentary system, not least because the Spanish parties were to be controlled
by the government and put into power by means of contrived elections.
At the local level, electoral manipulation was maintained by a patronage system know as *caciquismo,* whereby *caciques* (political bosses),
with the connivance and support of the government, ensured the outcome of elections. Employed by each of the dynastic parties, *caciques*
operated by personally dominating the administration and judicial apparatus of a locality. By doling out political favors and jobs to a select
group of constituents, the *cacique* wielded considerable influence within
a district, which in most cases enabled him to exercise virtual control of
the polls on election day.

Notwithstanding these glaring flaws in the democratic process, the
Cánovas system achieved—as the historian Joan Ullman has explained
in her valuable study of this period—something that had eluded previous administrations. By shifting the locus of power to political parties it
was finally possible to subordinate the monarchy, the church, and the
army to the Cortes.[2] The truly unique feature of the Cánovite party
system was that the two parties could alternate in political power. As
Raymond Carr points out; "This alternation of the dynastic parties (i.e.
those who accepted the monarchy) was called the '*turno pacífico*' and it
replaced the *pronunciamiento* as the instrument of political change."[3]

A significant feature of the Cánovite settlement was that the working
classes were, to all intents and purposes, excluded from it. It was not
until the Universal Suffrage Act of 1890—which did away with the
property qualification imposed by previous electoral laws—that workers were even eligible to vote. But this had little impact on the political
position they held. For without a strong party to represent them in the
Cortes, they remained beyond the pale of the Cánovite system of power
sharing.

From the time the constitution was adopted in 1876 until 1881, Cánovas remained in power. Then, after Martínez Campos defected to the Liberal camp, taking with him several other generals and thus the support of the army, the king called on Sagasta to form a ministry. Although the new administration by no means represented a radical departure from the Cánovas regime, it was nonetheless less rigid than its predecessor. Once in office, Sagasta began to slacken the reins of government control by introducing legislation that allowed for a greater degree of social and political activity among the public in general and the working classes in particular. A decree issued by the government on 14 February 1881, for example, pardoned the "penalties imposed on the periodical publications of all classes," and, by November, legislation was passed that restored to the working classes their old right of association.[4]

FROM BARCELONA TO THE SEVILLE
CONGRESS: THE BIRTH OF THE FTRE

The year 1881 also marked a turning point for the International movement in Spain. Having survived the hardships imposed by seven years of severe repression, the organization appeared to emerge from its clandestine life with little indication of regaining its former vigor. No doubt Sagasta's rise to power—which signaled a trend toward increasing political liberalization—influenced the Internationalists' decision to set about reorganizing themselves. During February, delegates at a regional conference in Catalonia discussed the fate of the FRE, and on 24 September, a general workers' congress was convened in Barcelona at which, according to Anselmo Lorenzo, a remarkable thing happened: the Spanish Regional Federation was formally dissolved and replaced by the Federation of Workers of the Spanish Region (Federación de Trabajadores de la Región Española, FTRE).[5] In one sense, the creation of the FTRE signified an end to the first stage of the International movement in Spain, for while the new organization was still to be regarded as a branch of the First International, it was distinguished from the FRE by its avowed commitment to a purely anarchist orientation. The most remarkable aspect of this conversion, however, was that it seemed to breathe life into a movement that had been on the verge of disintegration just a few months before.

As regards the different tendencies within the anarchist movement, the creation of the FTRE represented a triumph of the syndicalist forces.

With the Alliance to all intents and purposes destroyed, the syndicalists, as we have seen, were now in a position to assume control of the newly baptized heir to the old FRE organization. The preponderant influence of the syndicalists was most clearly manifested in the resolutions adopted regarding the organization of the FTRE. Rafael Farga Pellicer, José Llunas, and other syndicalist-minded veterans of the FRE made sure that the basic framework of the FRE remained intact. The five-man Federal Commission, for example, was to continue to function much as it had before. The commission was, significantly, composed entirely of pro-syndicalists: Antonio Pellicer Paraire, Francisco Tomás, José Llunas, Eudaldo Canibell, and probably Farga Pellicer. On another level, there was to be a district (*comarcal*) commission composed of three federation members, who were to be elected at the district congresses. They were to act as the liaison between the Federal Commission on the one hand and the local federations of each district on the other. At each level the primary function of these elected officials was to gather information relevant to the circumstances of the working classes. In this way, knowledge of planned activities—such as strikes—could be disseminated throughout the FTRE, thus making possible the united action of the entire network of federations.

Most important, the syndicalists were hoping to strike a balance between the demands of effective rule and the necessity of preserving the confederal character of the FTRE. They did not want a recurrence of "wildcat" strikes and other forms of independent action, which they believed to be counterproductive to the overall aims of an organized labor movement. To this end they sought to use the decision-making bodies, particularly the Federal Commission, as mechanisms for exercising some degree of control over the activities of the respective federations. They therefore endeavored, at this and other congresses until 1888, to direct the greatest attention to matters connected with trade union organization.

During the first years of the FTRE's existence, its ideological platform was in large measure defined and maintained by two publications, *La Revista Social* (1881–1885) of Madrid and *Crónica de los Trabajadores de la Región Española,* which was issued by the Federal Commission between 1882 and 1884. *La Revista Social* was by far the more significant publication of the two, not only because it became popularly identified as the official mouthpiece of the FTRE—for leading articles were often reprinted in the *Crónica*—but also because it rapidly attained the widest distribution of any working-class paper of the period: within the span of three years its circulation had climbed to an astonishing 20,000 subscribers.[6]

In these publications, the syndicalists attempted to set forth a policy for the FTRE already referred to above as "legalism." Despite its connotations to the contrary, they conceived of this as a plan of action which was consistent with the revolutionary aspirations of the anarchist movement. The notion of "legalism" itself, at least as it was understood by the syndicalists, bore no relation to the literal meaning of the term. That is to say, they did not interpret the policy as one which in any way bound the FTRE to the juridical system that granted these rights. Nor did the syndicalists follow reformist unionists, like the members of the Tres Clases de Vapor, in encouraging the workers to seek resolution of their problems through the legislative process. On the contrary, as anarchists, they were implacably hostile toward politics and unwaveringly committed to the idea of completely overturning the ruling system. For the syndicalists, a policy of "legalism" was nothing more than the most efficacious means of achieving this end.[7] In fact, the term held no real ideological significance for the syndicalists in that it was seen as referring to a practical way of implementing the long-range strategy they evisaged for the FTRE. What most syndicalists meant by such a policy was simply that they wanted to conduct their business openly and publicly without fear of government interference. The freedom to publish anarchist periodicals, the freedom for workers to read and discuss the ideas contained in them, and the right to demonstrate for more humane conditions for the working classes were among the more important objectives the syndicalists had in mind when they spoke of legalism.

Thus, notwithstanding its revolutionary content, the syndicalists' strategy represented a radical departure from the ultrarevolutionary line of conduct the anarchists had adopted during the period of repression. Evidence of this dramatic shift was most strikingly manifested in the syndicalist press. For example, in *La Revista Social* there is little of the apocalyptic rhetoric that characterized the underground periodicals like *El Orden*. Also noticeably absent were references to committees of war and acts of revenge, which had given place to talk about the tasks of building a trade union movement that was to be organized along the lines of anarchist principles.

Less than a year after the Barcelona Congress, the extraordinary regeneration of the labor movement was well underway. Between September and the end of 1882 there were at least eight public congresses convened by unions of similar crafts and ten regional or district congresses held by the FTRE.[8] The meteoric rise of organized labor peaked at the Seville Congress of September 1882. There the vitality of the recently founded Regional Federation (as it was commonly known) was clearly reflected in its numbers: 218 federations, 663 sections, with a membership of 57,934. These statistics are quite astounding when it is remembered that, before its dissolution in 1881, the FRE represented 7 district federations (*federaciones comarcales*) and 49 local ones, with approximately 3,000 members.[9]

Despite the impressive show of solidarity exhibited at this and previous congresses, the leadership nonetheless faced a number of problems even at this early stage of the FTRE's development. Above all they had to contend with the fact that the majority of the organization consisted of workers from the southern provinces. During the years of repression, the geographical boundaries of the International movement had shifted dramatically. Whereas during the 1870s the FRE drew its numerical strength from working-class organizations centered in Barcelona, Madrid, and Valencia, nearly two-thirds of the FTRE's membership resided in Andalusia—mainly in Málaga, Cádiz, and Seville. Significantly, though, the motivating forces of the International had remained fixed in Barcelona, Madrid, and other areas formerly dominated by syndicalists. One of the major problems created by these demographic changes was that until the workers in the south unionized, a significant gap would exist between the majority of the rank and file and the decision-making bodies of the FTRE. The syndicalists leaders themselves were of the opinion that this disequilibrium could be redressed by concentrating their efforts on organizing every kind of worker into one trade union structure, especially those who were notoriously difficult to organize, like the *braceros* (landless agricultural laborers) of the Jerez region.

The syndicalists' plan for implmenting their strategy differed little in form and content from that which had guided the leaders of the FRE in the early days of its development. Once again the importance of education, especially with regard to the task of inculcating the workers with the proper theoretical perspective, was stressed. Many of the syndicalists attributed the backwardness of the southern federations not just to the economic problems endemic to the region but also to the enforced ignorance of the proletariat. As a result, the congress expressly encouraged the creation of *escuelas laicas* (lay schools) in which the workers could learn the basics: reading, writing, and arithmetic.[10]

The syndicalists felt so confident that they were right in arguing for an open and legal trade union movement that they tended to be intolerant of any perspective that radically departed from the agenda they were setting for the FTRE. Considering that at the time they commanded the support of an overwhelming majority of the membership, it is hardly surprising that they did not hesitate to deal swiftly and firmly with recalcitrant opponents. When the Arcos section of western Andalusia railed against the syndicalist platform at the Barcelona Congress, for example, the Federal Commission responded by expelling its members.

By the time the FTRE convened its second national meeting at Seville in September 1882, it was becoming all too evident that dissension of this sort, instead of dying down as the Federal Commission hoped, was actually growing. Around the same time, other "grupitos" (tiny groups) of dissenters sprang up in and around Madrid and Barcelona. What all of these groups shared in common was their fierce opposition to the legalist orientation of the FTRE and their strong attachment to ultrarevolutionary practices, such as the use of propaganda by the deed. This was especially true among the Andalusian federations, many of which had conserved from the period of repression their commitment to violence and their propensity to work underground in small, disjointed groups.

Other signs of disquietude within the FTRE emerged at the congress when the ideological stance of the Federal Commission was challenged by a faction of anarchists led by Miguel Rubio from Montejaque. Directing his criticisms at José Llunas, the keynote speaker at the meeting, Rubio complained that to define the aims of the FTRE strictly in terms of collectivist economic principles as Llunas was doing was contrary to the Internationalist tradition in Spain. Rubio, who may well have been expressing the views of a number of other federations in attendance, pointed out that while the Alliance considered itself collectivist it had never advocated the adoption of only one type of economic system. For him, anarchism encompassed a variety of viewpoints, including the communistic idea that all the fruits of society belonged to everyone and not just to those who produced them. In the end, Llunas's view prevailed, although we shall see that this was by no means the last time that the collectivist orientation of the FTRE would be challenged. For, with the emergence of anarchist communism a few years later, this debate assumed much greater proportions.

THE "BLACK HAND" MYSTERY

While the syndicalists were able to consolidate their dominating position of power and influence within the FTRE at the Seville Congress, their success proved to be short-lived. Only a few months after the meeting, the FTRE was severely jolted by a scandal of massive dimensions that came to be known as the Mano Negra (Black Hand) affair. The repercussions of this event were felt for years afterward, but it had the more immediate effect of destroying the syndicalists' hegemony within the newly revived anarchist movement.

At the time, the Mano Negra episode created panic throughout Spain and Europe. Echoes of the affair have been heard down the years, such as when the distinguished sociologist Bernaldo de Quiros y Pérez was commissioned by the government in the late 1880s to investigate the Mano Negra, and it has recently been the subject of several historical studies.[11] As the details of the affair are readily available, we will confine ourselves here to a bare summary of the Mano Negra incident and then turn to a discussion of the significance it held for the anarchist movement itself.

The Mano Negra story actually began as a series of murders in Jerez between December 1882 and February 1883. The first of these occurred on 3 December. Late that night, a tavern owner, Juan Núñez, and his wife were slain during an encounter with a group of local *jornaleros* (day laborers). Next morning, the authorities rounded up seventy-five local workers, who were indicted as conspirators in the crime. After interviewing several witnesses, the police announced that a Juan Galán had been identified as the murderer.

Two months later—on 17 February—a Captain Oliver of the *Guardia Civil* in Jerez informed the authorities in Madrid of another murder. According to Oliver the victim, known as "El Blanco de Benaocaz," had been murdered—like the Núñez couple—on orders from a clandestine revolutionary organization: *La Mano Negra*. Oliver's startling discovery obviously had far-reaching implications. Among other things, it suggested that the recent murders were not unconnected phenomena but rather could be traced to a common source, namely, to a conspiratorial group based in the working classes whose tentacles stretched throughout the Andalusian region. Upon hearing Oliver's story, the government reacted at once by launching a vigorous campaign of persecution against this alleged secret body.

The unearthing of a network of underground terrorist cells was not anything new to Andalusia. During the previous decade, for example, the police and government had routinely attributed acts of vandalism to clandestine groups of the International. In fact, Oliver and the authorities were convinced that La Mano Negra had been in existence at least since 1878. Evidence of the society was first divulged at a trial held that same year. At this, the authorities supposedly produced the secret statutes of La Mano Negra, a document that described a society bent on "committing robberies, kidnappings and acts of vengeance."[12]

Meanwhile, Galán was tried and convicted for the murders of the Núñez couple, and La Mano Negra was eventually linked by the authorities not only to the "El Blanco de Benaocaz" killing but also to several other crimes in the region. Collectively these became known as the Mano Negra trials. As a result of these trials, hundreds of workers associated with the FTRE were either arrested or otherwise harassed by the local and national authorities.

Coming as it did on the heels of a spate of terrorist violence in Europe—namely, the anarchist-inspired bombings that had recently taken place in France, which climaxed with the celebrated Lyons Trial of 1883—the Mano Negra trials inevitably generated a wave of hysteria that extended well beyond the Spanish borders, resurrecting once again the timeworn theory of the existence of an extensive terrorist network organized by Internationalists. Spanish officials seized the opportunity to perpetuate these rumors by feeding the press with wild accusations, such as the baseless assertion that there were some 70,000 members of this subversive group, which aimed to terrorize and then to destroy the ruling classes by the most violent means. Having spuriously established a connection between violent crime and the organized labor movement, the authorities were able to "justify" their draconian treatment of the FTRE throughout the province of Cádiz.

From the beginning, the Federal Commission suspected that the government was determined to use the scandal as a pretext for attacking the FTRE. Several months earlier, the Federal Commission had grown suspicious that the authorities were plotting to disrupt its activities. In January, it was announced in the *Crónica* that the Federal Commission had received two leaflets from a revolutionary group calling itself "The Disinherited Ones" (*Los Desheredados*) of the Committee of War of the Spanish Region. The Federal Commission warned their audience that these mysterious publications were planted by the bourgeoisie in order to create the impression that the FTRE was connected to a number of illegal, ultrarevolutionary conspiratorial societies.[13] A few months later, the ever-mounting publicity about La Mano Negra prompted the Federal Commission to issue another proclamation, which categorically denied that the FTRE had any connection whatever with such a secret society:

[W]e must repeat again that our Federation has never been a party to robbery, arson, kidnapping, or assassination; we have never maintained nor do we maintain relations with whatever is called *La Mano Negra, La Mano Blanca,* or any other secret society whose object is the perpetration of common crimes. . . . We therefore have the right to ask the press to desist in its indignant propaganda and its lamentable attempts at confusion.[14]

Affirming that these organizations did not exist outside the imaginations of the authorities and the bourgeois press, the Federal Commission went on to declare that the Mano Negra scare was clearly being used as grounds for undermining the foundations of the legal trade union movement to which the FTRE belonged. To support its assertion, the Federal Commission reminded its audience that the government had in the past resorted to similar fabrications in its efforts to curtail the growth of a politicized labor movement. After all, the circular continued, during the previous decade the monarchy had branded all radical republicans as criminals.

The question of whether the secret body was real or imagined was academic once the police, landlords, and government troops combined their efforts to crack down on labor groups. Local federations of the FTRE, regardless of whether they had been linked evidentially to La Mano Negra, had to bear the full force of this campaign. Nearly every report emanating from Andalusian federations spoke of the rebirth of the Inquisition, under whose autocratic reign hundreds of innocent workers were being subjected to various forms of cruel punishment. Just how desperate the workers' plight was at this time is vividly evoked in a letter that a federation member from Jerez managed to smuggle out to *La Revista Social:*

This region, dear friends, has become a living hell. . . . The horrors of hunger have been succeeded by a reign of terror even more terrifying. The proletarians, and especially the farm workers, do not have a moment's rest. With the pretext of this or that crime, of the kind which are always committed in these parts, the police try by all sorts of illegal methods to secure confessions and documents from us. Our meeting places, our homes, our persons, even our beds are inspected at all hours of the day and night. And anyone unlucky enough to be found with a copy of *La Revista Social* . . . in his possession is considered to be the greatest criminal in the world and is thrown into jail.[15]

By angrily denying any affiliation with La Mano Negra or other underground societies, the Federal Commission was obviously trying to shield the FTRE from further reprisals. For some anarchists, though, the commission's attempt to divorce the FTRE from the scandal was a blatant act of betrayal. In their eyes, it was simply a way of abandoning the hundreds of Andalusian federations to the bleak fate that awaited them. And, indeed, in view of the widespread and indiscriminate campaign of persecution being waged against the working classes in the south, it was not surprising that the Federal Commission's repeated public condemnations of illegal activities found little echo not only among the some one thousand victims of this repression but also among those who felt strongly that the FTRE should never have gone to such great lengths to dissociate itself from La Mano Negra. Primarily for this reason, the Mano Negra episode was creating profound rifts within the FTRE; schisms that could not be easily papered over by the official pronouncements issued by the Federal Commission.

Did La Mano Negra ever exist? If it did, was it representative of the Andalusian federations that were radically diverging from the syndicalist policies advocated by the leadership of the FTRE? In recent years, both of these questions have been treated as historiographical problems. The first question cannot be answered with a simple yes or no. On the one hand, a group of historians represented by James Joll and Glen A. Waggoner have argued that La Mano Negra probably never existed. On the other hand, the chance discovery of a copy of one document purporting to be the official statutes of La Mano Negra has led the historian Clara Lida to claim that the society did exist, and that it was representative of a distinct ideological current within the anarchist movement. According to Lida, this form of society had as its antecedents the tiny secret societies of the International which sprang up in Andalusia during the seven-year repression. This particular form of organization was adopted by the Andalusians, she goes on to say, primarily because it was the "most suitable kind of organization the revolutionary Andalusians could find for their needs and situation. . . . [S]uch agrarian secret organizations became the melting pot for the tactics of traditional and radical anarchist ideology." The ideological tendency to which Lida refers is that of anarchist communism. She argues that, although this variant of anarchist thinking had not been formally introduced into the Spanish context at the time of La Mano Negra, the society nonetheless incorporated into its program many of the basic precepts of this line of thought.[16] For Lida, La Mano Negra can thus be regarded as one of the first groups in Spain to embrace an anarchist communist position. In so doing, it was also one of the first groups to challenge the reformist outlook of the anarchist collectivists who controlled the FTRE.

While Lida's scholarly investigations shed much light on the Mano

Negra affair, she does not conclusively prove either of her main conten-
tions: that La Mano Negra did exist and that it was also a manifestation
of an ideological shift in the anarchist movement. This is because Lida
confuses two historical problems. Whereas she argues that the emergence of La Mano Negra was bound up with the development of anarchist communism in Spain, the fact is that the question of the existence
of La Mano Negra can be answered without referring to the problem of
anarchist ideology.

Lida's first claim is founded on fragmentary evidence. Although she
does not acknowledge the possibility, the authenticity of the Mano
Negra "statutes" found years after the event is highly questionable, not
least because the document is not corroborated by any other. In view of
the International's long-standing feud with the authorities, especially in
the southern provinces, it is highly probable that the police could have
fabricated this in the same way in which they had faked so many of the
"documents" that were used to prosecute the labor movement during
the period in question.[17] Without further supporting evidence the question of the existence of the organization will have to remain open. In the
end, therefore, one is reluctantly obliged to accept the inconclusive
findings presented in Glen Waggoner's careful review of this matter:

> The Black Hand may have been concocted by Andalusian authorities as a
> pretext for attacking the anarchist movement in the south; or it may have
> existed as a secret cell of radicals within the *Federación* in Andalusia. The
> trials of alleged members of the Black Hand did not solve the question.[18]

As regards the ideological significance of La Mano Negra, Lida's
argument fails to take into account several significant facts. One is that
the other breakaway groups to which she refers adamantly refused to
acknowledge the existence of La Mano Negra. The Desheredados group
in particular asserted that La Mano Negra was a "force created by the
bourgeoisie and seconded by the Federal Commission."[19] What Los
Desheredados was implying here was that the Federal Commission was
not at all interested in dispelling the Mano Negra "myth." On the
contrary they believed that the Federal Commission was intentionally
using the scandal to discredit all of its ultraradical opponents within the
FTRE. Curiously, though, Los Desheredados, which had split from the
FTRE following the Seville Congress, is cited by Lida as an example of
the same ideological tendency to which La Mano Negra supposedly
belonged. Both extolled the virtues of violence, and both were, according to Lida, leaning toward anarchist communism. Even if we follow

her in accepting that such similarites did exist between them, it is not at all clear why a group that endorsed and presumably practiced terrorist tactics would have dismissed La Mano Negra as nothing more than a ruse. In this case, resemblance should not be equated with identity, for despite their apparent affinities it is highly likely that—if La Mano Negra ever existed—the two groups would have stood much further apart than Lida suggests.

If we look briefly at some of the salient qualities of La Mano Negra that are divulged in the "document" Lida discovered, these differences will become apparent. A peculiar feature of the infrastructure of La Mano Negra, for example, was the existence of a Popular Tribune (Tribuna Popular). Its function was to determine the targets for reprisals and the specific forms of punishment which were to be meted out to the victims.[20] The statutes of La Mano Negra strongly indicate that the *raison d'être* of the organization was to commit these acts of violence in the ongoing war with the bourgeoisie. Most important, the statutes also stress how vital it was for members to uphold a code of secrecy and loyalty: anyone caught betraying the society was automatically sentenced to death. This was, for example, how the police explained the murder of "El Blanco de Benaocaz." This is a significant distinction when one considers that the violent acts advocated by Los Desheredados and other radical groups were rarely directed toward individuals—especially other workers—but rather were aimed at a class of oppressors, the bourgeoisie, and usually took the form of destruction of property.

The fact that a radical organization like Los Desheredados shared a common vocabulary with La Mano Negra does not mean that they stood for the same doctrine or for the same kind of revolutionary practice. For in both form and function La Mano Negra bore a striking resemblance not to a working-class body imbued with anarchist principles but rather to a criminal organization not unlike the Mafia in Italy.

Underlying Lida's framework of analysis is the assumption that the growing splits within the FTRE can be explained in terms of regional differences. As we have seen, there is no doubt that the ideological boundaries of the anarchist movement were to some extent influenced by regional differences. An instance of this was the "terrorist" tendency, discussed above, which emerged during the period of repression. Nonetheless, Lida (and indeed many historians of Spanish anarchism from Gerald Brenan onward) is mistaken when she maintains that these differences can be defined in terms of "collectivism" versus "communism," especially in view of the fact that not all the federations in the south fell into the same ideological category. At the Seville Congress, Miguel Rubio may have been speaking for many Andalusian revolutionaries when he defended what amounted to an anarchist communist position against the collectivist line being promoted by José Llunas and the Federal Commission. Lida takes Rubio's rudimentary articulation of the communist position to be representative of dissident elements like Los Desheredados and La Mano Negra. By adopting anarchist communist ideas, Lida tells us, the breakaway groups were voicing their dissatisfaction with the official line set by the more conservative elements of the FTRE. It is true that Los Desheredados represented a radical tendency within the FTRE which urged the use of violent tactics and the need for revolutionaries to work clandestinely. But as far as its members were concerned, this did not imply the abandonment of anarchist collectivist principles.[21] Actually, contrary to what Lida's study intimates, none of the dissident groups formed around this time considered itself to be anarchist communist.

Another crucially important fact overlooked by Lida is that not all Andalusian federations were ultrarevolutionary. Temma Kaplan's researches into the Andalusian anarchists show that influential Andalusian unions, like the Union of Field Workers (Unión de Trabajadores del Campo, UTC) supported the Federal Commission's efforts to build a legal trade union movement:

> The UTC was exceptionally strong in Arcos, Grazalema, and other hill towns east of Jerez. . . . In July 1882, Andalusian UTC branches held a regional meeting in Cádiz, where they affirmed the collectivist principles laid down by the FTRE the previous autumn.[22]

Given the long history of violent class conflict in the Andalusian region, it would not have been unusual for societies like La Mano Negra to have sprung up from time to time. But since we know that such clandestine bodies predated the founding of the International in Spain, can we regard them as having formed part of the Internationalist movement? Possibly other dissident groups in Andalusia subscribed to principles similar to those embodied in the Mano Negra statutes. These would, however, have made up a tiny fraction of the overall number of federations in the region, and they therefore would not have been representative of the Andalusian International movement. Most of the federations that vigorously objected to the policies being promoted by the Federal Commission were not preoccupied with personal vendettas. As militant and volatile as the Desheredados group allegedly was, it nonetheless chose to air its grievances publicly through its mouthpiece, *La Revolución Social*.[23] For example, the lead article of the first issue inveighed against the Federal Commission for having deviated from the revolutionary line adopted at the Anarchist Congress of London held in 1881. As against trade unions, Los Desheredados proposed winning the hearts and minds of the rural masses through direct action tactics such as propaganda by the deed and other forms of open class warfare. That is why they so strongly denounced the Federal Commission, accusing it of having betrayed the interests of the thousands of workers in the countryside, for whom a policy of legalism must have appeared as meaningless:

> We are leaving the legal plane upon which we have been situated in order to carry out our activities illegally, which is the only road that will allow us to bring about revolution. . . . The persecutions of which every revolutionary press is a victim . . . demonstrates to us the need to organize a clandestine press.[24]

The point here is that Los Desheredados chose to voice their differences of opinion publicly in an apparent attempt to convince the anarchists of the correctness of their perspective. This was clearly not the style of an organization like La Mano Negra, which would presumably work surreptitiously and use the threat of physical intimidation to enforce its viewpoints.

Whether or not La Mano Negra existed, the affair itself had a profound impact on the anarchist movement. Above all, it directly caused the widespread destruction of many of the nascent trade union federations in the south, effectively crushing the FTRE in that region. The Mano Negra affair also created serious problems for the Federal Commission. Among other things, it revived with tremendous force the tactical debates that had plagued the anarchist movement during the period of repression. And, in so doing, it served to reinforce the divisions that already existed among the different federations, particularly those of the industrialized northeast and those of the latifundist districts in the south. The chief problem confronting the Federal Commission at this juncture was whether the FTRE should retreat from the public sphere for the time being or whether the organization should maintain at all costs its legal status, thereby running the risk of completely cutting off the recalcitrant militant sections in Andalusia and elsewhere. At the Valencia Congress of 1883, the Federal Commission clarified its position on this critically important issue.

THE VALENCIA CONGRESS AND THE
DECLINE OF THE FTRE

The extent to which the Mano Negra affair had decimated the southern sections of the FTRE was brought home at the Valencia Congress held in October 1883: in one year the reported number of federated sections had dropped nearly twenty percent, from 663 to 539, with most of the losses coming from the south.[25] The dwindling base of the FTRE did not appear to weaken the Federal Commission's resolve to whip the respective federations into conformity with its legalist policies. All illegal activities were roundly denounced and backed up with the threat of expulsion; and, indeed, a few months before the congress convened, several members who were identified as supporters of Los Desheredados, including Miguel Rubio, had been expelled.

Another nagging problem that arose at the congress was the issue of strikes. Ever since the emergence of the FTRE, strikes throughout Spain had been occurring with increasing frequency. The Federal Commission was thus concerned, as it had been during the early days of the International, with the ramifications of an unregulated strike movement. Strikes were, according to the statutes adopted at the Barcelona Congress, to be carried out only if they were *huelgas solidarias*—that is, strikes approved by the various unions affiliated with the FTRE. The Federal Commission argued that without this kind of inter-union support, strikes would only serve to sap the revolutionary strength of the FTRE. The fact is, however, that the dilemma facing the FTRE regarding strike action was insoluble, for there was no way in which the Federal Commission or any other body within the FTRE could enforce its views. Furthermore, in the opinion of Max Nettlau, the strike tactic presented a perennial problem because, "the FTRE was too weak to support each strike, and too proud to admit to this weakness."[26]

One of the important decisions made at the congress was to transfer the seat of the Federal Commission to Valladolid. There, it was thought, the Federal Commission could operate unencumbered by the squabbling that was rending the FTRE asunder in Barcelona, Madrid, and Andalusia. Significantly, the commission itself underwent a complete metamorphosis, with all the sitting members being replaced. The new ruling body included the following members: Indalecio Cuadrado, Toribio Villa, Santiago Gómez, S. González, and Miguel Lozano. The "old guard" of syndicalist leaders, perhaps fatigued by the internecine feuding within the FTRE, turned their attention to other projects. José

Llunas, while not entirely abandoning his political activities, increasingly divided his time between the FTRE and his publishing commitments to the satirical Catalán journal he founded and edited, *La Tramontana* (1881–1893), which was known for its biting anticlerical and pro-anarchist slant. Although it is not clear why, Francisco Tomás, who until this time had fiercely defended the policies of the Federal Commission as editor of the *Crónica de los Trabajadores,* severed his ties with the Barcelona group of syndicalists and moved to Madrid. While living there, he devoted part of his time to writing a historical account of the International in Spain.[27] The most prominent syndicalist in Barcelona, Rafael Farga Pellicer, also appeared to have lost interest in the politics of the FTRE. Instead, he immersed himself in several ambitious undertakings: he assumed the editorship of the journal of the typographical society in Barcelona, *La Asociación* (1883–1888), and began writing and editing books, the most notable being his popular study of Guiseppe Garibaldi and nineteenth-century liberalism.[28]

Changes of this sort were symptomatic of the general malaise that was gripping the anarchist movement at this time. In part this was due to the splits caused by the militant/legalist controversy mentioned above, but it was also attributable to the inroads being made by Marxists (the so-called *autoritarios*) and reformist non-Marxian socialists of unions like the Tres Clases de Vapor. Ever since the founding of the FTRE, the socialists generally had been slowly but methodically laying the foundations for a socialist-directed working-class movement. Although the Madrid Marxists had created the Spanish Socialist Party (Partido Socialista Obrero Español, PSOE) in 1879, it was not until Sagasta came to power that the socialist movement began showing signs of life. At a general congress held in Barcelona in 1882, the socialists' optimistic mood was reflected in their decision to found a national federation of workers, Asociación Nacional de los Trabajadores de España—although this particular plan never materialized, and a national union of this sort did not come about until the formation of the Unión General de Trabajadores (UGT) in 1888. Outside of Madrid, where socialist elements had established headquarters since 1871, socialism appeared to be making some headway in Catalonia. Despite a general crisis in the Barcelona-based cotton industry during the 1880s, the socialists were becoming more successful at recruiting workers than the anarchists, especially in the traditionally reformist unions of the textile industry. This was especially true after José Pamías, the popular leader of the important TCV, adopted the socialist program for his union. The fact is that the anarchists were no longer the predominant force among the organized workers, primarily because they had never recovered the ground they had lost to their rivals during the seven-year repression. By 1885, anarchist influence in the region had dwindled to the point that they were only managing to hold sway over traditional strongholds, such as in Sabadell.

The decline of the FTRE was accompanied by a decline in the fortunes of the syndicalist forces in the anarchist movement. Since the Federal Commission had moved its headquarters to Valladolid, the syndicalist tendency had lost its center of focus, and consequently, it had become ever more difficult for the leadership to regain the momentum they had managed to build up between 1881 and 1882. The fact that Los Desheredados began holding their own congresses after 1883 further complicated matters for the syndicalists. Apart from Madrid, where Juan Serrano energetically defended the legalist line in *La Revista Social*, Barcelona was the only other major city where the syndicalists still maintained their hegemony.

A severe blow to their efforts was dealt in the winter of 1883–1884, when Serrano y Oteiza became a casualty of the mounting bickering within the anarchist movement. Serrano decided to step down from his post as editor of *La Revista Social* and have the paper's editorial offices transferred from Madrid to Barcelona (Sans). In the months leading up to his resignation, Serrano and his paper had increasingly come under attack from several different antisyndicalists factions, including the group that published *La Autonomía* in Seville, and the ultradicals headed by Manuel Pedrote, from Cádiz, and Victor Daza, from Madrid. For the most part, these antagonisms were caused by the bitterness the dissidents harbored for having been expelled from the FTRE during the Mano Negra scare. The dispute was just reaching the boiling point when José Llunas arrived in Madrid to lend his moral support to the syndicalist cause. But in spite of this, Serrano succumbed to the pressures of his vituperative critics. As a result, the syndicalists lost an important battle in their ongoing rivalry with the extremists of the FTRE.[29]

This vicious circle of disputes weighed heavily on the Federal Commission, which was clearly at a loss as to how to bring the quarreling to an end. In September 1884, it convened an extraordinary congress in Barcelona to discuss the fate of the FTRE. The proceedings—which were conducted clandestinely owing to a government ban on public meetings—were no doubt permeated by a mood of despair, for the sixty-four delegates in attendance decided that circumstances no longer permitted the legal existence of their organization. Thus, reluctantly, they called for the dissolution of the FTRE and advised its members "to retreat to Mount Aventino until better times arrived."

In the end, the delegates decided not to disband the FTRE but rather to suspend its activities. Each member federation was to remain organized in whatever form possible. A faint hope echoed at the congress that as conditions improved it would be again possible to reconstitute the larger body. But very few delegates anticipated an early return to a legally recognized movement. That the Federal Commission was pessimistic about the future prospects of the FTRE is reflected in its decision to cancel a congress that was to be held in Madrid in the spring of 1885. Those who opposed this decision—notably, Serrano y Oteiza, who was still campaigning against the "illegalists" in the pages of the newly relocated *La Revista Social*—decided to celebrate their own congress. But as Max Nettlau points out in his history of this period, the meeting drew only those who were already sympathetic to Serrano and his supporters, and therefore it amounted to little more than a "monologue" of those who were already in agreement.[30]

By the end of 1885, the competition between the syndicalists and their rivals over who was to dominate the anarchist movement momentarily ceased, and, in any case, the FTRE showed little sign of regaining its former strength and influence. Without the syndicalists at the helm, the FTRE began drifting aimlessly and, as it turned out, irrevocably. This was primarily because the organization had been given shape and color by the syndicalist tendencies in the libertarian movement. It had been instituted by them as a legal trade union body that was to serve as a vehicle for advancing the workers' revolutionary ambitions. Under their direction, the anarchist movement had attained within two years a size and significance that could hardly have been predicted during the bleak days of the seven-year repression. The syndicalists' long-term strategy for the FTRE thus suggests that they had a realistic grasp of what was needed to build a mass base for their movement. Ironically, it was their dogged adherence to a policy of legalism that proved to be their biggest political liability.

Prior to the Mano Negra episode, the syndicalists' legalist program had proved itself remarkably successful. But the early successes of the organization had still not been consolidated at the time the scandal erupted, and for this reason the failure of their strategy has to be viewed against the background of this pivotal event. The Mano Negra affair affected syndicalist policy in several different ways. As the repression intensified in the south and the FTRE inevitably lost ground to its adversaries, the Federal Commission became increasingly obsessed with the question of legality, so much so that it lost the support of a significant segment of the anarchist community.

What the syndicalists' strategy had apparently failed to anticipate was the extent to which the FTRE was vulnerable to government repression. When the workers were sufficiently provoked to retaliate against the authorities—as they were in the wake of the Mano Negra espisode, for instance—the syndicalists told them to hold back, fearing that retaliation would jeopardize the legal status of the movement. Following the Mano Negra affair, the Federal Commission proved itself particularly ineffectual in dealing with dissident elements within the FTRE. Perhaps its greatest tactical error in this regard was to force the entire membership to toe a syndicalist ideological line. Through their control of the principal anarchist publications, the syndicalists attempted to place their policies above criticism by arguing that any form of dissension seriously endangered the true aims of the anarchist movement.

The inflexibility and intolerance shown by the ruling syndicalist factions may in the short run have preserved the basic trade union framework of the anarchist movement, but, in the end, they also had the more insidious effect of undermining a key pillar of the FTRE: the moral support it derived from rank-and-file anarchists. By persistently refusing to revise their strategy in the light of the Mano Negra scandal, the syndicalists soon found themselves unable to respond effectively in a leadership role.

CHAPTER VI

The Development of a Schism: The Origins of the Collectivist/ Communist Controversy

During the latter part of the 1880s and throughout the 1890s, the development of Spanish anarchism was dominated by an ideological conflict that profoundly influenced the course of the movement, not least because it divided the anarchists over the key issues of strategy and tactics. Known as the anarchist collectivist/communist controversy, this great debate generated an intense whirlwind of heated arguments, which arose in 1885 and did not completely subside until the turn of the century.[1] On one side of the dispute were the collectivists, a group consisting entirely of syndicalist-minded anarchists. Following the tradition laid down by the founders of the FRE, they sought to ground libertarianism on a legally recognized trade union structure, believing that once they had erected an extensive and powerful network of unions they could bring about a general social revolution. They were opposed by the heirs to the militant wings of the FRE and FTRE, namely, those who did not recognize, as the collectivists did, the value of centralizing economic power in the hands of organized workers. The communists argued that there was no purpose in maintaining a complex and cumbersome syndicalist apparatus, which in their eyes served only to retard the revolutionary movement. For them, revolution and violence were inseparable, and consequently, they professed faith only in conspiratorial and terrorist tactics. It therefore followed that when the majority of anarchists decided to adopt the communist position they were obliged to revise not only some of their theoretical principles but their revolutionary strategy as well. Significantly, this necessarily entailed abandoning the FTRE as the organizational framework for anarchist activity.

Although the protagonists of the collectivist/communist dispute can be characterized in this way, the intention here is not to present a simplified picture of a historical phenomenon that is quite complex. For even though it is possible to divide the arguments of the anarchists in the period from 1885 to 1900 into "collectivist" and "communist" categories, my intention is not to give a falsely black and white appearance to a debate whose real character was composed of various shades of both theoretical and practical differences. It would be wrong to suggest, for example, that the collectivist/communist debate simply brought about a polarization of the anarchist movement. To be sure, there were some, like Francisco Tomás, who never abandoned their faith in collectivism and remained throughout their lives uncompromisingly anticommunist. But there were also many anarchists who were not especially preoccupied with the dispute. The doctrinal differences that were so sharply dividing some ideologues probably had little significance for the ordinary anarchist worker. Still others refused to take sides and were instead content to regard anarchism in a wider sense as a doctrine that embraced a variety of different but nonetheless fundamentally related concepts. This perspective led some anarchists to formulate an anarchist school of ideas known as "anarchism without adjectives," about which we will learn more later. One should therefore bear in mind that during the course of the debate, what was really important for most anarchists was not whether they called themselves collectivist or communist but that they stood for the essential tenets of anarchist thought. In the words of a leading anarchist of the era, to be a libertarian one need only subscribe to "the ideals of no power, no authority, no subjugation to authority [of one individual by another]," and uphold "the equality of rights, obligations, and conditions among those constituting the social aggregate."[2]

There were two distinguishable phases to the collectivist/communist debate in Spain. The first one lasted for a period of three years (1885–1888), culminating with the dissolution of the FTRE. The second phase continued until 1897, when the anarchist movement was forced underground following the Montjuich affair.

THE COLLECTIVIST POSITION, 1881–1885

Until the mid-1880s, the vast majority of Spanish anarchists subscribed to the three cardinal principles of Bakuninism: antipoliticalism, atheism, and collectivism. While it is true that Bakuninist concepts formed the core of anarchist doctrine, it would be inaccurate to define Spanish anarchism solely in these terms. For it was also true that many anarchists had begun their political careers as Federals, and their thinking was also deeply influenced by the ideas of Proudhon and the person most responsible for popularizing his ideas in Spain, Francisco Pi y Margall. Pi, who translated into Spanish *Du principe fédératif* (Paris, 1865) and other seminal works by Proudhon, was the only thinker of the period to provide a coherent view of the theory of federalism. It was Pi's understanding of federalist doctrine that provided the conceptual link between federalism and Bakuninist collectivism. Both as a devoted apostle of Proudhon and as a theoretician in his own right, Pi helped to shape the ideas of several generations of anarchists, including such outstanding figures as Juan Serrano y Oteiza, Rafael Farga Pellicer, Gaspar Sentiñón, Fermín Salvochea, Anselmo Lorenzo, Ricardo Mella, and Fernando Tarrida del Mármol.

When he wrote *La reacción y la revolución* in 1854—a theoretic work that years later some anarchists came to regard as an early expression of Spanish anarchist thinking—one of the things Pi had attempted was to define the concept of revolution.[3] Pi explained that above all revolution meant the destruction of power. Most important, he conceived power as an entity that could be qualitatively altered by a process of dividing it and then subdividing it until it was completely eliminated. "I shall divide and subdivide power," Pi explained in his treatise, "I shall make it changeable and will go on destroying it." Within a social context, Pi thought this necessarily involved establishing a federalist system: an extreme form of decentralization in which power ultimately rested not with any centralizing agency but with the individual himself. After the revolution, he continued, society should be organized into "natural" social units—that is, extensions of the biological family—like the *municipio* (municipality) or *pueblo* (town). Binding together these units, as well as the individuals who lived in them, was the fundamental aspect of Pi's system: the mutual pact or contract (*pacto sinalagmático*). In common with Proudhon, from whom he borrowed the idea, Pi believed that the freedom of the individual would be safely guaranteed as long as he was permitted to enter into contractual arrangements with others. To be sure, these were not akin to the social contracts advocated by the Hobbesian school of thinkers, in which the personal independence of the individual was surrendered upon entering society. Nor were they to be legal contracts, which both Pi and Proudhon made a point of repudiating, but rather they were to be pacts based solely on the consent of sovereign individuals.

The scope of Pi's political philosophy encompassed a great deal more than what has been referred to here. His commitment to the Hegelian understanding of the dialectical process in history, for instance, was also fundamental to his thinking. But this dimension of his philosophy was never taken up by most anarchists. As we shall see, they did not follow the Hegelian tradition as interpreted by Proudhon (and, through him, Pi) but rather became the uncritical disciples of positivism as derived from the writings of Auguste Comte, Herbert Spencer, and Charles Darwin.[4] The anarchists followed the positivists in insisting that philosophy become more practical and scientific rather than metaphysical and speculative. Notwithstanding these epistemological differences, it was Pi's negative attitude toward authority as well as his abiding belief in the freedom of the individual which were most appealing to the anarchists. And, indeed, these two themes were generously incorporated into much of the collectivist literature during the late nineteenth century.

During the early days of the FTRE, Pi's influence was most clearly manifested in the political ideas of a prominent syndicalist whom we have already introduced, Juan Serrano y Oteiza (1837–1886). Serrano's writings, particularly his articles in *La Revista Social* and his posthumously published work *La moral del progreso* (1888), illustrate how federalist ideology was related to anarchist collectivism as it was interpreted in Spain. Born in Madrid into the modest home of a fan maker, Serrano took up his father's trade for a brief spell. As a youth, he was introduced to Federalist ideas, which led him to develop a keen interest in radical politics. After studying law, he eventually became a notary public.[5] In the early 1860s, he was associated with the Fomento de las Artes, where he often delivered lectures on the social and political theories of Proudhon. Anselmo Lorenzo, who frequently attended these talks, credits Serrano with having introduced him to the concept of revolution. Recalling an inspiring address Serrano gave in 1865, Lorenzo wrote in his memoirs:

> [O]n that occasion I heard for the first time the expression of the criterion of pure revolution, a principle that would some years later correspond perfectly to the ideas brought to us by Fanelli.[6]

When Giuseppi Fanelli founded the Madrid section of the International in late 1868, Serrano was one of the first to enlist in the organization, becoming shortly afterward a convert to Bakuninism. Like Pi, whose dispassionate approach to politics prompted some of his contemporaries to dub him "the man of ice," Serrano adopted a measured and analytical political attitude. All of his writings—be they polemical or not—were stamped by a quasi-legalistic style that relied on the force of rational argument rather than an appeal to the emotions to convince the reader of the correctness of his position. His abilities as a writer and polemicist were first tested in the pages of Morago's *El Condenado,* when he loyally defended the Bakuninist orientation of the FRE against the venomous assaults of the Marxist *La Emancipación.* During the repression that followed, he continued his involvement in the movement by contributing articles to the clandestine *El Orden* and *La Revista Social.*[7] By the time he took over the editorship of the latter paper from Viñas in 1881, Serrano was recognized as one of the leading spokesmen for the syndicalist wing of the anarchist movement.

As editor for *La Revista Social,* the mouthpiece for the FTRE between 1881 and 1884, Serrano defined an ideological stance for the organization which evinced his heavy intellectual debt to the Federalist tradition in general and to Pi y Margall in particular. The overall aims of the revolutionary movement which Serrano outlined in the first issue of the paper, for example, were strikingly similar to those set forth in Pi's writings:

> We want the autonomy of the individual, of the group or trade union section that individuals are able to constitute, and of the municipality. As a means of realizing these goals of autonomy we want legislative power to reside in the hands of the individual, in the trade union group or section, and in the municipality itself.[8]

The society envisaged by Serrano was patterned after the one first presented in *La reacción y la revolución* and later elaborated by Pi in his work *Las nacionalidades* (1876). In the passage just quoted, Serrano follows Pi in seeing the municipality as the social unit that is to serve as the apex around which the future society would be organized. Serrano in fact borrowed extensively from Pi's theories, incorporating many of Pi's basic concepts—like the belief that such values as morality and progress were the guiding forces in social development—into his own thinking.[9]

A casual glance at *La Revista Social* reveals that the origins of much of the political vocabulary employed by Serrano—as well as by other anarchist collectivists during the early 1880s—can be traced to federal ideology. For example, the Federalist term "municipio" (the "natural" social unit) was commonly found not only in Serrano's paper but in Internationalist circulars and newspapers from 1870 onward. This was especially apparent in the period following the Paris Commune and the cantonalist revolts of 1873, when the anarchists began enlarging the concept of *municipio* by identifying it with these commune experiences.[10] The word "autonomy" also recurs frequently in anarchist literature of this epoch, usually in association with other highly esteemed principles like "truth," "justice," and "moral progress." Some anarchists even went so far as to regard the word "autonomy" as being synonymous with "anarchism." Thus, despite the fact that he thought of himself as an anarchist, Serrano in particular tended to use the two terms interchangeably.

With reference to this last point, it should be made clear that in addition to the theoretical significance the collectivists attached to the term "autonomy," practical considerations may also have influenced them to substitute this word for "anarchism." Given that Serrano and other like-minded syndicalists wanted at all costs to preserve the legal status of the FTRE, it is highly likely that they deliberately avoided using potentially emotive terminology like "anarchy" or "anarchism" in order to project a more positive image of the International movement. Serrano himself was well aware of the negative connotations such terms conjured up in the public mind:

> [T]he material means of governing this society [of the future] are: autonomy, the covenant, and federation based on collective property, which is the just property principle. This is the society where order is permanent. This—and not the stupidities that are bandied about—is the anarchism that is hated so much.[11]

While certain strong parallels exist between the political ideas of Serrano and those of Pi and the Federals, there were also fundamental differences in their respective political ideologies. An obvious, but nonetheless crucial, distinction between their social theories was that they aspired to different ends. For Serrano, and indeed for all the anarchists, the ultimate aim of social revolution was not just to render government into the decentralized form visualized in Federalist theory but to bring about the complete abolition of the state.

The collectivists again differed from the Federals in their interpretation of the workers' role in the revolutionary movement and in their commitment to the economic principles of collectivism. While Pi and the Federals sought to bring about social change by means of a political party that was anchored in a mass movement, Serrano and the collectivists not only rejected political parties but also saw the working classes—and not middle-class intellectuals—as the principal agents for effecting the social and economic transformation of society. On this vital issue, the collectivists stood much closer to the viewpoints presented in Proudhon's *De la capacité politique des classes ouvrières* (1865) than they did to the Federals. Contrary to what Proudhon argues in this seminal work, the Federals did not see the respective political and economic interests of the working classes and the bourgeoisie as being mutually exclusive.

Although the collectivists retained some of the elements of the Federals' economic beliefs, such as the need for contracts of exchange in the future society, they vehemently rejected their view that it was possible under capitalism to harmonize the economic forces in society. Instead they argued that nothing short of a thoroughgoing social revolution was required in order to establish an equitable economic system. They also went beyond the Federals in calling for the collective ownership of property, insisting that each worker was entitled to the *integral* product of his labor. Later, with the introduction of anarchist communism, the anarchists advanced the logic of this economic argument one step further by demanding both the collective ownership of the means of production and the abolition of the wage system.

Another important point to consider is that, however freely Serrano and the collectivists adopted ideas from the Federals, they did not necessarily interpret them in the same way. This is best illustrated by Serrano's understanding of the notion of the pact, which was not only the basic premise for his social theory of anarchism but also the rationale for his belief in a policy of legalism for the FTRE.

Serrano followed Pi in holding that the mutual pact provided the basis for linking every element in society. Through it autonomous individuals were related to each other, as were the families that constituted the municipality, the different municipalities that made up a district or region, and, finally, the different regions (cantons) that collectively constituted a nation. Here, however, the similarity between their respective views on the pact ends. Serrano's understanding of the pact differs from that of Pi's in several respects. This difference was above all due to the fact that the underlying model for Serrano's political analysis was founded on different assumptions than Pi's.

Serrano developed his political theory on two levels. One was simply an argument that maintained that social revolution was necessary in order to bring about a genuine state of freedom. Significantly, this viewpoint was predicated on a moral proposition that was common to all anarchist thinking: the revolution was morally imperative because it was seen as the only way of destroying the corrupt system of economic and social values on which the capitalist system rested. The second dimension of Serrano's thinking was more complex, since it was derived from a quasi-scientific understanding of human society. The so-called natural scientific method of induction and deduction—rather than the dialectic method—was used by him to study social phenomena. Like so many anarchist thinkers of his day, Serrano believed that an analogy could be drawn between society and the world of nature. Man was seen as forming a part of a complex set of interrelationships, which existed not only between people but also between man and nature. It followed from this perspective that both society and nature were governed by the same laws, such as the law of evolution, which was understood as the principal dynamic for continuous change in the world. By viewing society in this way, Serrano believed that it was possible to demonstrate that anarchism was both a logical and necessary consequence of the development of society. To Serrano, then, the pact meant something more than just the social bond that Pi had talked about. In his view it also served as a mechanism for cementing the various components of society in such a way that they formed an organic whole and thereby allowed society to evolve naturally.

On another level, Pi's and Serrano's respective views on the pact differed insofar as the former broadly viewed the pact as a relationship arising from the needs and desires of all classes of individuals in society, while for Serrano the worker was the pivotal figure in the pact arrangements both in the present and in future society. Serrano thought he had found in the notion of the pact a way of reconciling the conflicting demands of effective collective action—that is, the trade unions—and the worker's individual freedom of choice. In the present society it was conceived as a way of protecting the natural rights—as against legislated rights—of the worker from the abuses of a system that was still subject to arbitrary authority. Under the anarchist system of the future, the pact was supposed to provide the worker with an equitable means to exchange the fruits of his labor and at the same time ensure that his individuality was preserved within the context of a larger producing unit.

Apart from some minor exceptions, the collectivism espoused by
Serrano in *La Revista Social* corresponded closely to the perspectives
of other leading syndicalists of the FTRE. While veteran anarchists like
José Llunas y Pujols and Francisco Tomás may not have accepted all
of Serrano's Federalist-inspired propositions—such as his insistence on
equating autonomy with anarchism—they were generally in agreement
with the thrust of his arguments. This was because the collectivists of
the period—whether their ideas were richly imbued with Proudhonian
qualities or were, like those of both Llunas and Tomás, more strictly
speaking Bakuninist—were united by a group of common assumptions
about the nature of the anarchist movement. A belief shared by all
collectivists, for example, was that it was necessary to erect the foundations of the future society before the day of revolution arrived. To this
end, in both theory and practice, they strictly adhered to the concept
of syndicalism as embodied in the traditions of the FRE and FTRE.
This slant was particularly evident in the writings of José Llunas.
Llunas was fond of saying that anarchism was nothing more than the
pure administration of things, and he saw trade unions as being at the
center of this administrative framework. In his *Estudios filosofías sociales* (Barcelona, 1883), as in all of his writings, Llunas pictures the
trade union federation as the embryo of the future society. As a result,
he stressed the urgent need in the present for building a working-class
movement organized in accordance with anarchist principles. The
FTRE, in his eyes, exemplified these qualities. It was an organization
in which power radiated from the bottom upward and which united
workers locally by crafts, regionally by a federation of different crafts
of an industry, and nationally under the umbrella of the Regional
Federation.[12]

From 1868 until the emergence of the FTRE in 1881, the collectivists
did not significantly modify their ideological beliefs. The only recogniz-
able shift in their thinking had to do with the adoption of the policy of
legalism during the seven years of repression, and this change of attitude
was prompted by practical rather than philosophical considerations.
Meanwhile, beyond the Spanish borders, anarchist thinking was rapidly
undergoing transformations rather than stagnating. The two most important changes that occurred in this period were the introduction of
the concept of propaganda by the deed, which I discussed earlier, and
the development of anarchist communism. By 1880, propaganda by the
deed had already made an impact on the Spanish movement, whereas
anarchist communism was still unfamiliar to the majority of workers.

Before examining the development of communism in Spain, we should pause momentarily to review the theoretical origins of the term.

THE ORIGINS OF ANARCHIST COMMUNISM

Like the concept of propaganda by the deed, anarchist communism originated outside of Spain. It evolved over a period of several years—between 1876 and 1880—and can be regarded as a product of the collective theoretical work of various anarchist thinkers. The use of the term seems to have begun simultaneously and separately in Geneva, Switzerland, among the anarchists associated with the Jura Federation, and in Naples, Italy, among the anarchists grouped around Emilio Covelli, Carlo Cafiero, and Errico Malatesta. According to Max Nettlau, however, the phrase "anarchist communism" first appeared in a pamphlet written—but probably never published—by François Dumartheray entitled "Aux travailleurs manuels partisans de l'action politique" (1876). Dumartheray, a refugee from Lyons who belonged to the "L'Avenir" group of militant anarchists in Geneva, was a close associate of Elisée Reclus, who may well have influenced him to write on the theme of anarchist communism. At all events, during the course of the next few months, "anarchist communism" was increasingly employed in the Jura's theoretical organ, the *Bulletin,* eventually replacing the word "collectivism" in discussions of the future society.

Elsewhere at this time, the Italian anarchists were also developing an anarchist communist perspective. Although it is not clear who first decided to use the term, the concept itself arose out of discussions among Covelli, Cafiero, and Malatesta over the question of the economic system of the future anarchist society.[13] On a theoretical level, the communists challenged one of the key concepts of collectivism, namely, that the worker was entitled to the integral product of his labor.[14] They argued that because this principle ignored the reality that there were those in society who, whether because of age, infirmity, or some other natural disadvantage, would not be able to produce and thus could not enjoy the fruits of their own labor, it failed as a criterion for establishing the just distribution of products in future society. The communists particularly feared that those who produced more might well develop into a new privileged class of rulers who arbitrarily determined the remuneration of labor. To resolve this dilemma the communists suggested the establishment of a communal system in which the wage system would be abolished altogether. Under this scheme, it was presumed that man's innate sense of solidarity would manifest itself, thereby ensuring that everyone would voluntarily produce according to his abilities and consume according to his needs. Hence, for the communists, a truly anarchist state was one in which everyone, including those who did not play an active part in the productive process, shared the wealth of society.[15]

The collectivists, and even Bakunin himself, had never addressed this question about the economic organization of the future society, possibly because collectivism for them implied a society in which workers would share their wealth with everyone, including those less fortunate members who—for some reason or another—would be unproductive. The only collectivist who even attempted to describe at length how a society would develop under collectivism was Bakunin's foremost disciple, James Guillaume. In a pamphlet written in 1874 but not published until 1876, Guillaume outlined the steps for bringing about the just distribution of social wealth after the revolution:

> The problem of property having been resolved . . . and the question of types of distribution and remuneration becomes secondary. We should to the greatest possible extent institute and be guided by the principle *From each according to his ability, to each according to his need*. . . . Everyone will draw what he needs from the abundant social reserve of commodities, without fear of depletion; and the moral sentiment which will be more highly developed among free and equal workers will prevent, or greatly reduce, abuse and waste. In the meantime, each community will decide for itself during the transition period [from capitalism and collectivism] the method it deems best for the distribution of the products of associated labor.[16]

By emphasizing the important role that the community—as opposed to the individual—played in determining the distribution of social wealth, Guillaume was providing a conceptual link between collectivism and communism. The communists, in fact, did not especially object to this depiction of the future society, but they did not see why it should any longer be regarded as collectivist. Their suggestion was to view collectivism not as an end in itself, as Guillaume had done, but rather as a transitional stage through which society would pass in its evolution toward a completely anarchistic (i.e., communistic) state of existence.

With regard to the day-to-day practice of anarchism, the communists were at odds with the collectivists over the organization of the revolutionary movement. The communists were intractably opposed to trade unions, which were viewed as essentially reformist bodies that were easily compromised by the antirevolutionary forces in society. Also in contrast to the collectivists, they saw trade unions as being invariably accompanied by the three most iniquitous features of capitalism: bureaucracy, hierarchy, and corruption. So far as they were concerned, the way in which the anarchist movement was organized should reflect the antiauthoritarian principles of their doctrine, and, consequently, they preferred to set up small, loosely federated groups composed of dedicated militants.

The communists' deep hostility toward trade unions was matched by their equally profound faith in the power of spontaneous revolutionary acts. Quite understandably, then, they tended to shun strikes and other forms of economic warfare in favor of violent methods, extolling above all the virtues of propaganda by the deed. This gave rise to the widepsread misconception that the concepts of anarchist communism and propaganda by the deed had sprung from the same source, when in fact they had developed independently. Nevertheless, from around 1878 on, communism and propaganda by the deed became inextricably linked in the minds of the anarchists and their enemies alike.

Between 1878 and 1880, the ideological drift toward communism was given impetus by two distinguished theoreticians, Peter Kropotkin and Elisée Reclus. Along with Cafiero and Malatesta, Reclus was one of the first anarchists to accept the principles of anarchist communism, and in addition he played an important part in developing this perspective through his collaboration with other influential anarchist thinkers. Kropotkin, who eventually became the most celebrated proponent of anarchist communism, seems to have been largely unaware of the communist ideas of the Italians until this time. Toward the end of 1879, he laid the formal groundwork for the new ideology in a series of articles in *Le Révolté* of Geneva, a paper he helped to found in February 1879. In these, Kropotkin argued that however minor the differences actually were between the two doctrines, communism nonetheless represented an advance over collectivism, and that it better expressed the overall aims of anarchism. By 1880, Kropotkin, along with most of the anarchists outside of Spain, had come round to accepting the doctrine. The classifying phrase "anarchist communism" was formally adopted by the international anarchist movement at a congress of the Jura Federation held at La Chaux-de-Fonds that same year.[17]

We should mention here that while some anarchists, notably Adhémar Schwitzguébel and his followers in the Jura Federation, were at first reluctant to adopt the communist label, the transition from collectivism to communism in Europe did not generate anything like the controversy that preoccupied the Spanish anarchists for the better part of two decades. This was due in large measure to the peculiar way in which anarchism had developed in the Spanish context. In the rest of Europe, the anarchists had never secured a foothold within the trade union movements. This was true even in countries where anarchism was popular—for example, in Italy, where the government's unrelenting war against the anarchists condemned libertarianism to a precarious existence. Principally for these reasons, collectivism was easily displaced by a doctrine like communism, which did not rely on the support of organized labor groups. In Spain, however, anarchist collectivism had from the beginning been identified with the trade union movement, and this identification persisted in spite of the frequent periods of repression during which union activity was conducted underground. Partly for this reason, and partly because the syndicalist wing of the anarchist movement retained its hegemony until the middle 1880s, collectivism survived in Spain considerably longer than it did elsewhere. Yet, when circumstances conspired against the syndicalists' attempts to continue working through the unions, collectivism increasingly gave place to the communist perspective.

THE EMERGENCE OF ANARCHIST COMMUNISM IN SPAIN

One reason Spain was for so many years impervious to communist ideas was that the Spaniards were isolated from the mainstream of the international anarchist movement. This was evident during the years of repression and especially after the collapse of the Alliance, when the bonds that had been established between the respective international anarchist groups and that had linked Spain to the movements in other countries were dissolved. As we have already seen, these connections were important avenues for the exchange of ideas. They also greatly facilitated the introduction of new tactics, the most notable example being propaganda by the deed.

There were other, more basic, reasons why communist ideas remained inaccessible to the Spaniards some nine years after it was first formulated by the French and Italians. The fact is that most Spanish anarchists were illiterate, and of those who could read only a tiny percentage knew French or any other idiom in which the communists were then writing. Translations of seminal communist tracts were slow in coming, and they did not regularly appear until after 1886. Hence, even though the communist position had first been expressed by Miguel Rubio at the Seville Congress in 1882, the doctrine itself was initially confined to a small reading audience whose knowledge of the theory was derived largely from foreign anarchist sources, especially in the pages of *Le Révolté* (Geneva), where articles by Malatesta, Kropotkin, and other leading proponents of communism frequently appeared.

Perhaps the only areas in Spain where anarchist communists could be found at this time were in Madrid, Seville, and Barcelona and its environs. Since the heady days of *La Gloriosa,* Barcelona had become a melting pot for foreign anarchists and revolutionaries, and it would seem that several Italian and German anarchist communists had been living there at least until 1883. Of all the foreign anarchists living in Spain, the French were by far the most numerous and most influential. French anarchists played a part in nearly every significant anarchist incident of the period 1871 to 1897. There is no way of knowing exactly how many of them were resident in Spain, but it would appear as though their community was large enough to support the limited circulation of several French publications, including *L'Audace, Le Révolté* (after 1887 *La Révolte*), *Revue Anarchiste Internationale,* and *Terre et Liberté.*[18] Apart from these tiny handfuls of radicals, though, the doctrine remained virtually unfamiliar to the mass of the rank and file affiliated to the FTRE. The first purely Spanish anarchist communist faction, the "Grupo de Gracia," was created in 1885 in the Barcelona suburb of Gracia. With the emergence of this group and the publication of its paper, *La Justicia Humana* in April 1886, communist ideas in Spain began to crystallize into a coherent body of doctrine. The penetration of communist ideas progressed slowly at first not least because collectivist principles were deeply instilled in the minds of the Spanish anarchists.[19] But, from 1887 onward, communist ideas began rapidly spreading throughout Spain, thanks in part to the proliferation of anarchist communist journals and to the growing number of translations into Spanish of the works of Kropotkin and other distinguished communists.

We mentioned above that in practice communism differed from collectivism in several ways, but most notably over the question of trade unions. Unlike the collectivists, who regarded trade unions as the channels through which the revolution would be realized, the communists did not see these organizations as being instruments of the revolutionary process. In Spain, this belief was manifest in the communists' deep-seated distrust of workers affiliated to reformist associations, like the Tres Clases de Vapor. Such associations were antirevolutionary, the communists claimed, because they increasingly sought reforms in the form of higher wages and the like within the established system rather than a radical solution to their problems. Worse still, the communists further charged, this group of workers was led by officials who were vile opportunists: they were willing to come to a secret understanding with the employers even if this meant betraying the interests of the working classes. Rather than rely on the trade unions, the communists placed great emphasis on building the revolution around small cells of self-sacrificing radicals. Stressing the importance of direct action tactics like "propaganda by the deed" and underscoring the constant need for the anarchists to maintain a revolutionary stance, the communists pictured themselves in a clearly defined relationship with the ruling classes: they were to have a decidedly militant public image so as to convince their enemies of the perpetual state of "class war" that would exist until the advent of social revolution. Their interpretation of the anarchists' role in society contrasted sharply with that held by the collectivists who, in spite of their antagonism toward the ruling classes, struggled to preserve the legal status of anarchist groups, fearing that a movement forced underground would never attract the mass following that they believed indispensable for a general revolution.

Another distinguishing feature of the anarchist communist tendency in Spain at this time was that it lacked intellectuals or leaders of any caliber. Neither Emilio Hugas nor Martín Borrás, the spirits behind the Grupo de Gracia, exhibited leadership qualities. It seems as though they both suffered from personality defects: Hugas projected a cold, unsociable image, while Borrás was reputed to be both ill-tempered and hot-headed. Moreover, in contrast to most collectivists, the communists took a perverse pride in maintaining a decidedly anti-intellectual stance. The editor of *La Justicia Humana* put it in the following way: "We are not literate, lacking the form and good style of diction . . . but insofar as we write for our *compañeros* the *desheredados*, we are confident that they shall understand us."[20] As far as the communists were concerned, to express oneself in a simple, unpolished style—that is, one that was unencumbered by the flowery, metaphoric expressions common to much of the popular literature of the period—was befitting to the true anarchist revolutionary. Above all, the communists believed that the directness of their language would allow them to express the authentic rebellious sentiments of the worker.

This insistence on anti-intellectualism also reflected the degree to which the communists were, unlike their collectivist counterparts, impatient for the revolution to begin. They maintained that there was no point in having either their message mediated through bodies like the Federal Commission or its content diluted by the opinions of others in general congresses. To the communists, the social and economic forces that gave rise to a revolution did not necessarily require a long period of gestation. Nor did the revolution demand that the proletariat absorb all the abstract tenets of anarchist doctrine. Instead they were convinced that a general insurrection could be incited by a vanguard of devoted radicals whose role it was to exploit the revolutionary potential of the masses by whatever means possible.

COMMUNISM VERSUS COLLECTIVISM

Previously we noted that, following the Seville Congress, dissident elements increasingly challenged the strategy of the "legalists," and began to enlarge the scope of their influence and activity by forming groups outside of the FTRE. By the end of 1884, the organization had split into at least three distinguishable tendencies: (1) those who supported the FTRE, (2) those who were willing to stay within the trade union movement but who did not support the "legalist" orientation of the syndicalists, and (3) those who were so violently opposed to the programs of the FTRE that they deserted it.[21] While not altogether rejecting the anarchist collectivist creed, the last two groups no longer saw the FTRE as the proper vehicle for taking the working class toward its revolutionary destination. Then, with the penetration of anarchist communist ideas from abroad, these dissident elements became the disciples of the new ideology.

Ironically, the communist viewpoint was first widely publicized by the collectivist *La Revista Social* of Sans. Provoked by several violently anticollectivist articles that had recently appeared in the *Revue Anarchiste Internationale* (Bordeaux) and *Le Révolté*, the editor set himself the task of rebutting the communist position. In a series of blistering articles that appeared in March and April 1885, presumably penned by Serrano himself, the differences between the two ideological tendencies were spelled out concisely and cogently.

No doubt Serrano felt compelled to defend collectivism in Spain because he strongly sensed that if anarchist communism took root there the fate of the FTRE would be sealed. Not surprisingly this sense of urgency affected the style of those articles, giving them an emotional tinge that was uncharacteristic of most of his writings. Wasting little time on an analysis of the finer theoretical distinctions between collectivism and communism, Serrano dealt directly with those issues that he felt were most pressing to the members of the FTRE. He began by castigating the communists for dogmatically opposing organizations of this type:

> [T]he anarchist communists do not accept any organization except that of a group, and therefore they do not have organized trade sections, nor do they have local federations, district federations or federations of trade or trade unions. . . . Their only and exclusive forms of organizations are the groups or circles of social studies among which there has not been established any pact or constituted any commission which can serve as a center of relations between the respective collective bodies that pursue the same ends.[22]

No less threatening to the syndicalist tradition of the Spanish anarchists, Serrano averred, was the communists' proposed line of conduct. He warned that they were eager to promote tactics that were fraught with disastrous implications for the revolutionary movement, not least because they would inevitably bring about the persecution of the proletariat. Rejecting strikes, boycotts, and similar economic weapons, the communists pinned their hopes on the efficacy of violent practices such as "propaganda by the deed"—which, as we have already seen, had been officially adopted by the international anarchist movement at the London Congress of 14–19 July 1881—as well as other acts that engendered a state of permanent insurrection. Besides strenuously denouncing such tactics on the grounds that they jeopardized the legal status of unions and thus imperiled the freedom of the working classes, Serrano also condemned them as being utterly unrealistic:

> To combat the bourgeoisie . . . by means of individual acts or allied groups appears to us [i.e., the collectivists] to be a form of self-sacrifice that borders on insanity. . . . We believe that individual actions—even if they employ thousands upon thousands of kilos of dynamite—will not succeed in any region, nor will they succeed in destroying the bourgeoisie or in bringing about the Social Revolution.[23]

Serrano attempted in his concluding article to discredit the communists by linking their doctrine to other branches of what he termed the authoritarian school of socialism. He labored to explain to his readers that all communists, including Plato, Campanella, Cabet, and Marx, were by nature authoritarian. Echoing the anticommunist sentiments he had absorbed from both Proudhon and Bakunin, Serrano declared that "Communism is the triumph of Authority over Liberty."[24] Accordingly, for him, the choice between the two doctrines was a clear one: to accept anarchist communism would be tantamount to breaking with the genuinely antiauthoritarian working-class tradition as it had developed in Spain, while to accept the principles of collectivism offered the only viable way of preserving it.

A significant aspect of Serrano's argument that is illustrated here is that he was presenting the collectivist/communist debate in terms of polar opposites. In doing so, he was setting the tone of the dispute: there was to be no middle ground or compromise struck between the adversaries. He thereby made it necessary for the worker to choose one philosophy over another.

As lucid and forceful as Serrano's arguments were, they nonetheless showed a narrowness of outlook. Above all, they did not address such key issues as the yawning gulf separating the federations within the FTRE. While content to restate the case for building strong trade union organizations, for example, Serrano neglected to take into account the fact that workers in the south were hardly in a position to follow such advice while they were struggling to overcome the debilitating effects of government persecutions. Flawed by this kind of parochialism—which was characteristic of the syndicalist perspective—Serrano's views inevitably failed to appeal to a wider audience.

Considering the FTRE's fragile state of existence, Serrano's urgent warnings can be seen as nearly desperate attempts to rally the syndicalists to respond to the ever-growing threat from their ideological rivals. By the time these articles appeared, however, the moderates had all but lost the battle against the forces of radicalism. For although they had not as yet embraced communist ideology, the militants, unlike the syndicalists, apparently found it too jarringly incongruous to continue calling for the establishment of a legally recognized anarchist movement while at the same time striving for the violent overthrow of the very political and economic system that accorded them this right.

In any case, Serrano's well-reasoned diatribes against the communists at first elicited little response from his reading audience. Even other collectivist newspapers, like the weekly *Bandera Social* of Madrid, exhibited little enthusiasm for taking up the cudgels against the communists, who, after all, had still not made any serious intrusions into Spain. Then, several months after Serrano's articles had first appeared in *La Revista Social,* the debate between the communists and collectivists began to show signs of life. During the second week of July 1885, the Centro de Amigos de Reus convened an exclusively working-class literary event known as the First Socialist Literary Competition (Primer Certámen Socialista). This event marked the true beginning of a long series of public discussions about the pros and cons of the rival theories of communism and collectivism.

Attended by both an ideologically and a professionally diverse group of labor federations that included, among others, carpenters, masons, shoemakers, and textile workers, the Primer Certámen Socialista may well have served as a forum for debating key doctrinal issues, but it also held another significance for the workers themselves. Above all, it was an outstanding example of the growing trend within the labor movement toward the establishment of purely working-class cultural traditions. As we will discuss this important social development in a later chapter, we need only mention here that the socialist competition was patterned after the *certámens,* or literary contests, which had formed a part of Catalonian cultural life for a number of years and were traditionally organized by and for middle-class intellectuals. These were celebrations at which promising young authors and poets would compete for prizes and the honor of representing their local social clubs. In the case of the working-class *certámens,* the contestants were judged by a panel assembled from the different *centros,* which were not only sponsoring the events but also responsible for awarding the winners various kinds of prizes. For a particularly well-written essay, a worker might receive a medallion with the name of his association inscribed on it, a gold pocket watch, or an expertly crafted bound book.[25]

The Primer Certámen had indeed provided the anarchists and socialists with a forum for exhibiting their intellectual achievements. And even if the well-presented essays might not have resolved any theoretical disputes, they nonetheless helped to introduce to the public a new and mostly younger generation of anarchist intellectuals, whose writings on the subject of collectivism and communism inevitably broadened the intellectual spectrum of anarchist thinking in Spain and thus raised the standard of theoretical debates. Three of the prize-winning essayists at the *certámen* were part of this generation of thinkers: Ricardo Mella, Teobaldo Nieva, and Fernando Tarrida del Mármol.

In the coming years, there emerged an ever-expanding community of libertarian intellectuals. Some of the most accomplished writers of this group were Ernesto Álvarez, Pedro Esteve, Antonio Pellicer Paraire, Juan Montseny y Carret (a.k.a. Federico Urales) and his *compañera,* Teresa Mañé (a.k.a. Soledad Gustavo), Teresa Claramunt, José Prat, and José Montenegro. Between 1886 and 1896, it was largely thanks to the efforts of these intellectuals that the anarchist movement managed to sustain the prodigious growth of a literary tradition.

CHAPTER VII

The Demise of the FTRE and the Emergence of Anarchist Associational Life

From 1885 until it was officially dissolved at the Valencia Congress of September–October 1888, the FTRE experienced an uninterrupted decline. The widespread repression of the anarchist movement in the south, combined with hard economic times throughout much of Spain at this time, inevitably took their toll on the organization, as did other equally important factors, such as the gradual ideological reorientation of the movement. The dwindling membership of the FTRE was the most telling sign of its deterioration. By the end of 1887, the organization counted only a few active federations, including those located in former strongholds like Andalusia, Murcia, Aragón, and New Castille. It was only in Valencia and Catalonia, where the trade unions had not been suppressed, that the FTRE was able to sustain membership in its local federations.

In the last two years of its existence, the FTRE continued to hold national congresses, which were perhaps called with the expectation of finding some way of reinjecting life into the nearly inert organization. Yet such slender hopes were soon disappointed. At a national congress held between 15 and 17 May 1887 in Madrid only sixteen delegates attended, furnishing an unequivocal index of how little interest there was in maintaining a national organization. The prevailing mood of the meeting was gloomy, and few proposals elicited any enthusiasm from the delegates. The Federal Commission's initiative promoting the idea of the eight-hour day, for example, was rejected, and the debate on whether it was necessary that only one federation exist in each locality was deferred until the next congress, slated to be held in Catalonia the next year.

Even though they still constituted a minority, the communists and their sympathizers were able to influence the outcome of the proceedings. When the delegates turned their attention to theoretical issues, for example, the communists brought up their objections to the collectivist principles embodied in the statutes of the FTRE. They particularly challenged the collectivist notion that the worker was entitled to the integral product (*producto integral*) of his or her labor, arguing that terminology like "integral" suggested a form of bourgeois individualism and not true anarchist values. In the end, the communists scored a minor victory when the congress decided that the word *proportional* should be substituted for the word *integral* in the official statutes.[1]

Although the rise of communist influence inevitably hastened the dissolution of the FTRE, other factors also contributed to this process. Perhaps the most significant of these was the sharpening of regional differences within the FTRE. As we have seen, regionalist sentiments were most pronounced in Catalonia, where the syndicalist-minded federations were largely preoccupied with their own affairs. From 1885 on, the Catalan federations became more and more independent of the nationally based FTRE, preferring instead to rely on their own network of unions—commonly referred to as resistance societies (*sociedades de resistencia al capital*)—to achieve their goals.

During the summer of 1887, the Catalan federations began taking steps that would ultimately give them more sympathy. The Barcelona section of the FTRE sponsored a series of conferences (Conferencias de Estudios Sociales) which, among other things, discussed the pros and cons of establishing a formal economic alliance among the societies of resistance of the region. The formation of such an alliance had obvious implications as far as the FTRE was concerned, not least being that there was no apparent need for parallel anarchist economic organizations to exist in Catalonia.

By the time the FTRE convened a general congress in Barcelona the following spring (19–21 May 1888), the Catalan federations had already agreed among themselves to set up the proposed economic alliance to be called the Federación de Resistencia al Capital (popularly known as the Pacto de Unión y Solidaridad). According to its statues, in each locality a federation of resistance would serve as the hub around which the various workers' societies would be organized. The collectivity of different professions was to operate along anarchist lines: there were no hierarchies and, most important, no stringent criteria for membership. This latter point was a reflection of the anarchists' concern to do away with ideological labels. To the Catalán trade unionists, the establishment of the Federación, or Pacto, was not associated with any ideological shift, for most of the societies affiliated with the organization retained their collectivist orientation. Nevertheless, the Catalán anarchists appeared anxious to end the cycle of theoretical bickering, which they believed had distracted attention from more pressing practical problems.

By opening the criteria of membership to all schools of thought, this group of anarchists was also hoping to attract workers from rival organizations. In the light of the recent upsurge in Marxist and reformist socialist activity in Catalonia, there is reason to believe that the anarchists may well have created the Pacto in order to absorb their ideological foes.

The main purpose of the new organization was to unite the various labor federations around economic issues, such as the demand for the eight-hour day and May Day demonstrations. It was meant to function in the following way. The Federación's central component, the resistance society, was to carry on the daily struggle by demanding improved working conditions and defending the workers' interests against the capitalists. Knitting together the different societies was the *libre pacto:*

> The pact has as its intention both a rational and practical objective; and, in addition to this, it has the aim of achieving the unity of all workers, for it has established a common denominator for all schools of socialism.[2]

Among the different societies of resistance, the pact was understood as a reciprocal contract that they entered into in order to provide mutual support for one another in the event of a strike or other form of revolutionary action. On another level, the extreme flexibility of the pact arrangements, which allowed any number of different trades to belong to the alliance, was seen as an advance over the FTRE, which imposed the restriction of having only one trade federation in each locality. Finally, the administrative work of this amorphous conglomeration of unions was delegated to a five-member commission that was to reside in Alcoy and that was to be elected at general assemblies. Of course this was not supposed to be a bureaucratic agency, but rather an administrative body that was to facilitate the collection of statistics and the distribution of communications among the various societies.[3]

Considering that the majority of delegates at the congress were from

Catalonia, it was natural that the resolution on the Pacto easily passed in the final voting. The alliance was to begin operating immediately, with the first national meeting scheduled for December 1889. The Pacto did in fact manage to hold congresses until it was finally forced to disband at the time of the Montjuich repression of 1896–1897.

Some anarchists, like the collectivist Ricardo Mella, were convinced that the establishment of the Pacto posed an obvious challenge to the FTRE, and by extension, to the national unity of the anarchist movement. The fact is that although the Pacto was supposed to be a nationwide organization, it was—and remained—an essentially Catalán-based movement, with only scattered membership in parts of Andalusia and Valencia. Three months after the Barcelona Congress, Mella began vigorously campaigning against the formation of the Pacto in *La Solidaridad* (Seville), a staunchly collectivist weekly that he launched in the summer of 1888. More than anything else, Mella perceived the Pacto as an insidious way of undermining the collectivist bloc within the FTRE. His contention was that, contrary to what its members claimed, the Pacto was not open to all theoretical perspectives, for it was actually an organization based exclusively on communist ideas. Considering that the members of the Pacto had repudiated commissions, statistics-keeping bodies, and all the other organizational forms associated with collectivism, Mella reasoned that communism would be the only acceptable ideological orientation for any federation desiring to affiliate with the new body.[4] Mella later warned his comrades that "any body bound by its exclusivity . . . will become an organism made up of fanatics, mystics, and men who are neither free nor genuinely revolutionary."[5]

Meanwhile, against the background of the steadily declining membership of the FTRE as well as the recent establishment of the Pacto, the anarchist communists escalated their war of words against the FTRE. Leading this attack were the Gracia communists grouped around the paper *Tierra y Libertad,* which began appearing in August 1888. None of the arguments being advanced by the Gracia communists was original. For, as usual, the Spanish communists were merely parroting the views of their French counterparts, especially those of the *La Révolte* group in Paris. We have already seen that, since 1885, *Le Révolté* had been reproaching the Spanish Federation for maintaining its so-called authoritarian trade union structure. The FTRE's commissions, they had argued, ought to be abolished because such bodies were "outlines of a new system of government." In any case, they believed that any officially constituted agency was redundant given that the anarchists already possessed periodicals and other forms deemed sufficient for "the necessities of maintaining relations with each other, for keeping statistics, for everything."

For their part, the Spanish communists decried the policies of the Federal Commission as "artificial formulae"—presumably a reference to the well-articulated procedures observed by the Federal Commission and the local federations. They complained that the ritual of adopting and implementing formal procedures acted as a brake on the revolutionary movement. The communists further contended that the revolutionary élan of the workers would inevitably be exhausted on reformist strikes and other antirevolutionary endeavors unless the cumbersome structure of the FTRE was replaced by a new form of organization, one that conformed to communist ideas. Because it represented a decentralized organization devoid of any substantive administrative infrastructure, the communists supported the creation of the Pacto—although, as we shall see, they were also intent on creating an organization that they themselves could control.

It was in these inauspicious circumstances that the Federal Commission summoned the remaining federations to a congress in Valencia so that the fate of the FTRE could finally be settled. At this historic meeting, held at the end of September 1888, the majority of delegates decided to abolish the FTRE. In the economic sphere this had already been accomplished with the advent of the Pacto. But, on another level, the FTRE was to be superceded by a political body that the majority of delegates believed gave fullest expression to anarchist ideals, the Organización Anarquista de la Región Española (OARE). Though not explicitly stated at the congress, the primary role of the OARE was to give the *sociedades obreras de resistencia al capital* a revolutionary orientation. Precisely what this relationship would entail was not made clear at the convention, but the communists later intimated that they wanted to see a "trabazón," or organic bond, formed between the two organizations:

> In truth there is some distance separating the Anarchist Organization from the Federation of Resistance to Capital, if we want to accelerate the advent of our ideal [i.e., anarchism], it is absolutely vital to abridge this distance.[6]

Like the statutes of the Pacto, those of the OARE made it clear that all schools of anarchism were to be tolerated among the membership so that no one was obliged to follow a particular line of conduct. Notwithstanding this commitment to nonsectarianism, in both theory and practice the

OARE was fundamentally a communist organization. The only vestige of the FTRE to be retained in the new organization was the existence of an administrative council, Centro de Relaciónes y Estadísticas—a body that had no executive powers and existed only as a liaison between the various *grupos*. This point was a crucial one for the communists. They explained that the Centro de Relaciónes y Estadísticas was to have a more limited role than the administrative bodies of the FTRE. Its sole purpose was to act as an intermediary between the *grupos* and the revolutionary movement, providing (the various anarchist groups with) facts and other vital information.[7]

The Valencia Congress determined not only the fate of the FTRE but also the outcome of the ideological conflict between the collectivist and communists. The death of the FTRE, which for nearly twenty years had been identified with collectivist ideas, meant that anarchist communism had finally emerged as the dominant ideology. Yet, even though the collectivists may have lost the ideological struggle, it was not because they failed to present a better argument than their opponents. The communists probably could never have consolidated their influence if they had depended on their numerical strength or the cogency of their rather stale and simplistic theoretical pronouncements. Ironically, what finally secured communist hegemony in the anarchist movement was the common ground its adherents shared with the Catalán syndicalists. Despite their ideological differences (for many of the Catalán federations remained collectivist after the Valencia Congress), both groups were united in their opposition to the FTRE, and both groups promoted the decentralization of the anarchist movement. It was this unspoken alliance of interests that had dealt the final blow to the FTRE.

THE COLLECTIVIST RESPONSE TO THE DISSOLUTION OF THE FTRE

The outcome of the Valencia Congress deeply troubled a small but determined group of collectivists, once again led by Mella. They seemed to believe that, despite the decision at Valencia to dissolve the FTRE, it was not too late to reconstitute it so as to accommodate the reforms demanded by both collectivists and communists alike. Mella himself was so profoundly committed to this notion that he rather quixotically refused to recognize the dissolution of the FTRE as a irreversible decision. In a series of articles published in *La Solidaridad* after the Valencia

Congress, he set forth a proposal that he hoped would demonstrate the advantages of resurrecting a reformed model of the FTRE:

> Alright; this organization . . . had and now has its defects; and who can deny it? As we have already made clear: the Statutes, as a contract of regional organization, conceded attributes that were excessive and unnecessary, trammeling the attributes of the autonomous organisms. . . . [F]or this reason we have decided to constitute something which is more in keeping with the law of contract. For this, reform is required. . . .
>
> The principal argument of the Regional organization, that which justifies and explains its reason for being, and one that all Spanish anarchists recognize—whether they are dissidents or not, or whether they are collectivists or communists—is that we live and we struggle within a society of organized authority. . . . [W]e are therefore obliged to combat these disciplined and well-constituted forces; thus we [must] organize ourselves in a manner that allows for the greatest amount of freedom but that has the cohesion and unity necessary to engage in an open conflict with disciplined forces and the ruling powers.[8]

Mella was obviously endeavoring here to reconcile the demands for reform being made by both rival tendencies with what he felt was the need to preserve a strong, nationally based union. He reasoned that this could be achieved by jettisoning the "authoritarian" aspects of the FTRE—such as the allegedly bureaucratic local and district federations—and by forming what he referred to as a *pacto de solidaridad* (solidarity pact) as a means of uniting organized workers of every school of revolutionary thought. Mella believed that the alliance he was advocating, offered, in contrast to the Pacto, the only realistic means of transcending the ideological barriers dividing the Spanish anarchists. Above all, Mella was desperately trying to convince those who had just abolished the FTRE that, unless they heeded his advice, the future of the revolutionary movement would be seriously jeopardized.

Despite his efforts, Mella's urgent appeals fell on deaf ears. But it was scarcely surprising that his recommendations were largely greeted with silence or puzzlement, for neither the communists nor the Catalán syndicalists could understand what purpose it would serve to reconstruct the FTRE along different lines. In fact, Mella spoke for only a minority of anarchists. Apart from a handful of anarchists in Seville, Madrid, and Barcelona, the majority of collectivists favored the idea of breaking up the FTRE. He therefore could not even count on the backing of his erstwhile ideological companions. We shall see in a later chapter that, although he sensed that his efforts to resurrect the FTRE were futile, Mella did not abandon his crusade against anarchist communism.

ANARCHISM AND WORKING-CLASS
ASSOCIATIONAL LIFE

The Valencia Congress marked an end to the First International in
Spain, and in so doing, inaugurated a new era of anarchist activity. No
longer rooted within the framework of a single working-class federation, the anarchists from then on operated on several different levels.
Instead of concentrating on building up their syndicalist base, they began laying the foundations of a proletarian society based on anarchist
values and belief. Their activities mostly centered around the broadly
based social institutions of the workers, the *círculos* (circles), cafes,
clubs, *ateneos,* and *centros obreros* found in the *barrios* of the cities,
towns, and the countryside throughout Spain. By working through
these institutions as well as their own, the anarchists eventually became
permanently integrated into the fabric of working-class society.

The important role these associations played in the socialization and
politicalization of the worker cannot be overemphasized. It may be
recalled that a specifically working-class culture began emerging during
the days of *La Gloriosa.* This was the period when the International in
particular actively sought to drive a wedge between the workers and the
middle classes by asserting its own hegemony within working-class
institutions—the Fomento de las Artes and Clavé's boys choir for
instance—which had formerly been supported and directed by the
Democrats and Progressives. By the 1880s and 1890s all of this had
changed. Now the workers were not only sharing social institutions
with the middle classes but also supporting their own associations: they
had their own clubs, cafés, publications, and, in some instances, lay
schools (*escuelas laicas*). Most important, these purely working-class
institutions gave rise to a distinct set of social values that tended to
reinforce class divisions.

The growing insularity of working-class life referred to here provided
an ideal breeding ground for anarchism, but this largely depended on the
ideological orientation of the respective workers' associations. Working-
class centers that were affiliated with reformist unions like the Tres
Clases de Vapor, for instance, were invariably antirevolutionary and
consequently had little in common with anarchist organizations. This is
illustrated by the fact that working-class cultural events that were sponsored by politically conservative unions were held independently from,
and sometimes in competition with, those of the anarchists and socialists.

Not only ideological influences but also regional differences played a role in defining the pattern of working-class cultural life. In the predominantly rural regions of Spain, particularly in the south, worker associations did not support as varied a cultural existence as their counterparts did in the industrial areas. Organizations that did exist were usually found in occupations that had a long tradition of association. Wine-cellar workers, coopers, and the building trades were by and large capable of sustaining their own *centros* and social clubs. Agricultural workers and peasants, especially those located in remote habitats, however, were less likely to have an intricate web of workers' institutions.

Notwithstanding these differences between urban and rural areas, it is essential to bear in mind that however primitive the associational forms were in the countryside, they played no less central a role in the social life of the worker. This was true primarily because the process of socializing and politicalizing the worker was much the same whether it was in a small town, a hamlet, or a big city. This point has also been made by the historian Tony Judt with reference to the French socialist movement of this same period:

> However rural the occupational pattern, [in Mediterranean societies] the context of life is remarkably urban. Communities live in closely-grouped habitats, existing and acting very much as communities, traditionally meeting in public to discuss problems of common interest . . . and frequenting societies and cafes where all manner of concerns are discussed in lively and open fashion.[9]

But in contrast to that in rural society, associational life in the urban centers tended to be highly diversified and organizationally complex, with various kinds of workers' organizations "organically" interrelated. Thus, workers may have belonged to a union that supported a *centro obrero,* which was, in turn, the living link to the neighborhood café or other social forms.

No group contributed more to this emerging pattern of social development than did the anarchists. A notable example of this was the prodigious growth of an anarchist literary tradition. In the period 1885–1900, no less than two dozen anarchist journals and newspapers were published. While it is true that many of these were ephemeral, the sheer number of publications indicates just how vigorous their literary efforts were. Some papers failed owing to poor financing, while a significant number had their lives cut short by repression. But because the anarchists knew how vital their publications were for keeping alive the spirit of revolution, they managed even in the most inauspicious circumstances to bring out at least a leaflet, circular, or some other form of communication.

Of all the anarchist publications that flourished during the period 1886–1896, two stand out as significant achievements of the libertarian cultural community: the monthly *Acracia* (Barcelona) and the weekly *El Productor* (Barcelona). The first to appear, *Acracia,* was by far the best anarchist theoretical journal of the decade. Founded in 1886 by Antonio Pellicer (Farga Pellicer's cousin) and his printer group, La Academia, *Acracia* was produced and directed by the most talented anarchist intellectuals of the period. Besides Antonio Pellicer, who was the chief editor of the journal, regular contributors included Anselmo Lorenzo, Ricardo Mella, Teobaldo Nieva, and Fernando Tarrida del Mármol. The word *acracia* was merely a euphemism for the word anarchy, for it also meant a society without government. But it held a special significance because the purpose of introducing the term was to promote the idea of anarchism without labels. The hope was that, by adopting a new anarchist term, workers would no longer be forced to choose between collectivism and communism. Thus, the journal aimed "to expose doctrines, to judge systems and opinions, and to give account of social progress that will be presented without exclusivity or preoccupation with a school of thought—although our intention is not to fall into an enfeebled state of eclecticism."[10] The social sciences were to provide the epistemological foundation of their ideas. Because of the "greatness and utility of its subject," sociology was thought to be the only method of analysis which could lay bare the complexities of society. The anarchists confidently predicted that by using sociology as an investigative tool, "the obstacles placed in the path of social progress will disappear."

Acracia quickly became the principal organ of the anarchist movement. Besides publishing articles written by the leading Spanish theorists, the journal provided translations of the writings of such important European thinkers as William Morris, Herbert Spencer, and Peter Kropotkin, all of whom were particularly popular among the Spanish anarchists. A valuable function of the journal was to circulate information that served as a means of connecting anarchists in the different regions. This included official communications from the FTRE, as well as news about working conditions, local strikes, and other relevant facts affecting Spanish workers. Details of labor activity in the United States, Latin America, and Europe also appeared regularly. In this way, it was possible to learn of significant developments in the international working-class movement, like the campaign for the eight-hour day in America, which, as we shall see, had a profound impact on the Spanish anarchists.

The successor to *Acracia* was the weekly *El Productor*. For nearly six years it, too, was regarded as the mouthpiece of the Spanish anarchist movement as a whole. Dedicated to exposing the views of every variety of anarchism, *El Productor* also replaced *Acracia* as the principal forum for the collectivist/communist debate. Indeed, its principal contributors— the collectivist Celso Gómis and the communist Pedro Esteve, for example—were strongly opposed to dogmatism of any kind. Given that the overwhelming majority of anarchist newspapers at the time rarely survived more than a few months, the longevity of *El Productor* meant that it provided a continuum of ideas and values over a significant period of time.

Anarchist literature consisted of more than just the newspapers and journals we have thus far examined. Plays, poems, songs, short stories, and novels were also used to convey the anarchist message. Often these appeared serially in the anarchist dailies and weeklies, although cheaply produced novellas and short stories were churned out with regularity as chapbooks or *folletos,* selling for only a few centimos. In view of the widespread illiteracy among the working classes, much of this kind of anarchist literature was purposely written in a simple and direct style so that it was easily grasped by even the unsophisticated reader. This so-called *obrerista* (working-class) literature was characterized by José Llunas as a genre that "lacked precise expression, sparkling characters, the cadence of prose that produces harmonious sounding notes." This was because anarchist publications were used both as instructional tools and as media for propagandizing anarchist doctrine. The plot of a typi-cal novella, for example, would revolve around the lives of workers who were struggling to liberate themselves from the chains of capitalist op-pression. The storyline was rather two-dimensional and populated by overdrawn stock characters, like the rich bourgeois banker who was portrayed as being greedy, gluttonous, and insensitive to the plight of the multitudes condemned to live in grinding poverty.

The low literary standards of anarchist literature can also be attrib-uted to the fact that there were very few professional writers within the libertarian community. Most, like Lorenzo, Mella, and Llunas, worked full-time at other occupations, and writing was something they accom-plished in their spare time. Given these circumstances, the real wonder is that there was such a prodigious output of their publications. Whatever its artistic failings, libertarian literature reached countless workers who might otherwise have been deprived of literature.

In addition to the writings by Spaniards—notably, Federico Urales, Anselmo Lorenzo, and Ricardo Mella—anarchist literature was enriched by the works of foreign authors. The stories and novels of Émile Zola, Eugene Sue, Jean-Marie Guyau, and Leo Tolstoy were frequently published under the anarchist imprimatur, sometimes in French or, more commonly, in Spanish. Among the Spanish intellectuals, Sue appears to have been both popular and influential, particularly his *The Wandering Jew* and *The Mysteries of Paris*.

Anarchist holidays, usually determined by red-letter dates in radical labor history, provided another outlet for expressing workers' literary and cultural achievements. These days were commonly set aside as occasions for staging festive pageants or holding literary contests such as the *certámens* I referred to earlier. For many years the anniversary of the Paris Commune was a popular celebration that took the form of large open-air meetings where workers were entertained by a diverse troupe of performers. On the fifteen anniversary of the Commune, for example, anarchist groups from Barcelona and the surrounding region organized an elaborate festival where choirs, working-class poets and playwrights, an orchestra, and actors and actresses provided the day's entertainment. Later, events like the Haymarket Tragedy of 1886–1887 and May Day were also celebrated, thus enlarging the scope of themes to be incorporated into the anarchists' constantly evolving cultural tradition.[11]

The anarchists' wide-ranging social and cultural activities engendered and promoted a network of affiliations among different working-class groups. Thus, for example, in the case of the anniversary of the Paris Commune just cited there was a convergence of working-class choirs, singing groups, and orchestras. Inevitably this kind of activity reinforced the community of interest among different cultural organizations regardless of what their respective political persuasions may have been.

Although there is no way of knowing the extent to which the anarchists influenced the associational life of the working classes, we do know that the anarchists sought to create their own social institutions and, where possible, to transform existing ones in accordance with their ideals. It is well known, for example, that at least some anarchist-dominated associations upheld a strict, almost puritanical moral code. Ricardo Mella is reputed to have remarked that anarchist values exercised so much influence over the workers belonging to the *centro obrero* in Seville that no worker would have dared to show up there intoxicated.[12] The distinctiveness of anarchist social forms is perhaps best illustrated by looking at the differences between libertarian cafés and bars (taverns or public houses) and those traditionally found in working-class neighborhoods.

The social life of the worker played a central role in shaping his political ideas. A vital component of the worker's milieu in late nineteenth-century Spanish society was the café or bar. This was true not least because of the miserable home life that the overwhelming majority of workers had to endure. Forced to live in homes that were poorly constructed—thus particularly uncomfortable during periods of inclement weather—workers often shared their cramped quarters with other families. The bar or café provided the most convenient and perhaps only escape from this bleak existence. In the mornings the worker would go there on his way to work in order to take his meager breakfast of hard bread, washed down with a small glass of wine. At the end of the day, he would return to the tavern in order to drink wine, converse with his friends, or while away the evening by playing games like cards, chess, and checkers.[13]

Working-class women, though—who represented a small but growing percentage of the overall work force—had very few social outlets. Barred from public houses and workingmen's clubs, women were obliged to seek other forms of socializing. Though many women maintained dual roles as wives and workers, their lives usually revolved around the family household and the church, the latter providing one of the few socially acceptable places where women could publicly meet. Less fortunate women had to spend what spare time they had begging alms on the streets for extra income. Still others were forced to degrade themselves through prostitution, even though they may well have spent fourteen or fifteen hours toiling at some other occupation.[14]

Recognizing the significance of the bar and café as socializing agents, the anarchists sought to alter these institutions qualitatively so that they would reflect anarchist values. In an anarchist café, then, one might find workers not only playing games but also educating themselves by reading books, periodicals, and pamphlets.[15] It should be noted here that the immense rate of illiteracy among the workers did not prevent the anarchists from using the café as an educational center. On the contrary, there was usually one or more *obreros concientes,* or enlightened workers, whose role it was to read the latest anarchist paper or lead discussions on political and educational topics.

The café also served as a setting for cultural events: theatrical sketches, musical recitals, and poetry readings were among the activities performed there. A distinguishing feature of the anarchist social institution was that both men and women participated in organized festivities. This is not to say that sexual divisions did not exist in anarchist social institutions, for on a daily basis cafés and taverns no doubt largely remained an exclusively male preserve. Nevertheless, both male and female anarchists were theoretically committed to the goal of breaking the ago-old mold of sexual prejudice. However patronizing they may have been, anarchist men did encourage women to free themselves from the yoke of male dominance.[16] Some women, like Teresa Claramunt, took the initiative and formed their own social circles. The fact is that anarchist women enjoyed an independence not matched anywhere else in working-class society.

As important as the cafés and bars were for promoting a libertarian life-style, they constituted only one facet of the wider context of working-class associations. The anarchists also operated in larger and more complex institutions, like the workers' *círculos* and *centros obreros*. Typically, the *centro* adopted a name that symbolized its inspiration and political orientation. Among the anarchists and politically progressive elements likely names were La Regeneración (Regeneration), Los Rebeldes (The Rebels), or Vía Libre (Road to Freedom). If large enough and financially sound, the *centro* itself would sponsor a variety of social and political activities, ranging from cultural conferences to the publication of a journal or newspaper. (*El Productor,* for instance, was brought out by the group La Regeneración.)

One anarchist intellectual of the period, Adrian del Valle (a.k.a. Palmiro de Lidia), has provided us with a first-hand account of how these institutions functioned as centers of anarchist activity. Adrian belonged to La Luz, one of the best known *centros* in Barcelona. Located on the Calle Ferlandina, La Luz served as a gathering place for those who were intellectually inclined. Not just workers but also young middle-class professionals who considered themselves freethinkers— that is, positivists, materialists, and republicans—would gather at the center in the evening to discuss the social issues of the day or engage in debate over theoretical topics. Interestingly enough, La Luz was predominately a republican club, although anarchists and socialists also belonged to it. Adrian claims that anarchist members such as Tarrida del Mármol, José Llunas, and Gaspar Sentiñón tended to dominate the intellectual atmosphere through their stimulating lectures and articles that appeared in the *centros'* paper. Through their association with such institutions, countless workers were exposed to anarchist thinking, and some, like Adrian himself, became converts. Adrian has described how the ambience of La Luz was instrumental in bringing about his own political conversion:

> In its principal salon, evening activities and conferences were held, and on "holy" Thursdays there took place a Bacchanal-like banquet, with the best known freethinkers of Barcelona in attendance. There was a local café where daily members of the club would gather, forming a meeting group [*tertulia*]. . . . In the daily *tertulias,* the discussions would revolve around social questions that were then the subjects of freethinking. There I began to form my libertarian perspective. . . . My republican ideas went up in smoke and the freethinkers were relegated to second place. Of the two theoretical tendencies that manifested themselves in these discussions, those of authoritarian socialism and libertarianism, the latter captured my sympathies. The idea of freedom, that is to say the *sentiment* of freedom, was then what it has been for me all my life: the most noble of feelings.[17]

Still another layer of anarchist social life consisted of the associations formed by the militant communists. These made up the core of the revolutionary movement and differed somewhat from the type of institutions mentioned above. Often referred to simply as *grupitos* or *grupos de afinidad* (affinity groups), these bodies were organized strictly along the lines of anarchist communist principles. For several reasons the communists believed that the group itself was the ideal medium for keeping alive the spirit and practice of revolution. According to one anarchist communist paper, "when one wants to carry out a revolutionary act of propaganda, etc., it is in the group that he will find others with whom he can easily establish the intimate relationships which are needed for its execution." Second, the communists thought that the individual could best develop within the context of a group because it was this form of social organization that best conformed to the ordering principles found in nature:

> When we base our organizations on natural units, it is not exclusively because this corresponds to our theory [of anarchist communism], but also because, as part of the natural order, we can better expose all social problems, and at the same time discover that which is stable.[18]

Even though these groups were supposed to function independently, in the opinion of the communists they were to be linked by their natural affinities, ideally combining to form an organic whole.

The *grupitos* consisted of nothing more than small circles of ardent radicals, numbering between five and ten members. Their activities were organized around the *tertulia*, which usually met at one of the numerous cafés found in every working-class neighborhood. There the workers belonging to a *grupito* met to debate politics, to hear the latest news—which was especially significant for those who were illiterate—or to plan their next act of reprisal against the bourgeoisie. Gerald Brenan has succintly described the purpose and daily activity of the *grupito:*

> Small parties or *tertulias* of people would meet everyday at some cafe to discuss the new ideas and to make plans, and at the centre of these would be four or five initiates, usually intimate friends, who held the secrets. These groups gave themselves names such as *Salut, Fortuna, Avant, Benvenuto,* and so on. Most of them confined themselves to discussion and propaganda, in which they were highly successful.[19]

As tiny as they were, one of the objectives of the *grupito* was to foster the education of the worker by maintaining small libraries at the usual meeting place so that one could learn to read and write. Whenever possible, they also tried putting out a daily or weekly newspaper, although these were usually so poorly financed that they rarely lasted for very long. There is no way of knowing for certain how many of these groups sprang up during the 1880s and 1890s. One contemporary writer, Gil Maestre, estimated that in Barcelona and its environs in 1896 there were around 502 "anarquistas de acción," that is, anarchists who were committed to the tactic of propaganda by the deed and therefore likely to be organized into *grupitos*.[20]

Patently rejecting the collectivist heritage of the FRE and FTRE, in which a formal bond of union existed among the respective federations, the anarchist communists argued that it was enough for each group to decide for itself what to do. Their emphasis on the complete autonomy of groups of individuals led to a pattern of revolutionary action which dominated the anarchist movement until the turn of the century. I am referring here to the series of bombing outrages of the late 1880s and 1890s that were chiefly perpetrated and sustained by communist cells. Above all the *grupito* existed in order to promote the revolutionary aims of the anarchists. Members of *grupitos* were not so much concerned—as were the anarchists associated with the institutions mentioned above— with constructing a parallel society, a counterculture that would replace the corrupt bourgeois society after the revolution. Instead, they gave primacy to violent revolutionary acts, believing that their most urgent task was to bring down the capitalist system.

Not surprisingly, it was the bomb-throwing anarchist communists who captured the public's attention, thus overshadowing the cultural activities and other substantive achievements of antiterrorist and pragmatic-minded anarchist groups. But more than just broadly tarring the image of anarchists, violent acts had the unintended but inevitable consequence of stunting the growth of working-class associational life. Already hard-pressed financially to publish their literature and sustain their institutions, the anarchists additionally faced the hardships imposed by government repression. Following a bombing incident it was common for the authorities to ransack anarchist newspaper offices and close down *centros* with which they were affiliated. For all the efforts of moderate libertarians like Fernando Tarrida del Mármol and Ricardo Mella, who continually sought to restrain their violence-prone comrades, terrorism remained a feature of the movement throughout the latter part of the nineteenth century.

CHAPTER VIII

Anarquismo sin Adjetivos

Beginning in 1886, the anarchists grouped around the Barcelona printers' association La Academia made a serious attempt to exorcise the Spanish anarchist movement of doctrinal disputes by espousing a nondenominational form of anarchism in the periodical *Acracia*. After two years, there were some tangible signs that their efforts were not entirely in vain. For a brief while, the term "acracia" itself gained currency among the anarchists, and in some instances it was actually substituted for the word "anarchism." However, most anarchist communists stubbornly resisted such attempts at compromise. *Tierra y Libertad,* for instance, loudly complained that introducing an imprecise term like "acracia" only served to confuse everyone. At the same time, the paper affirmed that the word "anarchy" should be retained since it unambiguously stood for revolution and the establishment of a society without government (*sin gobierno*).[1] Notwithstanding this kind of opposition, in the course of the next few years, other similiar expressions, like "acratismo societario," "anarquismo a secas" (indifferent anarchism) and "anarquista socialista" also began appearing with greater frequency in the libertarian vocabulary, and such phrases were not uncommonly used by the anarchists themselves to describe one's political orientation.[2]

After *Acracia* ceased publication in 1888, the campaign to eradicate sectarianism from the anarchist movement was taken up by several of the intellectuals associated with Antonio Pellicer's circle. Their collective efforts led to the formal articulation of a viewpoint that came to be known as *anarquismo sin adjetivos* (anarchism without adjectives). Considered by some historians to be Spain's only real contribution to anarchist theory, anarchism without adjectives was actually more of a perspective or an attitude than a set of specific ideas.[3] In its broadest sense, the phrase referred to an unhyphenated form of anarchism, that is, a doctrine without any qualifying labels such as communist, collectivist, mutualist, or individualist. For others, *anarquismo sin adjetivos* was simply understood as an attitude that tolerated the coexistence of different anarchist schools. The two Spanish theorists who were most responsible for developing this brand of anarchism were Fernando Tarrida del Mármol and Ricardo Mella. Because of the central role they played as expositors of *anarquismo sin adjetivos,* their major contributions to this tendency deserve close attention.[4]

FERNANDO TARRIDA DEL MÁRMOL: ANARCHISM PURE AND SIMPLE

The originator of the expression *anarquismo sin adjetivos* was the middle-class engineer and professor of mathematics Fernando Tarrida del Mármol. Born in Cuba in 1861, Tarrida came to Spain during the tumultuous days of La Gloriosa. His father was a prominent shoe and boot manufacturer who ran a large plant in Sitges (Catalonia). As a youth, Tarrida displayed an exceptional talent for mathematics, and he received a degree in the subject at the lycée of Pau. While studying in France, he also developed an interest in politics. A classmate of his named Jean Louis Barthou, destined later to become prime minister of France, eventually converted Tarrida to republicanism. Upon graduation, Tarrida returned to Spain, where he began his studies toward a degree in civil engineering at the University of Barcelona. He then accepted an appointment as professor of mathematics at the Polytechnic in Barcelona.[5]

Although he came from a well-to-do background, Tarrida never identified with his own economic class. Instead he was temperamentally and intellectually drawn to the working-class movement in Barcelona. He often frequented the working-class clubs in the city, where he would converse with republicans, anarchists, and socialists about politics and the plight of the workers. By his mid-twenties, Tarrida had become an anarchist, regarding himself as a collectivist steeped in the federal tradition of Proudhon and Pi y Margall. Through his inspiring lectures delivered at *centros* and *ateneos,* as well as his lucid writing on anarchist themes published in the leading libertarian publications of the day—

notably, *Acracia* and, later, *El Productor*—Tarrida earned the respect
and admiration of his fellow anarchists. With one of his mentors, the
veteran libertarian Anselmo Lorenzo, Tarrida formed a lifelong friendship. Tarrida's charisma and sincere personality also contributed to his
acceptance among the workers. A close friend and admirer of his recalled the following impression of him:

> Of his personal qualities it is impossible to speak too highly. It is no exaggera-
> tion to say that one felt better in his presence. His personal magnetism was
> wonderful. Endowed with an exquisitely tender nature, the sight of poverty
> in others was agony to him.[6]

That Tarrida came to be regarded as a bona fide representative of the
labor movement is attested to by the fact that in 1889 he was chosen by
an assembly of Barcelona workers to attend the International Socialist
Congress held in Paris.

Tarrida always thought of anarchism as an all-embracing philosophy
rather than as a narrow political doctrine. For him, anarchism was "the
natural and continuous development of all the vital integrating elements
contained in humanity, both in the individual and in the social groups."[7]
His mathematical training profoundly influenced his conception of anarchism. He often invoked equations and other mathematical formulae in
his explanation of anarchist principles. This was because he believed that
mathematics served not only to clarify with exactitude his own thoughts
on the subject but also to demonstrate the scientific validity of anarchist
propositions. Although his early contributions to anarchist theory were
written from the collectivist point of view, Tarrida never got entangled in
the collectivist/communist debate. Sometime in the course of his association with *Acracia*, he seems to have accepted Antonio Pellicer's notion
that it was possible for anarchism to be represented by a variety of
economic systems. Not long afterward, Tarrida took the next logical step
in this direction when he began developing a viewpoint that he referred to
as "anarchism without adjectives."

Tarrida first used the phrase in "La Teoría Revolucionaria," a public
address he delivered at the Segundo Certámen Socialista, held in November 1889 in Barcelona. Speaking as a representative of the "Benavento"
affinity group before an overflowing crowd of spectators who had gathered at the Bellas Artes palace to commemorate the Haymarket Tragedy
of Chicago (1887), he proclaimed:

> Of all the revolutionary theories that claim to guarantee complete social
> emancipation, the one that more closely conforms to Nature, Science, and

Justice, and that rejects all dogmas, political, social, and economic, and religious, is called Anarchy without adjectives.

Tarrida's public appeal for the acceptance of an ecumenical form of anarchism was obviously directed at both collectivists and communists, whose incessant quarreling over doctrinal issues still dominated the intellectual atmosphere of the movement. The crux of his argument was that the time had come for the respective factions to suspend their hostilities and show a greater tolerance for the different anarchist economic systems. In order to advance the revolutionary cause, he insisted, it was not necessary for one to adopt either a collectivist or a communist perspective; rather one had only to subscribe to the general principles of anarchism. Instead of arguing about the attributes of this or that system, he continued, anarchists ought to concern themselves with finding an accommodation of the various anarchist schools. He explained that this was possible since anarchists of all persuasions shared an aversion to any form of dogmatic thinking, since this violated one of the sacrosanct tenets of anarchism: the spirit of free choice. Tarrida therefore contended that, if anarchists were to remain consistent with their basic principles, they could never impose a preconceived economic plan on anyone.

Yet the intensity of the collectivist/communist debate was so great that it was not easily subdued even by Tarrida's conciliatory gestures. The next year he himself discovered this when he was challenged to defend his views on *anarquismo sin adjetivos*. The gauntlet was thrown down by the French communist paper *La Révolte* (Paris). In a series of scathing articles on the Spanish anarchist movement, the French communists censured the Spaniards for clinging to their collectivist heritage. This had obviously predisposed them, according to the French, to adopt authoritarian forms of organization. As far as the communists were concerned, the dismantling of the FTRE had not brought about the desired rupture with this past insofar as it had merely been replaced by two similar types of organizations: the Pacto de Unión y Solidaridad and the OARE.

Tarrida decided to reply to these accusations in a lengthy open letter, which was published in *La Révolte* in August 1890. While Tarrida agreed that both French and Spanish were divided over tactics, he pointed out that both movements were fundamentally in agreement as to the overall aims of anarchism:

All of us accept Anarchy as the embodiment [integración] of all freedoms, which it alone guarantees; as the impetus for and essence of human welfare.

Anarchy means neither laws nor repressions but spontaneous development, natural in all its manfestations. And it accepts neither superiors nor inferiors, neither governments nor governed.

What distinguished the French libertarians from their Spanish counterparts, according to Tarrida, were their differing approaches to the revolutionary struggle. He characterized the French anarchists as idealists, who upheld a puritanical view of strategy and tactics. In his opinion, this had blinded them to the realities of contemporary society. Tarrida argued that, no matter how closely their loosely constructed action groups conformed to the principles of anarchist social organization, these autonomous cells were largely ineffectual against the centralized forces of the bourgeoisie. Tarrida went on to predict that, as long as there were no formal bonds between the various anarchist groups, it did not matter how many acts of propaganda by the deed were committed, for, lacking a system of coordination, these could never amount to anything but random acts of violence.

Tarrida explained that the French revolutionary model sharply contrasted to that adopted by the Spanish anarchists. The latter's strategy, for example, promoted the formation of pacts between groups in the belief that the organized repression of the state could only be forcefully challenged by the organized resistance of the working classes. Tarrida thus defended the administrative bodies of the Spanish movement (which the French had so roundly condemned) on the grounds that they helped to reinforce the unity and strength of the respective anarchist organizations.

Tarrida also objected to the French communists' blueprint of future society, claiming that it was, like their revolutionary strategy, too rigidly defined. For this reason, he believed that the anarchist communist vision of the future was flawed in the same way as those advocated by such utopian theorists as Claude Henri Saint-Simon, Étienne Cabet, and Charles Fourier. According to him, their utopian systems had proved to be impracticable because they had been conceived as immutable models, which could not possibly adapt to the ever-changing social and economic circumstances. Tarrida argued, nonetheless, that it was impossible to predict accurately how society would evolve under anarchism, and it was thus essential for the anarchists to keep an open mind about the question of the economic organization of the future. "Anarchism," he told the communists, ought to be thought of as an axiom; where the question of economics "is only of secondary importance."[8]

Tarrida went on to admonish the French anarchists—and by extension their Spanish disciples—for attempting to impose a foreign style of anarchism on the Spaniards, whose movement had developed along different lines owing to different historical circumstances. He explained that in Spain anarchism had been nurtured and brought to fruition by the strong tradition of association among the workers. For this reason, Tarrida emphasized, the communists were wrong to condemn as authoritarian such organizations as the workingmen's circles, *centros obreros*, and *ateneos*, since for many years they had proved themselves indispensable to the growth of the Spanish revolutionary movement.

In one sense, Tarrida's letter to the French communists demonstrated that, unlike them, he had a sophisticated understanding of the nature of the political education of the Spanish worker. Because he grasped just how complex and intricate this process was, he was able to see that the question of organization was not a simple matter. Thus, for Tarrida, dismissing all forms of organization as authoritarian was more than just rash, it was wrongheaded. He recognized that in Spain the anarchist tradition had been transmitted by the very social institutions that the communists wanted to dispense with, and this fact convinced him that the communists were mistaken in their belief that the "French model" of anarchist communism could be successfully transplanted into the Iberian context.

Tarrida's letter also helps to explain why the Spanish were so resistant to anarchist communism. For anarchists like Tarrida, the adoption of communist ideas involved a great deal more than just changing ideological labels. As Tarrida intimated in his letter, Spanish anarchism was rooted in social institutions and traditions that were in many ways integral to its praxis. Therefore, while he may not have been opposed to the idea of communism, he would have none of the communists' plans to abolish indiscriminately working-class organizations that did not conform to their strict views.

By the same token, Tarrida and his adherents were opposed to the collectivists who refused to modify their strategy and tactics in the light of changing circumstances. That is why, for example, he did not feel impelled to argue for the continued existence of the FTRE. To his way of thinking, the organization had grown progressively bureaucratic in its last years and therefore had outlived its usefulness. Nevertheless, Tarrida was right to distinguish between the FTRE and forms of working-class organizations that were not, contrary to what the communists asserted, inherently collectivist.

RICARDO MELLA: COLLECTIVISM AND
ANARCHISM WITHOUT ADJECTIVES

Tarrida's attempts to transcend the collectivist/communist debate by adopting a flexible anarchist perspective attracted a small but growing audience within the anarchist community. Though some saw "anarchism without adjectives" as an alternative to choosing between collectivism and communism, others, including Ricardo Mella, interpreted it differently. Unlike Tarrida and those who followed his interpretation of *anarquismo sin adjetivos,* Mella stopped short of favoring the rejection of qualifying labels or recommending a synthesis of the different anarchist systems. Instead he promoted tolerance among competing anarchist factions, believing that this would allow for the rational experimentation and testing necessary to demonstrate which was the best system to adopt. What happened in Spain, in Mella's opinion, was that the collectivist/communist debate had degenerated into a contest between the forces of tolerance and openness on the one hand and intransigence and dogma on the other:

> All schools, all doctrines, all systems—whether political or religious—have been constantly undermined by two diametrically opposed tendencies, that of tolerance and that of intransigence. . . . With the people divided into parties and tendencies that disputed the supremacy of a closed dogma, an absolute, this division between those who were tolerant and those who were intransigent was quite natural and inevitable. The blind faith supporting dogma foments intransigence, whereas reasonable conviction breeds tolerance.[9]

Mella was also intensely preoccupied with preserving the collectivist heritage to which he belonged, and he thought that by promoting the idea of *anarquismo sin adjetivos* this would be possible. According to his understanding, then, a hierarchy existed among the different anarchist schools, with collectivism being the superior form of anarchism. This is not to say that he dismissed the significance of other brands of anarchism. After all, Mella's own anarchist philosophy owed much to Proudhon's mutualism. He was in fact constantly enriching his understanding of anarchism through his readings of other forms of libertarianism. Apart from French (*La Révolte*) and British (*Freedom* and *The Anarchist Labour Leaf*) anarchist journals, he avidly read the American anarchist press—particularly *The Alarm* (Chicago) and *Liberty* (Boston)—from which he acquired a knowledge of the mutualism of Dyer Lum, as well as of the individualism of Benjamin R. Tucker.

Mella lamented the fact that the anarchist community had fallen under the sway of communist militants, whom he blamed for inflicting others with their fanatical "spirit of jacobinism." Moreover, he perceived the rise of communist influence as a genuine threat to what he regarded as the quintessential qualities of Spanish anarchism. Under the communists, Mella wrote, there would be "no more peaceful or serious action; no more reflective propaganda; no more assemblies, meetings, literary contests, periodicals, journals, pamphlets, or books." Mella was so convinced of this that he felt compelled to devote his mental energies to the task of releasing the Spanish anarchist movement from the grip of his ideological opponents. In doing so, Mella was actually helping to perpetuate the controversy between communists and collectivists.

Of all the Spanish anarchist intellectuals of the last quarter of the nineteenth century, Ricardo Mella stands out as the most original and eloquent thinker. Mella distinguished himself primarily through his numerous essays and articles, which were published over a thirty-year period and which covered a wide range of topics. While the bulk of his publications were contributions to anarchist theory, he also wrote on other themes, such as education and science. One of his outstanding contributions to the sociological debates of the era, for instance, was his study *Lombroso y los anarquistas* (Barcelona, 1896), in which he set himself the task of refuting the famous Italian criminologist's thesis that anarchists were born criminals. In addition, he wrote short stories and was an accomplished translator. In the course of his political career he translated into Spanish key anarchist tracts from the French, Italian, and English, including Bakunin's *God and the State* and the American G. C. Clemens's *Primer of Anarchy*. In this way, he played a significant part in enriching the anarchist literature available to the Spanish reading audience.

A number of historians—notably, Juan Díaz del Moral, Diego Abad de Santillán, and Max Nettlau—have called Mella the most gifted of anarchist thinkers. Gerald Brenan wrote that Mella "was the only Spaniard to make any contribution to Anarchist theory." His intellectual achievements were also recognized by his contemporaries and by several generations of anarchists. The Catalán anarchist thinker José Prat and the Asturian anarchosyndicalist Eleuterio Quintanilla were two of his better-known pupils. Surprisingly, though, comparatively little has been written about his personal life or his political ideas.[10] Mella's contribution to anarchist theory and practice has been obscured for several reasons. One is simply that, except for a few works that were rendered into French and Italian at the turn of the century, none of his major writings has been translated; consequently, his ideas are known only to those who read Spanish. There were personal reasons why Mella's reputation has not received much attention. Modest and self-effacing to the extreme, he never aspired to become a popular leader among the working classes. Perhaps he shunned the limelight because he lacked the personal warmth and charm of his good friend Tarrida del Mármol, and was therefore not temperamentally suited to be a public figure. A fellow anarchist, Juan Montseny (Federico Urales), claimed that Mella was by nature a critic, who tended to be rather cold and something of a complainer.[11] In any event, he preferred to retreat to the background, devoting himself partly to his profession as a topographical engineer, partly to his large family, and partly to his writings on anarchism. In contrast to anarchists like Anselmo Lorenzo and Juan Montseny, Mella never wrote an account of his personal experiences, and therefore we know little of the details of his personal involvement in the anarchist movement. What have survived are his theoretical writings, and through them we have a clear and powerful expression of anarchist ideals.[12]

Mella's political philosophy did not radically shift over the thirty-year period he wrote on anarchism, for he consistently fashioned his social-political theory according to the perspectives he adopted as a young man. Born in Vigo (Galicia) in 1861, Mella grew up in a family of artisans. His father ran a modest hat shop, though Mella himself seems to have had little interest in following in his father's footsteps. At age fourteen he began working at the maritime agency of Vigo, where he not only got a firsthand view of the town just as it was rapidly expanding into an important port city but also witnessed the exodus of thousands of emigrants who embarked from Vigo on their way to the Americas.

Like so many Spaniards of his day, Mella began his political education at an early age. As a boy he was introduced to the writings of Pi y Margall by his father, who was himself an ardent Federalist. By the time he was sixteen, Mella was already a member of the Federal party. In 1881, Mella, along with other young republicans, began publishing *La Propaganda,* a weekly journal of Federalist ideas which aimed to "defend the interests of the working classes." At this early juncture in his career, Mella promoted the politicization of the working classes, believing that politics could be used to further their interests:

> There remains for the worker only one road: that of politics dignified and honorable. . . . The worker has to bear in mind that to stray from this path is to invite his own death, it is to run wildly and precipitately toward certain suicide.[13]

Mella, however, possessed only a fleeting attachment to politics. His personal encounter with a local *cacique* named José Elduayen was a demoralizing experience, causing him to lose faith in the political process. By the time he was twenty-one, he had converted to anarchism, largely because of the impact *La Revista Social* had on his thinking. Mella had evidently found in this journal a political philosophy that appealed to him, not least because its synthesis of Proudhonian mutualism and Bakunist collectivism corresponded to his federalist background. Mella particularly admired the writings of Juan Serrano y Oteiza, for whom he quickly developed a profound respect. This was later manifested in Mella's own writings, which in both style and substance bore the hallmarks of Serrano's dispassionate and logical approach to theoretical topics. Perhaps, then, it was no coincidence that after Mella moved to Madrid in 1882 to begin his apprenticeship as a topographer, he became a close friend of Serrano and even fell in love with his daughter, Esperanza, whom Mella married in 1887.

Under Serrano's tutelage, Mella soon became an anarchist collectivist, an ideological standpoint with which he became identified for the remainder of his life. Mella gained his first experience as an Internationalist at the Seville Congress of 1882, at which he represented the local federation of Vigo (Galicia). The next year he began contributing regularly to *La Revista Social*, writing articles and providing translations of such anarchist classics as Bakunin's *God and the State*. Then, in 1885, he got his first real opportunity to exhibit his intellectual talents when he participated in the Primer Certámen Socialista. His "El problema de la emigración en Galicia" (written the previous year) won a prize, but his polemical article on the differences between collectivism and communism, "Diferencias entre el comunismo y el colectivismo," attracted the most attention. From both his father and Serrano, Mella had inherited anticommunist sentiments. This was amply reflected in the latter essay as well as in most of his writings on anarchist communism. It is essential to note that Mella, like Serrano, did not distinguish between different forms of communism. Thus the communist ideas found in Plato's *Republic* were, for him, fundamentally the same as those found in the writings of Marx and the works of anarchist communists like Kropotkin, Malatesta, and Elisée Reclus.[14]

MELLA'S CRITIQUE OF COMMUNISM

The analysis of communism which Mella developed in his writings is predicated on his sociological perspective. He held, like all anarchists of his day, a positivist view of society. Like Peter Kropotkin, the famous Russian anarchist thinker who attempted to provide anarchism with a scientific basis, Mella thought that human society was analogous to the world of nature. It therefore followed for them that society could be understood in similar terms. As a social theory, anarchism was seen as an articulation of the scientific view of sociology as formulated by Auguste Comte and Herbert Spencer. Mella himself subscribed to the main features of Spencer's so-called synthetic philosophy. Briefly, this was an attempt to account for all natural and social phenomena in a single scientific theory. Of particular interest to the Spanish anarchists was Spencer's concept of evolution. Spencer had found the theory of evolution a useful conceptual tool in his quest to combine the study of the organic and inorganic worlds. To his way of thinking, the forces governing social change followed the same pattern as those in nature: the tendency of growth or progress was toward increasing differentiation, from the simple to the more complex. Spencer's rather mechanistic view of evolution also posited that underpinning the development of nature and society was a fundamental law, namely, that the universe and all that it contained was moving toward a state of equilibrium.

It is important to bear in mind that all those who accepted Spencer's epistomology were confident that, as long as they used scientific terminology, they were dealing in certainties. The belief was that anyone who applied the scientific method to the study of human society was able to emancipate himself from traditional metaphysics, which had long dominated the intellectual community in Spain. Because the anarchists believed that science enabled them to transcend the limits of speculative thinking, they thought it could be used as a means of verifying their social theory of anarchism. Mella's understanding of revolution as a function of social evolution illustrates this point. According to this:

> [T]he inevitability of revolution is absolute, as absolute as the laws of nature, without which human progress would be a concept devoid of meaning. . . . If, then, evolution is a biological law of social development, then revolution is the decisive element by which this law fulfills its function.[15]

Viewed in this way, revolution was conceived as an unavoidable consequence of social development.

Mella's early writings on communism were thoroughly imbued with this scientific interpretation of society. In "Differencias" we find an attempt to prove "scientifically" that the concept of communism is a primitive one, dating back to the earliest stages of civilization. At that time, Mella explained, communism was the prevailing form of social and economic organization; everything was communally owned and everyone shared the fruits of nature. Yet society had long since evolved to a higher (i.e., more complex) state, making communism irrelevant to contemporary social conditions. The retention of communist ideas in current social theory, Mella concluded, was therefore a form of theoretical atavism.

Mella went on to say that the collectivist theory first formulated by Proudhon and then elaborated by Bakunin stood at the opposite end of the evolutionary scale of ideas. He took as evidence of this the fact that, in contrast to communism, the theory of collectivism had only recently emerged. More important, though, he regarded anarchist collectivism as the zenith of social development, the state of equilibrium toward which society was inexorably moving.

There were other aspects of communist theory which equally disturbed Mella. He argued, for example, that communism tended to inspire authoritarianism because latent in all communist systems was an autocratic form of social organization. This tendency could be traced from Plato's *Republic,* which describes a hierarchical society organized along communist lines, through the utopian writings of Thomas More, Gabriel Bonnet de Mably, Morelly, and Fourier, and finally, to the communistic system expounded by Karl Marx. To Mella, the ultimate aim of communism was the establishment of a society where

> everything belongs to everyone, where everyone works for the good of the whole, and where everyone is able to satisfy his personal needs by taking from the communal base formed by everyone. It is a dreamworld organization in which equality is an absolute ... it is the principle, the method and the aim of all things, it is, in the final analysis, the preponderance of the State for the sake of sacrificing the individual.[16]

From another standpoint, Mella tried to prove in his writings that communism offered an unsatisfactory explanation of how the economy of the future would successfully function. According to the communists, Mella pointed out, the distribution of social wealth was to be determined by the axiom: from each according to his abilities, to each according to his needs. But who, Mella asked, will determine the strengths and needs of each person? "Who will work to the fullest of his abilities once it is known that the remuneration for work, whether one works a great deal or just a little, will be proportional to one's needs, a ratio that could be either directly or inversely related to work?"

Whereas such fundamental problems apparently could not be resolved by communism, Mella believed that they could be accommodated by the collectivist formula. Under this system, private property also disappears, but, significantly, each person receives the integral product of his labor, the incentive that all collectivists thought was essential to galvanize the production process. The equitable distribution of goods is thus realized through an exchange system based on labor, whereby a worker can exchange his products for the goods and services of others. Mella never provided in his writings the details of the infrastructure of the collectivist economy. But given that his economic ideas were entirely derived from Proudhon and Bakunin, it is likely that the collectivist system Mella had in mind would have resembled the models developed by his predecessors. A feature of the economic system Mella envisaged might have been, for example, a people's bank similar to the one Proudhon founded. In this system, labor credits earned by producers would serve as the basis of exchange. The value of these would be calculated partly on the basis of the nature of the work performed and partly on the number of hours required to produce a commodity. Finally, the bank itself would serve as a clearinghouse for distributing the interest-free labor credits.

ANTICOMMUNISM AND ANARCHISM WITHOUT ADJECTIVES

When he began writing for *Acracia* in 1886, Mella adopted another tack in his campaign against anarchist communism. In keeping with the spirit of the *Acracia* group, he began calling for tolerance among the different anarchist schools of thought. Mella may well have been sincere in this, but there can be no doubt that his call for tolerance was seen by him as a way of preventing the communists from completely imposing their views on the Spanish anarchist movement. In his most significant article on the subject, "La reacción y la revolución," Mella argued that to state categorically, as the communists did, which form of economic system should be installed in the future society was an example of the worst form of dogmatic thinking. Because he equated dogmatism with reaction, Mella insisted that the development of a true revolutionary movement had to spring from a different perspective, "one open to . . . proceed according to whatever traditions and customs best suited the circumstances at hand."[17] As it was impossible to determine what these would be after the revolution, Mella contended that it was absolutely necessary to leave open for debate the question of economic organization.

In the following years Mella continued to develop his interpretation of *anarquismo sin adjetivos* from this perspective, with the crystallization of his theory finally being achieved in his novella, *La Nueva Utopía*, which was written in 1889 for the Segundo Certámen Socialista. The leitmotiv of his interesting and imaginative story is the social and economic organization of the future society. Because it is in *La Nueva Utopía* that Mella most clearly articulated the central themes of his anarchist philosophy—particularly his views on anarchism without adjectives—it is necessary to pause here to examine this work.

Mella's fable is set in a tiny fishing village along the shores of the Cantabrian Sea in northern Spain. Before the establishment of La Nueva Utopía, the inhabitants of the hamlet had been deprived of well-being and enlightenment. Enslaved by superstition and the fear of the unknown, weakened by excessive work, and lacking proper food and intellectual stimulation, these miserable people lived as true pariahs. Then, following a profound social revolution, a new community arose. (Curiously, Mella does not say here or in his other writings precisely how the revolution would come about.) Now, with the advent of La Nueva Utopía, the inhabitants "enjoy all the comforts that they desire and live in complete harmony with one another, never disturbed by the agitations so familiar to previous generations and other manners of living."

The nucleus of workers who founded La Nueva Utopía faced enormous obstacles, not least being the reorganization of the economy and the complete moral rehabilitation of the people. After several centuries and the painstaking work of numerous generations of villagers (whose efforts were guided by science on the one hand and the ideals of liberty and justice on the other), the new material and moral order finally emerged. Mella believed, as did many anarchists of his day, that the technological age held great promise for the future of mankind. In his utopia, not only have arduous and debilitating tasks been abolished by machines but pollution and other evils of the former epoch have also disappeared: "The distinctive characteristics of the great city are iron and electrical power applied prodigiously to all of the combinations of the marvelous machine." The landscape and architecture of the village evoke the mathematical precision of the Renaissance utopias. For throughout Mella's ideal setting, symmetry reigns supreme. The wretched living quarters of the villagers have given way to "great buildings perfectly aligned, separated by gardens where the neighborhood children happily play." At the apex of the city are public facilities such as schools, business, social exchanges, medical buildings, libraries, museums, and other recreational establishments. "One section of the city is devoted to living space, while in the other part one sees immense manufacturing plants, workshops, outdoor agricultural enterprises, large markets, combined with that beautiful and grandiloquent manifestation of human activity, labor."

THE SOCIAL SYSTEM OF LA NUEVA UTOPÍA

The social system of La Nueva Utopía is grounded on two fundamental principles: liberty and equality. Natural resources—that is, the forests, oil, gas, and iron ores, as well as the bountiful fruits of the soil—now belong to everyone, for private property has disappeared. When asked how the people live in La Nueva Utopía, one of the imagined residents replies, "We live in the middle of equality and justice, where the achievement of greater personal freedom makes for a more solid and more firm social order."[18]

The citizens themselves are related through a system of reciprocally binding pacts (*pactos*) of the kind described in both Proudhon's and Serrano's writings. These vital links, which are the only means by which individuals form economic and social relationships, are highly flexible in that they can be rescinded or annulled at any time.

Another unifying force in society is the general feeling of social solidarity. No longer plagued by politics, religion, and other sources of social friction, which formerly divided society into opposing factions, the people of La Nueva Utopía need only worry about the general welfare of society. Out of the feeling of solidarity, for example, there arises the obligation to cure sickness, and thus in La Nueva Utopía Mella made provision for the creation of hospitals known as "casas de corrección medica."[19] That Mella envisaged such a social institution proves that, contrary to what some of his critics have suggested, his concept of anarchism did not ignore the interests of the weak and old in society. On the contrary, he believed, like all anarchists, that once society was liberated from the bonds of capitalism and its attendant ethical system people would no longer be guided by their self-interested passions (i.e., egoism) but rather would act out of feelings of solidarity for the good of everyone.[20]

EDUCATION IN LA NUEVA UTOPÍA

Mella emphasized that the proper education of the citizens of La Nueva Utopía was of utmost importance. In the story, education is regarded as a means of molding person's character, a way of preparing him or her for life in the "ideal" state. The educational program Mella depicts in *La Nueva Utopía* is not confined to the schoolroom or any single setting but rather permeates every level of society. In order to instruct children without restricting their freedom, teachers will introduce letters of the alphabet, geometrical theorems, and facts about natural history into their games and diversions. Football (soccer) provides an interesting example of how teaching would be coupled with playing. The ball itself serves as an illustration of geometric spheres, and its motion serves to demonstrate the law of gravity as well as other physical laws. At each stage of the child's development he or she will be introduced to another level of scientific understanding, and this learning process was supposed to continue throughout the life of an individual.

Still another dimension of the ideal society which Mella developed in his fable has to do with the conduct of the citizens. A common concern for all anarchist theorists was to explain how crime and other "social diseases" would disappear under anarchism. For his part, Mella claimed that even though La Nueva Utopía is not "populated by angels," it is generally free from criminals because "with the disappearance of the causes of delinquency, delinquency itself disappears." Yet, later on in the story, Mella admits that while there are no longer any sociological reasons for crime to arise in a reformed society, there always remains the possibility of a crime's being committed. He explained that this was because

> In nature there are rare phenomena, rare exceptions to the general rule; and these phenomena, these exceptions are no more predictable than any physical, intellectual, or moral imbalance. At times nature breaks with her regular pattern, or, rather, is perturbed by the intervention of some outside agent.[21]

Mella considered all social phenomena, like crime, to be a form of illness, and therefore he believed that it was possible to correct or "cure" the problem. He explained that the only obligation society should arrogate to itself was to discover this agent or sickness (*enfermedad*) in order to destroy it and thereby reestablish social equilibrium.

The society that emerges in Mella's tale is one that in nearly every way conforms to the principles of all anarchist schools. It is not, for example, dominated by a particular kind of economic system—although Mella

makes it clear in the story that collectivism is without question the superior form of economic arrangement. Men and women are free to choose
whatever form of exchange they are predisposed to: "[If the worker]
wishes to reserve the right to exchange the products of his labor, no one
will impede him; if he wishes to donate his products to the community at
large, no one will stop him; if he wants to turn them over to a cooperative,
he is free to do so."

That Mella seemed to be advocating a "mixed" libertarian economy
was precisely why his novella was so highly regarded within the entire
anarchist community. Even his most pertinacious critics grudgingly accepted it as an admirable synthesis of the different anarchist systems.
Another reason why *La Nueva Utopía* had a wide appeal was the
optimistic spirit of revolutionism it conveyed. In the book, Mella had
not just sounded themes that all anarchists could endorse; he had, above
all, succeeded in conjuring up a vision of anarchist society which appeared to be eminently realizable.

LA NUEVA UTOPÍA IN THE UTOPIAN TRADITION

Mella's fictional piece is not easily classified since it represents a
mixture of utopian traditions: the elements of the positivist tradition are
clearly present, but so, too, are the elements of the moral utopias of the
distant past. From the posivitists, including, among others, Auguste
Comte, Saint-Simon, and Spencer, Mella had inherited two basic tenets:
faith in science and its ability to explain the progress of human society
and the belief in the perfectibility of mankind. Mella followed the positivists in holding that science was the key that unlocked the mysteries of
these tendencies; for by using the scientific method of investigation, they
believed, it would be possible to determine accurately not only the laws
that governed social development but also the direction in which it was
evolving. And, as we have also seen, science was regarded as the pana-
cea for all social ills, enabling man to eliminate such things as poverty
and crime.

Although science serves as the deus ex machina that Mella invokes as
a means of providing the material comforts of his utopia, it does not
mean that he was concerned mainly with the material well-being of
society. Rather, his vision of human progress focused on the intellectual
and moral improvement of mankind, which could not be attained by
material means alone. In this sense, Mella's *La Nueva Utopía* strikingly

parallels William Morris's *News from Nowhere* (1890), as well as the utopian literature of the Renaissance period.

In *La Nueva Utopía,* Mella set forth a dynamic view of society. Like the world of nature, society was constantly evolving. The "utopia" itself was merely a blueprint or model of what this state of being would be like if society were allowed to develop in accordance with its natural tendencies. Implicit in his view of social change is the belief that it is equally possible that society could regress to a more primitive level of development, and indeed, this is something that Mella frequently talked about in his writings. More specifically, he warned that the adoption of the atavistic economic ideas of the communists would inevitably result in a retrogressive state of affairs.[22]

The influence of the French philosophes of the Enlightenment can also be readily seen in Mella's work. Like them, he believed that social institutions reflected the state of man's moral development. Mella perceived the moral degeneracy of contemporary society as a function of the bourgeois social forms that had developed under capitalism. Above all, these institutions had given rise to a society afflicted with class divisions, where one class was pitted against another in a bitter struggle for dominance. To Mella, the prevailing ethics of such a social system was fundamentally egotistical, and consequently, it was irredeemably bankrupt. But under anarchism—that is, in La Nueva Utopía, where institutions developed spontaneously and uncorrupted by bourgeois values—Mella thought it would be possible to establish harmonious relationships between man and man and between man and nature.

In writing *La Nueva Utopía,* Mella was not attempting to define anarchism as a form of utopian thinking as it was then understood by social theorists. At the time, "utopia" was used to refer to a perfect state of affairs, one that was impossible to realize. The Marxian socialists in particular used the term in a pejorative sense; it was a label they attached to the social and economic programs of their political opponents. To be utopian was, at least for the Marxists, to be unscientific. Anarchists like Mella, however, interpreted their utopian fiction differently. For them, this genre could be used as a vehicle for discussing the abstract concepts of their doctrine, something they believed could not easily be conveyed in other literary styles.[23] Moreover, they did not believe that their literature was "unscientific." The fact is that Mella's work satisfied most of the criteria by which Engels and other Marxists differentiated between utopian and scientific thinking. Like the so-called scientific socialist literature described by the Marxists, for example, Mella's utopia emphasized the primacy of class conflict and the working classes' historical mission to establish socialism.

One of the main reasons for writing a fictionalized account of anarchist society was that it served to illustrate how good life could be if society were ordered according to anarchist beliefs and principles. If Mella's vision of the future lacked precision it was because his intention was not to construct a rigidly defined system but rather to sketch out in broad strokes the social and economic arrangements that lent themselves to a much-desired state of existence. By painting an appealing picture of what anarchism potentially held for mankind, Mella was not only holding up a mirror to what he perceived as the degenerate society of his day but also giving the common man a goal to work toward. As such, stories like *La Nueva Utopía* also served an important ideological purpose.

THE LEGACY OF *ANARQUISMO SIN ADJETIVOS*

To what extent Mella's writings on *anarquismo sin adjetivos* actually helped to sustain the collectivist/communist debate is difficult to determine. We do know, however, that between 1888 and 1889, when he was editor of *La Solidaridad* (Seville) and its successor *La Alarma* (named after Dyer Lum's Chicago paper), Mella was a leading protagonist in this dispute. After 1889, however, his role changed. While Mella believed that theoretical debates provided a healthy stimulus for the development of anarchist thinking, he was opposed to the internecine character of the collectivist/communist rivalry. By advocating a non-denominational form of anarchism, he hoped to change radically the terms of a controversy that had assumed the form of a life-and-death struggle, from which only one ideology could emerge victorious. This outcome is precisely what Mella sought to avoid.

Over time, Mella grew increasingly tolerant of communist ideas. This was evident in *La Nueva Utopía,* where he suggested that different economic systems could coexist in future society, and in later books and articles. In *Lombroso y los anarquistas* (1896), Mella eloquently defended anarchist communism against the spurious views of the noted Italian criminologist Cesare Lombroso, and in his essay "La cooperación libre y los sistemas de comunidad"(1900) he again echoed the theme of economic cooperation. Perhaps the closest Mella ever came to endorsing anarchist communism was when he consented in 1912 to translate into Spanish and write a prologue for Kropotkin's *Modern Science and Anarchism,* a work in which the Russian social theorist skillfully summarized his understanding of the scientific basis of anarchism. But, no matter how sympathetic Mella may have been to Kropotkin's arguments, he never fully embraced the philosophy of anarchist communism. This is partially borne out by the fact that, when he was approached in 1922 to write an introduction to Kropotkin's study of the evolution of ethics, Mella refused to do so. It may have been that Mella, who agreed with much that Kropotkin said, felt uncomfortable endorsing a book written from an anarchist communist perspective.

For the next few years, Tarrida continued preaching his brand of anarchism, not so much through writings but through his talks at workingmen's clubs and circles. Often sharing the lecture platform with well-known representatives of other anarchist schools, such as the communist Pedro Esteve, Tarrida extolled the virtues of adopting a nonsectarian form of anarchism. Toward the end of the 1890s, he once again rose to prominence in the anarchist movement, although not in the role of theoretician. During the notorious Montjuich affair of 1896–1897 Tarrida gained international recognition for exposing the barbarous tortures of the Spanish government, of which we shall have more to say later.

Although Tarrida and Mella each offered a different interpretation of *anarquismo sin adjetivos,* both were striving toward the same end. As it turned out, their campaign had a lasting impact on the movement. In the following years, more and more anarchists began calling for a moratorium on the communist/collectivist dispute and the adoption of *anarquismo sin adjetivos.* Among this growing group of converts were prominent anarchists like Ernesto Álvarez, Anselmo Lorenzo, and Federico Urales (pseudonym of Juan Montseny), who promoted this brand of anarchism in the paper *La Anarquía* (Madrid). In fact, after so many years of bitter quarreling among the anarchists, the terms "collectivism" and "communism" had acquired negative connotations to many. Thus, an anarchist from Cartagena wrote to his comrades in the anarchist communist paper *La Controversia* (Valencia) that "one cannot be an anarchist, nor by extension a free-thinking man, by upholding dogmas. For this reason my cry is that of ¡*Viva la anarquía sin adjetivos!*"[24]

Finally, it is noteworthy that *anarquismo sin adjetivos* as developed by Tarrida and Mella also influenced the anarchist movement outside of Spain. Eventually, Errico Malatesta, Elisée Reclus, Max Nettlau, and other eminent international libertarians also adopted the view that sectarianism violated the true spirit of anarchism. The notion of anarchism without adjectives was even spread by Spanish émigrés who settled abroad. After moving to Buenos Aires in 1891, Antonio Pellicer cautioned the workers against becoming dogmatic, and urged them instead to adopt an open anarchist perspective on theoretical and practical matters. But perhaps the greatest representative of "anarchism without adjectives" outside of Spain was the American Voltairine de Cleyre. In his biographical study of her, the historian Paul Avrich writes that when Tarrida met De Cleyre in London in 1897, he deeply impressed her. The fact that she later developed an anarchist theory also known as "anarchism without adjectives" testifies to the profound influence Tarrida had on her thinking.[25]

CHAPTER IX

The Haymarket Tragedy, the Origins of May Day, and Their Impact on the Anarchist Movement

Although the ideological and organizational unity of the Spanish revolutionary movement had been shattered as a result of the collectivist/communist rivalry and the disintegration of the FTRE, there were two events that briefly revived a feeling of solidarity among the anarchists: the Haymarket Bombing Affair of 1886–1887 and the invention of the May Day tradition. The repercussions of these events were felt for many years afterward, the most enduring legacy being the celebration of May first as a working-class holiday.

The trial of the Chicago anarchists who were accused of throwing the bomb in Haymarket Square in May 1886 provoked an outcry from around the world. This protest movement reached a crescendo following the execution in November 1887 of four of the eight men who had been convicted of the crime. At the time, anarchists, socialists, and progressives throughout Europe united in a chorus of dissent, decrying what they saw as a blatant miscarriage of justice. While the Haymarket Affair also became a *cause célèbre* for the entire Spanish left, the episode deeply impressed the libertarians, inciting them to escalate their radical activities. In their eyes, the deaths of the Chicago anarchists were more than just personal tragedies, for, above all, the hangings underscored the revolutionary significance of the eight-hour campaign and the celebration of May Day.[1]

THE EIGHT-HOUR CAMPAIGN AND THE
ORIGINS OF MAY DAY IN SPAIN

The revival of the campaign for the eight-hour day in the United States during the 1880s was accompanied by a tremendous upsurge of labor radicalism. The labor struggles in America found resonance in Europe, infusing life into working-class organizations that had been largely dormant since the death of the First International. Of all the European countries, though, it was perhaps in Spain that this campaign exerted its greatest influence on the development of the working-class movement. This was in large measure due to the important position anarchism (and to a lesser extent socialism) held among the workers.

As early as 1885, the eight-hour movement in America was being closely monitored by the Spanish anarchist press. Of particular interest to them was the growing number of anarchist-inspired May Day demonstrations. By the next year, the idea of an eight-hour movement had generated so much enthusiasm among the anarchists that they decided to form an Internal Commision of Eight Hours to investigate the possible means of obtaining this objective. Founded in Barcelona on 12 September 1886, the commission consisted of some sixty-eight delegates representing fifty-seven organizations. Although it later became associated with the nonrevolutionary segments of the Spanish working-class movement, the campaign for an eight-hour day initially aroused considerable alarm among the authorities. For example, Indalecio Cuadrado was imprisoned for four months because he dared to publish an article demanding the eight-hour day in the collectivist weekly *El Grito del Pueblo* (Barcelona), and the paper was forced to close down for good. The government's swift and severe response to Cuadrado's article can be explained by the fact that the anarchists themselves made it clear that their demand for a reduced workday was not a recantation of their revolutionary doctrine, which was in principle opposed to piecemeal reforms. Rather, for them, the eight-hour campaign served as a powerful inducement for the workers to advance the revolutionary movement. Above all, the anarchists thought that it heralded the dawn of a new era:

> The workers do not understand that they have initiated this movement in order to reach a state in which it is normal within an eight-hour day to earn a salary with which one can attend in a dignified manner to the necessities of civilized man; this is a true utopia. [In doing so] the workers propose to conduct war against the bourgeoisie, to produce disturbances, in short, to inaugurate a revolutionary period that has as its end the abolishment of all wages![2]

We saw earlier that by the mid-1880s most anarchists had lost faith in the strike tactic, not least because strikes seldom yielded any concrete results for the revolutionary cause. With the advent of the eight-hour campaign and the celebration of May Day, however, collectivists and communists alike began reassessing the revolutionary potential of strikes. In the end, both groups agreed that certain types of strikes, namely general and insurrectionary strikes, were the principal weapons the proletariat had at their disposal to "lash out against the capitalists." One anarchist journal announced the anarchists' reborn enthusiasm for the general strike:

> We dare to affirm that nearly every school of anarchism is united in the belief that it is necessary to abandon the futile routine of staging strikes—unless they are revolutionary strikes, that is to say, it is imperative to leave the vicious circle of [reformist] strikes in which our revolutionary strength is exhausted by chasing the illusion that the worker's lot will be improved merely by shortening the workday or augmenting his wages.[3]

To the anarchists, May Day and the eight-hour struggle were the rallying points, not just for the Spanish proletariat but for the working classes in all countries. "We, the workers of the world, must prepare ourselves," proclaimed *Víctima del Trabajo* (Valencia), "since the first of May is the day designated everywhere for presenting the bourgeoisie with an ultimatum for the eight-hour day. We must hasten to this call and seize the opportunity to stage a universal strike."[4] Hence, like their American counterparts, the Spanish anarchists came to regard May Day as an occasion for conducting violent protests, usually in the form of a revolutionary general strike.

The fact that the anarchists attached a revolutionary significance to the eight-hour campaign and the celebration of May Day distinguished them from the socialists and the unrevolutionary sections of the working classes, most of whom placed their faith in legal reforms as a way of furthering the workers' cause.

THE CHICAGO MARTYRS AND THE CELEBRATION OF NOVEMBER ELEVENTH

Certainly the acceptance of the idea of May Day in Spain was given tremendous impetus by the Haymarket affair of 1886–1887. For it was following this celebrated incident that the eight-hour movement in America became the focus of labor groups and radicals around the world. The Haymarket affair itself represented, in the words of the

historian Paul Avrich, "the culmination of a decade of strikes and agitation" in this campaign. As the details of the affair are well known, there
is no need to recount them here. Suffice it to say that although the
Haymarket bomb explosion alone created quite a sensation (especially
among the middle classes), what primarily disturbed the international
working classes was the manifestly unjust punishment meted out to the
eight Chicago anarchists who were held responsible for the bombing.
On 11 November 1887, against a background of worldwide protests,
the State of Illinois put to death Adolph Fischer, George Engel, Albert
Parsons, and August Spies.

In Spain the deaths of the Chicago anarchists had a two-fold significance. On one level, their executions served to reinforce the revolutionary connotations of May Day, primarily because the four men were
generally identified as martyrs of the eight-hour movement. Yet, quite
apart from their association with May Day, the Chicago martyrs collectively became a symbol of the revolutionary struggle for Spanish workers of all schools of thought.

For the anarchists, the hangings illustrated graphically what they had
long argued in their antistatist credo, namely, that the state was by
nature repressive—whether it was the autocratic kind found in Russia
or the democratic republic (*república modelo*) as represented by the
United States:

> Authority and obedience are terms that are incompatible with human dig-
> nity; no matter what kind of political regime it may be and in whatever
> manner it may have been established, some men are obliged to obey them.
> The scaffold of Chicago is our irrefutable proof of this.[5]

But the executions in Chicago did more than just provide the anarchists
with a pretext for asserting the validity of their doctrine. Perhaps more
significant, the incident had the immediate effect of inflaming the tem-
pers of the Spanish anarchists, thereby giving fresh impulse to their
revolutionary movement. Obviously outraged by what had happened,
the anarchists declared their determination to avenge the "legal murders" of their comrades, who were now being referred to as the "Chicago Martyrs." Even moderate libertarians, like the highly respected
intellectual Ricardo Mella, were moved to make incendiary speeches. In
one of his widely read pamphlets, Mella proclaimed defiantly that "the
terrible tragedy of Chicago was the bloody harbinger of the definitive
triumph of the proletariat." Again and again, Mella's sentiments were
echoed in working-class clubs and meeting halls by those who cried,

"Eternal praise to the Chicago Martyrs! Long live Anarchy! Long live the Social Revolution!"[6]

Within a year, the date November eleventh had acquired the status of a worker's holiday, and it was commonly recognized as being as important an event as the commemoration of the Paris Commune.[7] Reporting in the London anarchist journal *Freedom,* a Spanish correspondent explained its significance in the following way:

> This date [11 November] is in Spain a workers' holy day, and also an occasion for Anarchist demonstrations and propaganda. In all of the great cities, and in many country towns, the people commemorate the death of the noble workers, whose martyrdom instead of degrading them, glorified the instrument, at the same time that they view with horror the disgusting and untimely social institutions which now exist.[8]

If we piece together the various accounts found in newspapers and journals of the period we can get a good idea of how the eleventh of November was typically celebrated by workers throughout Spain. The ceremonies of the "holy day" were commonly held in the evening, when, after having toiled a full day, workers would gather at their trade union *centro* or other commonly used meeting place. For the evening's festivities, these halls would be temporarily transformed into shrines for the "martyrs" of the anarchist cause. The walls were adorned with brightly colored red and black banners that encircled large portraits (*retratos*) of working-class heroes: the Chicago Martyrs, Spanish anarchists who had sacrificed themselves to the class struggle, and such venerated figures of the socialist movement as Pierre-Joseph Proudhon and Michael Bakunin. Such use of iconography undoubtedly produced a powerful emotional response from the audience, giving these gatherings—to paraphrase the historian Gerald Brenan—the air of an American revivalist meeting. Following several brief introductory speeches about the significance of the date, the meeting was given over to readings of prose and poetry pieces dedicated to the memory of all those who had fallen victim to state persecution. Although a somber atmosphere prevailed over these proceedings, toward the end of the evening the solemn mood was abruptly broken when the audience rose to its feet and burst into spirited songs and verses espousing the glory of the Chicago Martyrs and the emancipation of man by man.[9]

The Chicago Martyrs continued to arouse considerable interest among the anarchists for the next several years. The revolutionary spirit engendered by the Haymarket Tragedy was kept alive not just by the annual memorials referred to above but in a variety of ways. For example, anarchists raised money to be sent to the families of the Chicago Martyrs, devoted whole issues of their periodicals to the subject of the Haymarket affair, and even gave their affinity groups such names as "The Martyrs of Chicago" and "The Eleventh of November." Perhaps the greatest tribute ever paid to the Chicago anarchists was the celebration of the Segundo Certámen Socialista, to which I referred earlier. This event, which was dedicated to the memory of the Chicago martyrs, may have been the largest working-class literary event to take place in Spain during the nineteenth century. Over 12,000 workers representing a wide range of trades attended the ceremonies at the majestic Palace of Fine Arts (Palacio de Bellas Artes) in Barcelona.

Meanwhile, the celebration of May Day itself was growing in importance among other segments of the Spanish working classes, especially among the socialists. After 1890, the socialists began celebrating May Day as their own labor holiday, and this created a great deal of anxiety within the libertarian community. More than anything else, the anarchists feared that, under socialist influence, May Day would inevitably lose the revolutionary orientation it was assuming under their own direction. According to one anarchist critic, the socialist May Day celebration was not a day of working-class protest but rather "a day of ritual, of cults, of idolatry."[10] Considering that the anarchists themselves incorporated iconography and other forms of quasi-religious rituals in their commemoration of the Eleventh of November, this uncharitable observation may well have appeared ironic to the socialists. But what this anarchist was referring to was the fact that the socialists, having committed themselves to a different revolutionary strategy than that of the anarchists, refused to use May Day as an occasion for staging violent demonstrations. As a result, from 1890 on Spanish workers began observing May first in different ways.

MAY DAY AND THE SECOND INTERNATIONAL

The revival of the European socialist movement in the late 1880s and early 1890s and the birth of the Second International were events that owed much to the struggle for the eight-hour day in America. At the founding congress of the Second International held in Paris in July 1889, it was decided to follow the American example and adopt May first as an international workers' holiday. Thus, 1 May 1890 was designated as the Second International's first official May Day celebration.

As far as the socialists were concerned, May Day was meant to serve several purposes. Besides demonstrating the solidarity and political effectiveness of the international working-class movement, it was a way of giving dramatic expression to their resolve to reduce the working day by law to eight hours. The Spanish delegate Pablo Iglesias spoke for many others when he stated that May Day should be recognized as a universal public manifestation by all those who suffered under the yoke of "the oppressing classes." He went on to declare:

> For this reason, because it affirms the class struggle so powerfully and announces to the proletariat their certain triumph, the May 1st demonstration is more than just an occasion full of pomp and beauty—it is an action that possesses supreme utility for the working classes.[11]

For all their apparent enthusiasm for staging May Day demonstrations, the socialists could not agree on the specific form of action that was to be taken on this holiday.[12] Some, like the Austrians and the majority of the French delegation, advocated a complete stoppage of work on the first in order to display the economic leverage that lay behind workers' demands. The Germans, who represented the largest and best organized section of the Second International, did not share this view, and therefore they refused to pledge themselves to any tactic that implied strike action. Lacking a consensus on how May Day was to be celebrated, the congress finally adopted a resolution that left this decision to the respective socialist parties: "The workers of the various countries will have to accomplish the manifestation under the conditions imposed on them by the particular situation in each country."[13]

MAY DAY AND SPANISH SOCIALISM

In order to understand the impact May Day had on Spanish socialism, one has to bear in mind several facts about the early development of the movement. It may be recalled that since its foundation in 1879, the Socialist Party (Partido Socialista Obrero Español, PSOE) had endured a miserable existence. The party's efforts to attract a following among the workers had met with little success except within certain unions, like the printers union in Madrid (Asociación General de Arte de Imprimir)—which was predominantly Marxist—and the reformist labor groups in Barcelona, principally the textile association Tres Clases de Vapor (TCV). During the 1880s, the socialists passed through a phase that the socialist historian Juan José Morato likened to "crossing the desert." Even Pablo Iglesias later publicly confessed that, as compared to other working-class organizations at this time, the PSOE was an insignificant party: "It included only a small number of groups, with no more than two hundred members."[14] The only developments of the period that augured well for the movement came in March 1886, when the PSOE began publishing its own mouthpiece, *El Socialista* (Madrid), and in August 1888, when a trade union branch of the party, the Unión General de Trabajadores (UGT), was established in Barcelona.

The early evolution of socialist ideology was a crucial factor in determining the position socialism held among the working classes. Deeply influenced by the French Marxists, the Spanish socialists maintained a doctrinaire view of politics and particularly of their relationship to other labor groups. On a practical level, this entailed eschewing political alliances with the bourgeoisie on the one hand and rejecting the ultrarevolutionary tactics of the anarchists on the other. Thanks to their persistent refusal to abandon this ideological stance, the socialists remained, during the first part of the Restoration (1875–1899), isolated from the mainstream of the labor movement.

It was of course quite natural that once they adopted May Day as an official workers' holiday, the socialists were keen to avoid confusing their celebrations with those of their chief rivals on the left, the anarchists. It therefore followed that their May Day demonstrations had to be conducted along different lines. Because they maintained an unshakable faith in political methods, the socialists seriously questioned the efficacy of using strikes and other economic weapons as a means of advancing the social revolution. Their goal was to achieve control of the local and national governments through electoral organization and propaganda. Only after the proletariat had conquered political power, according to the socialists, would it be possible to mount a revolution in which the existing capitalist system would be overturned and replaced by a worker's state. As regards May Day, this meant that the socialists favored the idea of holding strikes as long as their overall aim was strictly limited to improving working conditions (*las huelgas parciales*). They would have none of the anarchist concept of the insurrectionary general strike (*la huelga general*).

As the first socialist-sponsored May Day (1890) drew nearer, it became increasingly evident to the socialist leadership that they could not coordinate the demonstrations in the different regions. Socialist strength and influence was, as we have seen, negligible in most areas, and even in Madrid, the headquarters of the PSOE, there was no mass base for the movement. However, in Barcelona, where the UGT had been founded, socialism was more advanced. Ever since the mid-1880s, the socialists there had come out in favor of the eight-hour day, and had even supported the anarchist-inspired Internal Commission of Eight Hours created in 1886.

Given the uneven development of their movement, and given their uncertainty about how both the workers and the bourgeoisie would react to their call for May Day demonstrations, the Spanish socialists decided to hold their first May Day events on two different days, May first in Barcelona and May fourth in Madrid.[15] Both occasions reflected the cautious attitude adopted by the socialist leaders. Antonio García Quejido, the popular head of the UGT, led the demonstration in Barcelona, while the leading lights of the PSOE, Pablo Iglesias and Matías Gómez Latorre, presided over the one in Madrid.

The May Day activities of the socialists in Barcelona were overshadowed by a paralyzing general strike that had been called by the anarchists. Refusing to involve themselves in the strike—which dragged on for another four days—the socialists proceeded with their own demonstration. They convoked a meeting in the Tivoli Theater, after which an estimated 20,000 workers marched to the office of the governor general to present him with a petition of workers' demands. Then, without a hint of disturbance, the procession broke up and the workers returned to their homes. Just how many of those in attendance were marching in favor of socialism is impossible to say. Nonetheless, the fact that so many people turned out for the May Day protest suggests that the socialists had, if not very many official members, a considerable number of sympathizers.

In contrast to Barcelona, in Madrid May Day events took place in a relatively tranquil atmosphere. Some 2,000 workers assembled at the gardens located in the Buen Retiro, where they listened quietly to speeches delivered at the Liceo Reus. When this meeting concluded, the gathering joined up with a crowd of several thousand others and marched to the Council of the Presidency. Upon reaching their destination, the orderly demonstrators waited while a small delegation presented the liberal Prime Minister Sagasta with a list of their demands.[16]

Elsewhere in Spain, socialist-sponsored May Day celebrations were of little consequence, for as a rule they were conducted benignly, much like any other working-class holiday during which families spent the day picnicking and listening to public speeches. A notable exception to this pattern of events was in the Basque city of Bilbao, where the May Day demonstration touched off an impressive strike. Although during the 1880s socialist ideas were only beginning to penetrate the mining districts of the north, by 1890 it was becoming increasingly apparent that socialism had found an echo among the militant miners. This was abundantly manifested in Bilbao following the massive workers' parade held on Sunday the fourth. In response to the miners' show of solidarity, the owner of the La Orconera mine dismissed all of the workers belonging to the socialist group called La Arboleda. On the twelfth, miners from several pits replied by downing their tools. Apart from wanting their fellow workers reinstated, the miners demanded improved living conditions (the mine owners were responsible for building the shoddy barracks in which the miners and their families lived), and the reduction of the workday from between twelve and fourteen hours to ten. By the fifteenth, over 15,000 miners and approximately 12,000 other workers (including carpenters, cabinetmakers, and marblecutters) from the neighboring towns and villages had joined the strike. Then, just as the strike movement was gaining momentum, government troops were called in to crush the workers' resistance. Not long afterward, the general strike collapsed.[17]

It is noteworthy that the Bilbao strike had not been planned by the socialists, and, more important, it was clearly an example of the general strike tactic, which in principle had been rejected outright by the leadership. Nevertheless, the propaganda value of the strike was not lost on figures like Pablo Iglesias, who joined others in declaring it an important socialist victory. He pointed out, for instance, that as a result of the miners' action their workday was reduced to ten hours and their abysmal dwellings (*cuarteles*) were declared by the authorities to be unfit for habitation. With respect to the socialist movement, the strike itself was to have lasting significance. Perhaps more than any other form of action during this period, it served as an impetus for the growth of socialism in the Basque region.

THE LEGACY OF MAY DAY

Although occasionally interrupted by a strike like the one in Bilbao, the nonrevolutionary pattern of activity established at the socialists' May Day demonstrations of 1890 remained unbroken in the coming years. Until the late 1890s, the anarchists too continued their practice of using the holiday as an occasion for staging general strikes and other insurrectionary activities. Because it was bound up with the issue of the eight-hour day, May Day provided both socialists and anarchists with a potentially powerful rallying point for their respective movements. In another sense, though, it was also true that the introduction of May Day, far from promoting solidarity among the diverse groups of Spanish workers, simply threw into sharper relief the ideological boundaries that were dividing them into opposing camps.

The issue of the revolutionary general strike presented the biggest obstacle in the process of reconciliation between anarchists and socialists. The socialists, while willing to admit that limited strikes served to radicalize the workers and thus foster solidarity among them, never tired of preaching about the shortcomings of the general strike tactic, calling it the product of "wooly thinking" (*un pensamiento descabellado*). Yet, as it happened, one violent or highly disruptive strike—such as the one that occurred in Bilbao—probably did more to advance the socialist cause than did years of carefully orchestrated and pacific demonstrations held on May Day.[18]

Even though the anarchists never lost their faith in the *huelga general* as a means of generating revolutionary momentum among the workers, after 1892 it became increasingly difficult for them to mount large-scale strikes on May Day. This was largely because the anarchists themselves were abandoning the trade unions, and instead were turning more and more toward individual acts of violence, or "propaganda by the deed," to oppose the ruling classes. The attendant upsurge in violent activity inevitably brought on government repression, which became progressively harsher during the heyday of anarchist violence, 1892–1896. Thus, while the emotional force and symbolic significance of May Day demonstrations were never wholly dispelled for the anarchists, by the mid-1890s they had ceased regarding them as effective vehicles for advancing the revolutionary movement.

CHAPTER X

Terrorism and the Anarchist Movement, 1892–1894

In the early days of its existence, the Spanish section of the First International was generally identified as a source of revolutionary violence, a connection that was reinforced by the Paris Commune of 1871 and the cantonalist unrest during the summer of 1873. Violence at that time, though, had sprung from the collective action of the International and was predominantly in the form of strikes and small-scale social rebellions. This was no longer true once the anarchists adopted the tactic of "propaganda by the deed." During the late 1880s and the 1890s, the period when acts of propaganda by the deed peaked throughout Europe, anarchism became associated with a wide-ranging spectrum of direct action that was mostly violent and that was not necessarily linked to strikes or other forms of organized labor resistance. Because robbery, vandalism, political assassination, and bombings were all at one time or another sanctioned by the anarchist community as legitimate expressions of propaganda by the deed, anarchism was inevitably equated with terrorism in the public mind.

Of course anarchist-inspired violence was not confined to Spain. In Europe and the Americas, too, the sensational acts of a few determined radicals commanded the headlines of newspapers and periodicals of nearly every shade of political opinion, giving rise to the popular image of the anarchist as the incarnation of death and destruction. When reading the popular press of the era, one finds the anarchist commonly portrayed in cartoons and stories as a shadowy and fiendish figure with a bomb in his pocket and a dagger in his hand. Anarchists were, according to these accounts, the "miscreants who are now aspiring to terrorize the world: the very dregs of the population . . . despicable desperadoes already under the ban and always subject to close surveillance."[1] This somewhat colorful and largely inaccurate description of the typical anarchist proved to be an enormous liability for the movement, not least because the image of a violence-prone anarchist was exploited by their enemies. The bourgeois press in particular was highly successful at fanning the flames of the public's hysteria and ardent resentment of the anarchists, thereby tarnishing the reputation of all libertarians, even those who openly opposed terrorism.

Nor did terrorism improve the Spanish anarchists position vis-à-vis their more circumspect political rivals, the socialists and reformist trade unionists. As regards the socialists, for example, the anarchists gradually began to lose ground to them after 1890, and this was in no small way due to the anarchists' commitment to violent tactics. The socialists themselves, who had been slowly but methodically building up their strength and popular support by concentrating on developing a well-defined and organized trade union movement, deplored the use of violence. Consequently, they were not stigmatized with the label of terrorism, and they rarely suffered the full force of repression, which invariably followed an outburst of anarchist violence.

Antianarchist legislation was enacted in every country where they were considered a threat. The Spanish authorities, especially, took extraordinary measures in their campaign to eradicate anarchism. Following a series of bombings in the early 1890s, for example, a special police unit, *Brigada Social*, was created to investigate bombings and to prosecute terrorists. In addition, special legislation was passed in 1894 and 1896 which was designed to stamp out terrorism, but which was also used as a pretext for disrupting the activities of all anarchists, including those affiliated with legal working-class organizations. This was by far the most serious consequence that the tactic of propaganda by the deed had on the development of anarchism.

THE TACTICS OF REVOLUTIONARY
TERRORISM

Although it is true that the negative image of the anarchist was largely molded by a hostile bourgeois press and the authorities, the anarchists themselves were partly responsible for their own unpopularity inasmuch as a significant number of them stubbornly refused to abandon violent methods. The anarchist communists' attitude toward violence helps to explain the persistence of the tactic of propaganda by the deed.

As a rule, the Spanish communists followed their French counterparts in regarding propaganda by the deed as representing any act of force against the bourgeoisie. During the 1890s this usually meant endorsing individual acts of sabotage, the destruction of private property, assassinations, and bombings, that is, any tactic that aimed to shock, intimidate, or kill the class enemies of the proletariat.

The principal reason the communists advocated violence was that they saw it as being integral to the revolutionary process. They held, like Bakunin, an apocalyptic conception of the final struggle: the end of capitalism was envisaged as a bloody confrontation between the workers and the ruling classes. The communists also believed that the intensity of this struggle was directly proportional to the state of misery and repression that existed in the present. Violent acts were therefore seen as a necessary means of agitating the workers so as to awaken them from the apathy thought to be the result of centuries of oppression.

It must have struck many of their contemporaries as ironic that, as a matter of principle, the communists rejected the concepts of violence and force on the ground that these forms of activity were anathema to all they stood for. This was because the communists maintained two distinct moral standards. One applied to contemporary society, where capitalism reigned supreme, and the other applied to society after the revolution. While the communists predicted that these twin social evils would disappear with the advent of anarchism, in the present they pictured themselves in a life-and-death contest with the middle classes. And in this so-called struggle for survival, the anarchists resorted to violence and force because they were viewed as necessary means to an end.

The communists' theoretical defense for a policy of terrorism was predicated on their conception of bourgeois society. In their judgment, the ruling classes of this social order used force to maintain control over the means of production as well as the conditions under which the proletariat lived. Because the proletariat were enslaved in this iniquitous system of oppression, the communists claimed that the worker had no choice but to use violence as means of liberating himself. To illustrate their reasoning, they adduced the bourgeois institution of private property. Following Proudhon, they saw property as the greatest source of social injustice under capitalism:

> From no point of view can we admit or in the least way believe that property as it exists today can signify even one atom of justice. . . . Yet this social illness [i.e., property], this unheard-of crime, is sustained thanks to force; so how peculiar is it, then, for one to use force in an attempt to dislodge this other force, which is so antihuman, antisocial, and dishonorable to civilization, to justice, and to human reason?[2]

Anarchists generally were so convinced of the immorality of property that they were ready to condone any kind of crime committed against the bourgeoisie. Robbery and the destruction of property, for example, had long been thought by many to be a fitting means of expressing propaganda by the deed. Then, just as these manifestations of violence appeared to be dying out in the late 1880s, anarchist terrorism assumed a new and far more serious form with the advent of dynamite.[3] Because it was, despite its dangerous volatility, relatively simple to manufacture and as easily transported by one as by two or more individuals, dynamite proved to be an effective and powerful weapon with which the radicals could arm themselves in their assault upon the bourgeoisie. Dynamite was thus seen, as one socialist historian put it, as "the poor man's weapon. It was the power that science had given to the weak to protect them from the injustice of tyranny."[4]

The mere possession of dynamite gave the anarchists an added aura of power, both in their own eyes and in those of their class enemies. To some militants, dynamite symbolized the salvation of the revolutionary movement, a way of equalizing the forces engaged in class struggle. In their newspapers, they openly published articles advocating the use and even the different methods of manufacturing dynamite. The Spanish communist paper *El Eco de Ravachol* boldly declared the significance of the explosive to the revolutionary movement: "Force is repelled by force, and that is why dynamite was invented."[5] Whether intended or not, this was a form of "psychological terrorism," which signaled to the bourgeoisie that the anarchists were seriously preparing themselves for the final day of reckoning.

In practice, however, the potential destructive power of dynamite was seldom exploited by Spanish anarchists of the late nineteenth century. Of all the bombing incidents of the period, very few actually caused death and large-scale destruction. As we shall see, one was the *attentat* committed by Paulino Pallás in 1893, which killed two people and wounded several bystanders, and another was that of Santiago Salvador French, who threw a bomb into the stalls of the Liceo theater in Barcelona the following year, killing some twenty people and wounding many others.

The anarchist communists' abiding belief that resorting to violence was a legitimate means of furthering their cause was not the only reason why propaganda by the deed became a permanent feature of the anarchist movement. An obvious advantage of the tactic was that it kept alive the spirit of revolution by providing the intemperate radical elements with a means of challenging the authorities. Bombing outrages also drew attention to the anarchist movement as a whole, sometimes greatly exaggerating its real size and strength.

The emergence of a cult of violence among the extremists associated with *grupitos* also helped to perpetuate anarchist terrorism. This cult doubtless fed on the publicity generated by revolutionary outrages, perhaps artificially elevating the status of the lonely militant who might otherwise have been relegated to complete obscurity. It is therefore likely that propaganda by the deed was sustained not just by the self-righteous few who were committed to abstract principles but also by a personality type that was attracted to a seemingly romantic revolutionary life-style. This sort of anarchist did not take directives from anyone and existed as a maverick, forming a subculture with other like-minded militants that was isolated from the mainstream of the organized labor movement. There is, in fact, some evidence that *grupitos* were formed expressly for acts of reprisal. Two created in Barcelona in 1888, Sin Nombre and El Destructor, had as their slogan "The ends justify the means," leaving little doubt as to their intention with regards to propaganda by the deed.

Much like the terrorist groups of the late twentieth century, *grupitos* of this variety took their inspiration from the fanatical adherents of the revolutionary cause, especially those who fell victim to what the anarchists perceived as social and governmental oppression. During the 1890s, the infamous French anarchist assassin, Ravachol, was a highly venerated figure, as were others who had sacrificed themselves while waging the revolutionary struggle. The hero worship of these "martyrs" was manifested in a number of ways, but typically the communists' publications and affinity groups paid homage to them by adopting such names as *El Eco de Ravachol* and *Mártires de Jerez*.

While the Spanish collectivists (and a select few communists, like Pedro Esteve) saw violence as inevitable in the revolutionary movement, they strongly disagreed with the communist view that sanctioned any form of violence as an expression of anarchist propagandism. At an anarchist conference held at the Paris International Exhibition in 1889, and attended by several leading European anarchists, this issue drew heated debate from the delegates.[6] Some, like the Italian anarchist communist Salverio Merlino and the Spanish representative Tarrida del Mármol, held that even though robbery was justifiable for the poor vis-à-vis the rich, it was not an affirmation of anarchist principles. Furthermore, Merlino expressed reservations about condoning robbery because there was always the danger of criminal elements taking refuge in the ranks of anarchists. Tarrida del Mármol went beyond Merlino in protesting against the use of violence and robbery as a means of anarchist action. He strongly challenged the prevailing view among the communists that such tactics were either justifiable or efficacious.

In the end, Tarrida's views prevailed at the meeting.[7] Significantly, though, there was no way of enforcing the proposal. By now the international anarchist movement had no formal organizational links, and, in any case, the movements in the respective countries were dominated by autonomous militant groups. Thus the interpretation of "propaganda by the deed" ultimately rested with individual anarchists.

The views expressed by Tarrida and Merlino were representative of a large group of anarchists who subscribed to a different style of thinking on the issue of violence. To be sure, some forms of violence were understood as necesary elements in the daily struggle, and in the final battle of the social revolution. Where they departed most radically from the apostles of propaganda by the deed was in their interpretation of how violence was to be manifested in the revolutionary struggle. They adamantly rejected individual acts of terrorism—especially criminal activity and bombings—whereas strikes, sabotage, civil disobedience, and similar forms of collective action were regarded as legitimate ways of challenging the government and capitalists.

Unlike the communist "purists," the collectivists gave morals an explicit role in the process of social development, holding that it was not possible to divorce ends from means in the revolutionary struggle. Because they also believed that the radical transformation of capitalism into an anarchist society must be accompanied by the moral regeneration of the people, they thought that one's behavior in the present ought to conform as much as possible to the anarchist ideals of justice, freedom, and good. It was this belief that also distinguished them from most communists and that accounted for their revulsion toward the arbitrary use of violence.

During the 1890s, the issue of violence remained a complex one, particularly for the collectivists. Not least of their problems was the need to formulate a viable revolutionary strategy that did not rely on individual acts of reprisal. In fact, the anarchists' increased reliance on propaganda by the deed revealed the growing impotence of the revolutionary movement in Spain. As May Day demonstrations and general strikes became more and more difficult to stage, the anarchists lost their ability to orchestrate large-scale demonstrations against the authorities. As we shall see, this was most apparent in areas like Andalusia, where transient, casual laborers, who lacked any well-defined organizational framework, could only ventilate their hostilities through spontaneous risings, such as crop burnings and other acts of sabotage in the countryside. Following the notorious Jerez rising of 1892, libertarians of every school, including moderates like Ricardo Mella, became incensed by the authorities' sweeping campaign to persecute the anarchists and to suppress organized labor activity in the south. Even though escalating government repression caused the collectivists to grow increasingly strident in calling for the violent overthrow of the existing social order, they never went so far as to endorse propaganda by the deed.

There was a further reason why anarchists like Tarrida and Mella rejected terrorist-inspired violence. Mella himself—quite rightly as it turned out—feared that such acts would ultimately alienate the masses from the anarchist movement. Without popular support, he warned, the revolution was doomed to failure. Writing on this theme during a wave of anarchist bombings at the turn of the century, Mella implored his comrades to think of the consequences of their actions: "It is necessary that we are not ourselves auxiliaries to the current of opinion which regards dynamite as synonymous with anarchism."[8]

In the urban centers, anarchist violence usually took the form of bombings. With few exceptions—like the plot, mentioned below, to blow up the Cortes in 1892— these acts did not appear to be intended to bring about significant political changes. This was especially true during the late 1880s, when bombings or bombing attempts became commonplace in Madrid, Barcelona, and other major cities.

Most bombs caused little harm, for many of them were only crude instruments fashioned from an odd assortment of materials, such as tin cans, coffee grinders, metal pipes, or just sticks of dynamite. Usually placed outside the front entrance to a church, public building, or well-known haunt of conservative politicians, very few ever discharged properly. Even when they did explode, they seldom injured anyone.

Because bombings became a popular form of protest at this time, it was not always possible to know who was responsible for the deed. Thus, when the target was not overtly political, it was difficult to distinguish genuine acts of propaganda by the deed from other forms of protest that were not politically motivated. For example, in January 1889 a spate of random bombings in Madrid prompted a reporter for the London *Times* to write:

> A good deal of exaggerated importance has been given in the foreign Press to the recent explosions in various quarters of Madrid. The fact is, these machines have in no instance been of a dangerous character. . . . The one exploded last was made of an old shoe. Perhaps a senseless practical joke is intended; but the matter has certainly no political significance.[9]

While the majority of these explosions caused no serious harm to the general public, they were still dangerous acts that had to be dealt with by the authorities. In order to demonstrate their apparent effectiveness in combating terrorism, the police would occasionally announce the unearthing of a conspiracy and then proceed to round up suspects. The arrests and trials that followed rarely brought anyone to justice but rather served to bolster the government's claim of the ever-present threat posed by both the domestic and international anarchist movement.

Who, then, were the bomb throwers and conspirators? Some were the fanatical members of anarchist communist cells to whom we have already referred. Numerically, this group was quite small, representing the fringe of the anarchist movement as a whole. At least some of the masterminds behind bombing conspiracies were drawn from the community of foreign anarchists who had since the days of La Gloriosa found Spanish soil a fertile ground for conducting their revolutionary campaigns. Such was the case in April 1892, when a Frenchman named Devas and a Portuguese named Ferreira were detained by the police just as they were preparing to discharge a bomb in the Cortes.[10] Their plot was foiled, according to one source, because the police had had the men under surveillance for some time. Ferreira in particular was being closely watched as he was a suspect from a previous bombing incident; only shortly before his arrival in Madrid he had reportedly set off a bomb at the Spanish Consulate in Lisbon.

Although the authorities were sometimes successful at discovering bombing conspiracies, more often their detective work came to nothing. This was apparent even following the creation of the Brigada Social, which quickly acquired a reputation as an incompetent and corrupt body. In its attempts to destroy anarchist revolutionary cells, the

Brigada would enlist the help of underground gangs and paid informants. These unreliable and undesirable types employed a variety of
methods while in the service of the police. Some would gather information by gaining entry to anarchist groups, while others would act as
provocateurs, planting incriminating evidence in anarchist circles or
discharging bombs themselves in order to justify police action against
leftist working-class organizations.

There were other reasons why propaganda by the deed proved to be
a tactic that was nearly impossible to suppress. First of all, given the
fragmented state of the anarchist movement, it was especially difficult
for the authorities to pinpoint the source of terrorism. And since few
people were required to put it into effect, it was nearly impossible for
the authorities to stamp out completely the ephemeral, tiny revolutionary cells that proliferated throughout Spain. Hence, unlike the general
strike, which could be suppressed through, say, direct military intervention, propaganda by the deed was a tactic that permitted the anarchists
to continue operating—albeit on a small scale—even in the most unpropitious circumstances.

REBELLION AND REPRISALS: THE JEREZ
INCIDENT OF 1892

During the 1880s and 1890s, the roles of the protagonists and an-
tagonists in the world of the Spanish working-class movement never
changed. On the one side were the anarchists and—to a lesser extent—
the socialists, both of whom ceaselessly struggled to mold a working-
class consciousness according to their respective ideological beliefs. On
the other side stood their sworn enemies, the authorities—especially the
Guardia Civil—the landlords, and all others who were viewed as representatives of the prevailing system of economic and political oppression.
It deserves mention here that this polarization of society into those who
felt subjugated and those who were perceived as the tyrannizers was not
an abstract problem but rather was visible at every level. The *Guardia
Civil,* for example, were ubiquitous in the cities, and they even operated
in the tiny hamlets in the mountains and countryside. Perhaps more
than any other official group, they came to symbolize the brute force of
the state that was so often used to break the resistance of protesting
workers. In the words of Gerald Brenan, "every Civil Guard became a
recruiting officer for anarchism, and, as the anarchists increased their
membership, the Civil Guard also grew. One has to have lived in

Andalusia to understand the kind of warfare that went on between them."[11]

As far as the anarchist movement was concerned, the focus of this ongoing war was forever shifting. At one point, the movements in Barcelona and Madrid would come alive, either because of massive May Day demonstrations—which were frequently accompanied by crippling strikes—or because of a series of widely publicized *attentats*. At other times, the focus would shift to the south, especially to Andalusia, where the friction between the social classes was visibly acute. The so-called Jerez rising of 1892 serves as an outstanding illustration of what is being referred to here. According to Ricardo Mella, Jerez had become by the 1890s the apex of working-class discontent primarily because the polarization of the classes there had reached its end points. In this land of stark contrasts, he wrote, it should surprise no one that the workers and peasants were constantly hovering on the brink of rebellion:

> The land of Andalusia is a land of liberty. . . . But the land of Andalusia is also a land of despotic government and capitalism, it is a land of great wealth and great poverty, where rich and poor live in a state of nervous tension that frequently leads to the most brutal form of tyranny on the one side and to constant sedition on the other. The extremely fertile soil is monopolized by the few, the privileged few, whereas the vast majority of people find themselves stripped of all means of living and are condemned to the tortures of hunger. There where the soil can produce the best of fruits, there where there is an abundance of everything and nothing is lacking, so that there ought to be enough for all, thousands upon thousands of poor creatures go for days without eating and eat badly when they do get to eat.[12]

Like the Mano Negra episode of the previous decade, the Jerez rising was to exercise a profound influence on the course of the workers' movement. While most historians have referred to it as an archetypical anarchist insurrection or as a classic example of a millenarian revolt, the fact is that the Jerez "rising" cannot be so easily classified.[13] Moreover, because there are several conflicting accounts of the incident, the task of characterizing it is very difficult. Were the events at Jerez revolutionary? If they were not, what did happen that fateful night of 8 January 1892?

The events that formed the immediate backdrop to the Jerez rising began on May Day of 1890. It may be recalled that since 1886, Spanish anarchists had recognized May first as a day to stage protests and demonstrate their collective strength in the revolutionary movement. In the Cádiz region the mounting successes of these demonstrations were obviously causing considerable alarm among those who feared the growth of anarchism. Not surprisingly, when a large crowd turned up in Cádiz for the May Day activities of 1890, the authorities resolved to take steps to stem the rising tide of worker radicalism in the region. The police, who since 1883 had been repeatedly invoking the specter of La Mano Negra as a pretext for disrupting labor groups, began their campaign by rounding up suspected rabble-rousers and others whom they considered potential leaders of demonstrations. In view of this, it was probably no coincidence that, just days before the planned May Day events of 1891, the police permanently shut down the printing presses of the popular anarchist tribune *El Socialismo* (1886–1891) and then arrested its editor, Fermín Salvochea.

A well-known figure in the Cádiz area, Salvochea was also widely recognized as the unofficial spiritual leader of the Andalusian anarchist movement. Even among the working classes elsewhere in Spain, Salvochea enjoyed immense popularity, and he was looked on by many of his comrades as a paragon of anarchist virtues. Born in 1842, the son of a fairly well-to-do merchant in Cádiz, Salvochea spent part of his youth in England. While studying abroad, he was introduced to the socially progressive ideas of such English thinkers as Robert Owen, Thomas Paine, and Charles Bradlaugh. By the time he left England, Salvochea had become a socialist. Returning to Spain during the 1860s, Salvochea eagerly embraced the Federal Republican cause. Despite his middle-class background, he championed the interests of the lumpenproletariat during La Gloriosa. Two years after he was elected mayor (*alcalde*) of Cádiz in 1871, Salvochea spearheaded a Federal revolt, and thereafter he became identified as a revolutionary with strong anticlerical and antimilitarist feelings. Later, when he abandoned the Federalist cause and became an anarchist, his fate was sealed. Until his death in 1907, the authorities, who did not underestimate the significance of Salvochea's reputation among the anarchists, relentlessly harrassed him.[14] But this did not put an end to his political career. For even though Salvochea was continuously in and out of prison, he managed during brief periods of amnesty to play a leading role as a revolutionary agitator. Perhaps his greatest contribution to the anarchist movement was made during the time he edited and directed the highly regarded *El Socialismo*.

In the meantime, Salvochea's detention in April 1891, far from dampening the spirits of May Day demonstrators in Cádiz, actually spurred on the day's activities: thousands of demonstrators marched into town on May first. Celebrations in other parts of Andalusia also attracted large crowds. At the Plaza de Toros in Córdoba, for example, Ricardo Mella, Ramón Montejano, and Miguel Rubio addressed an audience of some 3,000 workers.[15] Through these impressive demonstrations, workers were announcing to their adversaries that their movement was not easily intimidated by strong-arm tactics.

Shortly after May Day, two bombs exploded in Cádiz, killing one worker and injuring several others. The incident sparked off a wave of reprisals by the authorities, in the course of which over 157 anarchists were arrested. Salvochea, who had just been released from jail, publicly denied that anarchists had had anything to do with the bombings. Though he insisted that the deed had been the work of *agents provocateurs,* his efforts to exonerate the anarchists were to no avail. Salvochea himself was viewed as a suspect, and consequently, the authorities incarcerated him as well. That the police were using the bombings as an excuse to harass the workers is strongly suggested by the fact that they not only failed to produce any evidence linking Salvochea or the anarchists to the crime but also arbitrarily closed the *centros obreros* of the city.

While in prison, Salvochea evidently maintained contact with anarchist organizers, and it has been claimed—even by anarchist sympathizers—that he met with the leaders of the Jerez revolt several days before it occurred. According to his good friend and biographer, Pedro Vallina, Salvochea advised the workers to wait for the arrival of Errico Malatesta, who was accompanying Pedro Esteve and Tarrida del Mármol on a lecture tour of Spain and was due in Jerez sometime during January. Given his revolutionary experience, Malatesta was, in Salvochea's opinion, the person who could best determine whether or not such a rising would be successful.[16]

It is noteworthy that Malatesta himself seems to have had no prior knowledge of the impending Jerez rebellion. Having given several public addresses across Spain commemorating the deaths of the Chicago Martyrs, Malatesta was surprised to learn of the rising.[17] It would appear as though Jerez was scheduled to be the next stop in his journey, but this had to be abruptly cancelled in view of the circumstances. Risking certain arrest if he was recognized, Malatesta nevertheless made his way to Andalusia disguised as an Italian businessman. What precisely the nature of his trip was and whether he met with other anarchists involved in the Jerez incident are not known. But, judging from all the available evidence, it is reasonable to assume that Malatesta played no role in the planning of the rebellion.

The belief that Salvochea met with the Jerez leaders on the eve of the revolt gave rise to the widely held view that the Jerez rising was part of a grand anarchist conspiracy to spread the fires of revolution throughout the Andalusian region. In any event, we shall see that the police and government officials never satisfactorily established this crucial link in the chain of events that led to the Jerez insurrection.

Just before midnight of 8 January 1892, several hundred workers entered the town of Jerez crying, "¡Viva la revolución!, ¡Viva la anarquía!" Armed with only rocks, sticks, scythes, and other simple farm implements, the mob marched toward the city jail with the evident intention of releasing all of its prisoners. It is significant that many of them were political prisoners, victims of the government's antianarchist campaign, which had been vigorously waged since the Mano Negra affair. The feeling of solidarity among the workers was running so high that they apparently invited the soldiers stationed at the nearby garrison to join their march to free their imprisoned comrades. Surprisingly, the soldiers did little to contain the hostile gathering, though they did fire at random a few shots in the general direction of the workers.

By then the angry mood of the workers had reached such a pitch that the crowd was clearly running out of control. As they made their way through the town, the workmen passed by the theater just as the evening's performance was ending. Two men emerging from the theater were seized. After examining their hands for the presence of callouses—the telling signs of one's profession—the workers declared the men to be bourgeois enemies and then set upon them viciously. Pausing only momentarily, the mob continued their march to the jail, leaving in their wake the dead bodies of the two men. Arriving at their destination, the demonstrators were met by the warden's daughter, who tried to fend them off by firing several rounds of her pistol into the crowd. When the shooting was over, it was discovered that she had wounded at least one worker and had killed another.

The remaining workers laid seige to the jail, but despite their great number, they failed to take the building. As dawn approached, some workers began leaving, while others began showing signs of their growing weariness. Then, with the arrival of a calvary regiment, the rump of the crowd was quickly dispersed. The frustrated agitators thus returned home with no further disturbances taking place.

By the next day, news of the incident had spread far and wide. The domestic and international press was, as usual, presenting it as a full-scale working-class rebellion with international implications.[18] In the course of the following week, the authorities arrested scores of workers, including those who were supposedly responsible for having plotted the conspiracy. Two of the alleged ringleaders, El Lebrijano and Busiqui, were accused of having murdered the two bystanders. Not long afterward, a Félix Grávalo (a.k.a. "El Madrileño"), another suspect who was to play a pivotal role in the subsequent trials, was also arrested. Other leading anarchist figures of the region were soon rounded up and jailed on the flimsiest of pretexts. Because the authorities considered the Jerez event an act of sedition, a trial was arranged under the auspices of the military. By the beginning of February, the courts were ready to pass sentence on the accused. While most of them received harsh prison terms, four were condemned to death and executed on 10 February, a little more than a month after the Jerez revolt. Salvochea, who had been in jail in Cádiz during the entire episode, was convicted on the testimony presented by Félix Grávalo and sentenced to twelve years in prison for allegedly having been the mastermind behind the Jerez disturbance.

THE AFTERMATH OF THE RISING

Was the Jerez rising a carefully planned anarchist revolt aimed at overthrowing the local government? If it was, were the men convicted guilty of the crimes of which they were accused? What the government needed to justify the trials and executions, as well as their sweeping campaign to destroy the network of working-class federations affiliated with the anarchist movement in the region, was hard evidence of a planned revolt. But what evidence was there of such a conspiracy? For all the rumors that circulated in both the official and bourgeois press about the discovery of caches of dynamite, weapons, and other damning "proof" of such a conspiracy, no one ever produced any concrete evidence at the trials. The material basis for the government's case hinged on two highly dubious premises. One was the testimony of Félix Grávalo, the man whom the anarchists accused of being a police spy. The contention that Grávalo was a paid informant is partly borne out by the fact that it was his testimony which led to the arrest of dozens of anarchists. Once in prison, the anarchists managed to smuggle out letters to *El Productor* and other anarchist newspapers in which they spoke of the insidious role Grávalo played as a police spy. According to these letters, there could be no question that he was in collusion with the authorities. Their claim was partly substantiated by the fact that Grávalo alone escaped the cruel punishment everyone else was forced to endure. For example, all the other anarchist prisoners were crowded into tiny cells, where sanitary conditions were so appalling that some men collapsed and had to be immediately hospitalized. Many of the survivors were then subjected to brutal beatings with whips and wooden rods, which were administered in order to extract confessions.[19]

While being tortured, a handful of prisoners confessed to planning the Jerez rising, and it was these highly dubious testimonies that provided the authorities with the additional material proof needed for obtaining convictions during the hastily contrived military trials. Given that the authorities lacked the proper evidence they needed to prove their case, there can be no doubt that the anarchists convicted and sentenced were merely scapegoats.

Making extensive use of the bourgeois press (e.g., *El Imparcial*) as well as the official records of the trials, the historian Temma Kaplan has examined the circumstances surrounding the Jerez rising. While she accepts the validity of much of the documentation presented in the official version of the Jerez incident, her investigations ultimately revealed a welter of contradictory evidence. Kaplan concluded that there is no way of knowing for certain whether or not the Jerez rising was intended as an anarchist insurrection:

> The Jerez Insurrection that occurred on the night of January 8 may at least have been what the local authorities had feared, a revolution to seize the entire Jerez region and establish an anarchist community like that the Sanlucar workers tried to create in 1873. There were, in fact, simultaneous uprisings in Arcos, Lebrija, and Ubrique the night of the Jerez Insurrection, and rumors of aftershocks in Bornos, Benaocaz, Montejaque and Grazalema in successive weeks. On the other hand, the 1892 Jerez Insurrection may have been intended primarily to free the prisoners. It is also possible that, as in so many earlier uprisings, workers simply have been using violent political means to assert the right to associate.[20]

It is hardly surprising that the anarchists' account of the Jerez rebellion bore little resemblance to the official version. First of all, they did not accept the view that the rising at Jerez was actually a seditious act, that is, a premeditated insurrection. According to Ricardo Mella, who published a detailed study of the rising of 1893, as well as others writing in the two most important anarchist papers of the period, *La Anarquía* (Madrid) and *El Productor* (Barcelona), the incident was nothing more than a riot or large-scale social disturbance in which the poor and desperate people of Jerez were expressing their dissatisfaction with a manifestly unjust social and economic system. They argued that it was the government as

well as the bourgeois press which had blown the event all out of proportion so that they could freely go about the business of persecuting the
working classes. Second, the anarchists claimed that the evidence used to
obtain convictions in the trials was provided by workers in the pay of the
bourgeoisie and by police informants such as Félix Grávalo, Ángel Torre,
and a Frenchman named Fernando Poulet.[21] Mella maintained that the
rising itself had been provoked by these outsiders to the anarchist movement. To justify their interpretation, the anarchists pointed to a number
of factors that were either glossed over or never brought out in the official
accounts of the incident.

An interesting point made by Mella in his carefully researched *Los
sucesos de Jerez* (1893) was that not all of the men who had been
accused of murdering the two *jerezanos* were anarchists (still popularly
known as Internationalists). This had been purposefully overlooked by
the press and the courts, Mella suggested, because the government was
eager to promote the view that all criminal activity could be traced to
the anarchists. Indeed, that was precisely why La Mano Negra was
continually invoked by the authorities; for if the officials could convince
the public that this criminal body was still at work then they had carte
blanche to persecute any and all anarchists. It therefore stood to reason
that, by branding everyone involved in the Jerez episode as anarchists,
the government was trying to give credence to the theory that the rising
was connected to a massive anarchist conspiracy afoot in Spain.

Unlike the military prosecutors, the anarchists asked some probing
questions about the circumstances surrounding the affair. In *La Anarquía,* for example, a correspondent attempted to refute the claim that
the anarchists had provoked the revolt. To show that the rising had not
been planned, he pointed out that the workers themselves possessed
only the crudest of weapons when they launched their "attack" on the
town. The author further noted that the communication lines that connected Jerez to the outside world had not been tampered with: no
telegraph wires had been cut, nor had the railroad track been dam-
aged.[22] Given that it was well known that a garrison of soldiers was
located in the vicinity, this would have been a remarkable oversight by
anyone preparing for a full-scale rebellion.

Overall, the anarchists steadfastly held to the view that the events in
Jerez had not amounted to an anarchist-inspired insurrection. For them,
the violent protests of the destitute *braceros* could not be solely ascribed
to anarchist agitation, for they believed that the root cause of such
actions stemmed from the iniquitous social and economic system that

existed under capitalism and was especially harsh in southern Spain. For this reason, most anarchists unhesitatingly endorsed the interpretation put forward by the independent Madrid paper, *El Heraldo:*

> It is only misery without hope of relief that can give rise to such an abhorent deed. Because of this, it is in vain that the authorities look for culprits. They can shoot some of these aforementioned instigators, just as they hanged the seven men when there was the *Mano Negra,* but the true perpretrator of these crimes will not be eliminated, for this is hunger and desperation, and hunger is something you cannot kill with bullets but rather requires prudent measures and knowledge, that is to say, something that is contrary to the conduct of the present government.[23]

There are several additional observations about the Jerez episode which should be made before leaving the subject. First, it seems odd that the workers would have intentionally staged an insurrection so late at night and at that time of the year. After all, for at least two years May first had served as an effective rallying point for working-class demonstrations everywhere in Spain, and surely this would have provided a better occasion for mounting a revolt.

The fact that the Jerez rising took place when it did suggests strongly that the anarchists were right in saying that it had been spontaneous and that its true origins had more to do with perennial economic problems of the region than with political causes. This point is significant when one bears in mind that seasonal economic factors largely determined the ebb and flow of the working-class movement in Andalusia. Strikes and other forms of protest were generally most effective not in the middle of winter but during the summer or after a rich harvest. For these were the only times of the year when the withholding of labor directly threatened the profits of the landowners. Moreover, during the hard times of the winter months, the reservoir of unemployed *jornaleros* swelled dramatically. Thus, it is not hard to imagine that at that time of year the discontent and frustrations of a large number of idle workers could have been easily incited either by *agents provocateurs,* as the anarchists claimed, or simply by the workers' own pent-up anger over the way in which the authorities were treating their politically motivated comrades.

Finally, considering that the authorities were already in the process of repressing the labor movement in the south, the anarchists elsewhere stood to gain very little by playing down the anarchists' role in the Jerez rising. It is therefore significant that the anarchists held a nonrevolutionary interpretation of these events. Instead of seizing the opportunity to use the rebellion as an example of, say, propaganda by the deed—for this would have enabled them to broadcast their message throughout Spain and wherever else it had been reported in Europe and the Americas—the anarchists presented Jerez simply as another explosion of the working-class discontent that seemed to occur with cyclical regularity in the latifundist districts of the south.

The Jerez rising later inspired the writer Vicente Blasco Ibáñez to revive the memories of that epoch through a fictionalized account of the controversial event. We find in his *roman à clef, La bodega* (1904), a description of the revolt which is sympathetic to the anarchists.[24] In particular, the author accepts the view that the rising was not contrived by the anarchists—who supposedly cautioned the workers against taking such precipitate action—but rather was instigated by *agents provocateurs* like the inscrutable El Madrileño:

> And the overseer spoke to his son of the great mass meeting that the workingmen were going to hold on the following day upon the plains of Caulina. Nobody knew who had given the orders, but the call was being circulated from mouth to mouth through the countryside and the mountain district, and thousands upon thousands of men would get together. . . . "A genuine revolution, my son. And at the back of it all is a stranger, a young fellow they call the *Madrileño,* who speaks of slaying the rich and dividing up all the city's treasures. The people seem to have gone crazy; they all believe that to-morrow victory will be theirs and that poverty will be a thing of the past."[25]

While this embellished reconstruction cannot be taken as fact, it does suggest a millenarian interpretation of the Jerez event, which has been accepted by historians such as Juan Díaz del Moral, Gerald Brenan, and Eric Hobsbawm. Hobsbawm, for example, sees the rising as a classic example of millenarian behavior. In *Primitive Rebels,* he describes the Andalusian anarchists as modern-day secular mystics, who, like the millenarians of the Middle Ages, were guided by the irrational belief that it was possible to will profound social change. Accordingly, Hobsbawm maintains that Jerez and similar risings were partly revolutionary in that "overwhelming change was their sole objective"; but they were also millenarian inasmuch as the insurrectionists "were not themselves makers of the revolution."[26] Hobsbawm's explanation of the Jerez incident can be summarized as follows: it was the result of the anarchists' commitment to a primitive understanding of the nature of revolution. Unable to grasp the complexities of the economic and political structures that dominated their lives, the farm workers were attracted to a simplistic theory, one that told them that by spontaneously rising up en masse it was possible to overthrow the forces of repression and usher in the new millenium.

From what has already been said, however, the Jerez incident cannot be explained in terms of this model. What the millenarian view fails to do in this instance is to credit the workers with the ability to define their own political goals. This is not to deny that there were millenarian aspects of the rising, for the mob action of the workers on the night of 8 January indicates a degree of irrationalism that is consistent with millenarian behavior. But, as we have seen, the agitators seem to have had a clear motive in mind when they rose: they sought to release their comrades from the local jail and thereby demonstrate their defiance of the government's incessant persecution of the International movement. However clumsily and crudely they expressed their grievance, the workers were patently aiming to achieve this objective and not to overthrow the local government in order to inaugurate the birth of a libertarian society.

Whatever the true origins of the Jerez rising may have been, there is no doubt that it provided the authorities with a convincing excuse for suppressing the labor movement that was, thanks to the successful celebrations of May first, beginning to gain momentum in the region. It is likely that the government's swift and harsh response to the Jerez revolt was connected to this fact. For a brief time, May Day had given a fresh impulse to the revolutionary movement in the Cádiz region and, indeed, throughout Spain. But as the government repression following the Jerez rebellion clearly demonstrated, the authorities were not going to tolerate for long the growing threat of working-class resistance.

FROM JEREZ TO BARCELONA: THE *ATTENTATS* OF PAULINO PALLÁS AND SALVADOR SANTIAGO

Like the Haymarket Tragedy of 1886–1887, the Jerez episode generated a wave of reaction within the anarchist community. Frustrated and angry at what had happened to their comrades, many began calling for violent reprisals as a way of avenging the victims of repression. Their call was soon answered. Not quite a year after the four anarchists were garroted in the town square of Jerez, Paulino Pallás, an anarchist immigrant from South America, sought retribution in the form of a bombing outrage.

Paulino Pallás was thirty years old when he attempted to slay the capitan general of Catalonia, Arsenio Martínez de Campos. Born in Cambris (Tarragona), Pallás had led an itinerant existence for most of his troubled life. While still a youth, his family moved to Argentina. During his apprenticeship as a typesetter in Santa Fe, Pallás developed an interest in radical politics, eventually becoming an anarchist communist. In 1891 Pallás, who was by then married and supporting a small family, moved to Brazil. It is not clear whether this was done for professional reasons or because he wanted to pursue his revolutionary ambitions. Whatever the case, within a year he was involved in a bombing incident. During the May Day activities of 1892 held in Rio de Janeiro, Pallás hurled a petard into the Alcantara theater, crying "¡Viva la anarquía!" Apparently the small bomb was meant to register protest rather than to cause serious damage, for, according to one source, Pallás's act was greeted with cheers and applause by the crowds taking part in the May Day demonstrations.

In October of that year, Pallás, along with his wife and three young sons, emigrated to Spain. Although he arrived after the Jerez incident, Pallás seems to have been deeply moved by the repression that followed in its wake, and he was especially disturbed by the summary executions of the anarchists. Once he resolved to seek revenge for the "judicial murders" of his comrades, all that remained for Pallás was to find the appropriate moment to strike out. He finally decided to use the military parade held in Barcelona on 24 September 1893 as the occasion for a bombing. On the day of the ceremony, Pallás situated himself close to the street where the head of the procession of military figures and prominent local officials would be traveling on their journey through the city. As the leading military guard passed by him, Pallás flung his handmade bomb in the direction of the capitan general, Martínez de Campos. But his timing was off. The device exploded under Campo's horse, killing it instantly but only wounding the general himself. The explosion was so powerful that it killed at least two others, as well as seriously injuring twelve soldiers and spectators. Unable to escape, Pallás was immediately seized and thrown into jail. Like the Jerez anarchists, Pallás was swiftly convicted by a military court and sentenced to death. He was executed on 6 October 1893 outside the Montjuich fortress. Defiant to the end, his last words were that his own death would be avenged. His dying prediction proved to be accurate.[27]

The execution of Pallás was widely reported and commented on in the anarchist press. As regards the bombing itself, the anarchists held differing opinions. Those who refused to condone his action still portrayed Pallás himself as a martyr to the revolutionary cause. Others, like the Spanish émigré paper *El Despertar* (New York), explained that Pallás's act of revenge was an example of propaganda by the deed, a tactic that, despite its shortcomings, should not be condemned. The Spanish anarchist communist paper *La Controversia* (Valencia) went even further by applauding his violent deed:

> It is certain that in commiting the *attentat,* our comrade Pallás had as his objective more than just the killing of some general or the other—behind whom there are plenty of others who would like to take his place. By throwing the bomb, Pallás was attacking all that society and its institutions stand for; his act was an immense protest against all the social crimes, infamies, and stupidities.[28]

It was the latter image that had the profoundest and most immediate impact on the anarchist community as whole. Such was the case with Santiago Salvador French, a young anarchist who had been converted to anarchism largely through his brief personal association with Pallás. "The death of Pallás produced in me a terrible feeling," Salvador was reputed to have said,

> and in order to avenge his death, as a tribute to his memory, I conceived of a plan in which it was possible to terrorize those who had enjoyed killing him and who believed that they had nothing to fear. . . . I did not ponder over it nor did I vacillate about it; . . . I only meditated about the form of the deed; it had to be something that would make a great deal of noise.[29]

Not quite a month after the execution of Pallás, Salvador was present at the opening performance of the opera *Guillermo Tell* at the Liceo Opera theater in Barcelona. Attended almost exclusively by the rich and well-to-do citizens of Barcelona, the opera was, understandably, an ideal target for the act of revenge Salvador had in mind. For here were assembled the most distinguished members of Barcelona high society, the haute bourgeoisie whom Salvador not only had accused of mocking him and his fellow workers but also blamed for taking the life of his friend, Pallás. Salvador waited for the first act to end before he stood up and threw two bombs from the fifth floor of the opera house. Upon landing, one bomb exploded with trememdous force, rocking the entire building. It instantly killed fifteen patrons and seriously injured some fifty others. According to one report, the other bomb failed to detonate because its fall was broken when it landed on top of a woman. The interior of the Liceo lay in shambles, and for Salvador that night Pallás's death had not been in vain.

The next day the entire city was in a state of panic over the bombing. Dozens of known anarchists or suspected radicals were detained by the authorities. The queen-regent, Christina, issued a decree declaring a state of emergency and suspending the constitutional guarantees of the city. In this atmosphere of fear and repression, rumors about the bombing spread fast and furiously. At first the press speculated about a vast conspiracy, naming a José Codina as the culprit and ringleader. The police were confident that the case was closed when, two months after the bombing, they arrested Santiago Salvador. Salvador confessed to the crime, insisting, however, that he had acted alone. The attitude of the police toward terrorism was such that while they were willing to believe that Salvador had thrown the Liceo bomb, they refused to believe that he had no accomplices. Several of the prisoners already in custody, including a Cerezuelo who was arrested after Codina had been named as the chief culprit in the bombing, were tortured and forced to sign confessions implicating themselves in the plot.[30] Shortly afterward, six prisoners were condemned to death and then executed, and four others were sentenced to life in prison.

Meanwhile Salvador himself was far from languishing in jail. He was receiving a great deal of publicity for having supposedly renounced his anarchist beliefs in favor of Christianity. The Barcelona press as well as the Church eagerly publicized Salvador's dramatic conversion, reporting, among other things, that his cell had been virtually transformed into a religious shrine, with books of devotion lining his bookshelves and sacred images adorning the walls of his tiny cubicle. Upon hearing of his planned execution, Salvador gave up this elaborate charade, telling the newspaper reporters that his conversion had been nothing more than his way of playing one last joke on the bourgeoisie. This may have been true, but it may also have been the case that Salvador feigned his conversion in order to escape the infamous torture chambers of Montjuich prison. In the event, Salvador went to his execution without showing any remorse for his deed. He was garroted in the courtyard of the fortress on 21 November 1894.

Neither Pallás nor Salvador seemed to be aware of the appalling toll their outrages took on the lives of people and on society generally. Most of their victims were not guilty of anything more than belonging to a supposedly hostile class. Ironically, in some cases, workers themselves were the ones killed or injured. The fact that very few of the victims had been prison executioners or military judges, or had in any other capacity been directly involved in persecuting the anarchist movement, did not seem to concern the anarchist terrorists. For they believed that "civilian" casualties were both justifiable and inevitable in a class war. Yet, even though the terrorists accepted the legitimacy of their abominable tactics, they never stopped to consider how effective such violent actions were in furthering the revolutionary cause. The repression that invariably followed terrorist acts also claimed many victims among the anarchists, including those who adamantly rejected terrorist methods. Not only were many anarchists and their sympathizers imprisoned or deported—fates that significantly diminished their ranks—but libertarian newspapers, cafés, and other associations were targets of government harassment. Hence, whatever symbolic importance bombings may have had for some anarchists, the reality of terrorism was that it always had a devasting impact on the anarchist movement. As we shall now see, in no case was this more apparent than in the Montjuich affair of 1896–1897.

CHAPTER XI

The Aftermath of Repression, 1894–1898

As a result of the upsurge of anarchist violence that began with the Jerez rising, the authorities stiffened their resolve to crush the anarchist movement once and for all. They slashed at the very roots of the movement by arbitrarily harassing all anarchists, even those legitimately affiliated with working-class associations, newspaper publishing, and similar enterprises. Although this wave of repression was widespread, it was applied unevenly. The anarchists outside major cities, for instance, were not as hard-pressed as their comrades in Barcelona, where a virtual state of siege existed. There, the authorities were attempting to extinguish all traces of anarchist social life, whether terrorist or not. Accordingly, in 1893 the presses of two important anarchist publications that did not promote terrorism, *La Tramontana* and *El Productor,* were forcibly shut down. The disappearance of the latter publication was a terrible blow to the anarchists throughout Spain, for it had served for several years as an unofficial mouthpiece of the libertarian movement.

Another significant consequence of the government's sweeping campaign was that it precipitated the exodus of the anarchists themselves. Although small at first, this migration began to swell—perhaps climbing into the hundreds—as the repression intensified. Some of those fleeing were the ablest of anarchist leaders—Pedro Esteve, for instance—who eventually found refuge in countries like Argentina, Mexico, and the United States, settings that seemed to afford them better opportunities for continuing their revolutionary activities.

Even in this climate of persecution, though, the anarchists showed a remarkable resilience and even defiance. Between 1894 and 1899, the printer and former director of *La Anarquía,* Ernesto Álvarez, managed to publish the theoretical journal *La Idea Libre.* With the suspension of such key publications as *El Productor* in 1893, *La Idea Libre* became the principal forum for anarchist thinkers. Some of the notable figures contributing to it were José Prat, José Lopez Montenegro, Soledad Gustavo (a.k.a. Teresa Mañé), Ricardo Mella, Fermín Salvochea, and José Martínez Ruiz, the future "Azorín."

The next year *La Ciencia Social,* another pro-anarchist weekly, was launched by Anselmo Lorenzo in Barcelona. This journal, which professed its adherence to a sociological tradition that included such diverse thinkers as Proudhon, Darwin, Marx, and Bakunin, published the articles of a varied group of talented writers and noted theorists from Spain and abroad. Among the contributors were the Frenchmen Auguste Hamon and Fernand Pelloutier and the Spaniards Pedro Dorado and Miguel de Unamuno.

What is particularly noteworthy about these two journals is that, in spite of the prevailing hostile environment in which they found themselves, their anarchist publishers succeeded in upholding an exceptionally high standard of writing and editing.

Backed by special legislation passed in July 1894 giving them extraordinary powers to prosecute terrorists, the authorities had some success in curbing the bomb-throwing elements in the anarchist movement. In fact, a brief respite from terrorism at this time gave libertarian intellectuals an opportunity to combat the negative image that all anarchists were now saddled with. Two publications that appeared between 1894 and 1896 were significant contributions to this campaign. One was a collection of articles by Antonio Pellicer entitled *En defensa de nuestros ideales* (1894). Originally published serially in *El Productor* several years earlier—Pellicer had emigrated to South America in 1891—these essays attempted to prove the practicability of anarchism as a social doctrine. Far more important was the publication of Ricardo Mella's *Lombroso y los anarquistas* (1896), a short polemical treatise that convincingly demonstrated that, contrary to the spurious scientific claims of criminologists like Lombroso, anarchists were not born criminals.

While there is no way of knowing for certain, these writings probably did little to alter the thinking of an already deeply prejudiced public. And, even if Mella and other like-minded writers were making some headway in salvaging the reputation of anarchism, their efforts were completely overshadowed in the summer of 1896 by another sensational bombing incident in Barcelona. The bombing and the series of events it set in motion marked a turning point in anarchist development. The Montjuich affair, as these events came to be known, effectively brought to a close the nineteenth-century movement and, in so doing, signaled the beginning of another phase of anarchist history.

THE MONTJUICH AFFAIR OF 1896–1897

On 7 June 1896, during one of Barcelona's most important religious celebrations, the festival of Corpus Christi, a bomb thrown at the tail end of the procession exploded, killing at least six people and seriously injuring about forty-five other bystanders.[1] Before long the incident sparked off a public scandal of enormous proportions. The main source of this controversy, though, was not the bombing itself—although this was generally deplored everywhere—but rather the ferocity of government repression that followed in its wake. The Montjuich affair provoked a public uproar and general feeling of indignation at the Spanish government's savage treatment of those held accountable for the crime. So hideous were the brutalities that the expression "the revival of the Spanish Inquisition" became a popular phrase. From all the available evidence produced at the time, such an indictment was not misplaced. Not only did survivors of the horrifying tortures provide living testimony of the charges being leveled against the authorities, but many of those unjustly imprisoned as a result of the bombing and who later found asylum abroad attested to the abominable treatment of prisoners.

Most of the details of the bomb throwing itself are well known. As the cortege of ecclesiastical, military, and civil representatives was passing through the Cambios Nuevos throughfare—one of the widest streets in Barcelona—suddenly and without any warning whatever a bomb was tossed into the roadway.

A curious fact about the incident was that none of the dignitaries leading the procession, among whom were General Despuyols and the bishop of Barcelona, was injured, for the bomb was thrown after this group had passed. That the majority of victims were common people gave rise to the speculation that the bomb thrower must have been either an amateur anarchist or an *agent provocateur* planted by the police.[2] At the time, the anarchists themselves were divided over the question of who was responsible for the bombing. Some thought the crime bore all the hallmarks of police work, while others, particularly Ricardo Mella and José Prat, thought the culprit might have been a misguided anarchist.[3] Several years after the incident, the revolutionary journalist Luis Bonafoux advanced a hypothesis that gave further credence to the theory that the bomb thrower was an anarchist. From information he obtained from the Italian anarchist Mataini, Bonafoux, who was himself particularly well-informed about the Spanish anarchist movement of this period, named a French anarchist called Jean Girault as the perpetrator of the *attentat*. According to Mataini, Girault had confessed his guilt during the brief time he was hiding out in Mataini's home. After successfully eluding the police, Girault fled to Argentina, never to return to Spain.[4]

The officially endorsed theory as to who was responsible for what happened on 7 June was circulated in all the major Spanish newspapers during the Montjuich trials. This can be summarized as follows. The ringleaders of the bombing plot were the anarchists Tomás Ascheri, José Molas, and Antonio Nogues, all of whom had been arrested immediately following the explosion on the 7th. Apparently the Cambios Nuevos assault came about as a result of a previous failed bombing attempt. The group had initially planned to detonate several bombs on May first as a way of propelling a much-anticipated strike movement. As no strikes materialized on May Day, the anarchists aborted their plan. At this point they decided to use the Corpus Christi celebrations in June as the occasion for their bombing campaign. On the fourth, Nogues and Molas were supposed to set off several bombs just when the religious procession was scheduled to leave the Barcelona cathedral. At the last moment, though, they balked, leaving their bombs (still unexploded) at a nearby garbage dump. (The next day these were supposedly found by a dustman.) Meanwhile, Ascheri had assumed command of the band of conspirators. After chiding his friends for lacking the courage to follow through with their project, Ascheri resolved to finish the task himself. On the morning of the seventh, he intended to contact a Francisco Callis, yet another anarchist in on the plot. But when Callis failed to show up, Ascheri made his way alone to the spot where the bomb had been placed the night before. It was hidden on the Calle Arenas, located at one corner of the Cambios Nuevos. From this position, Ascheri waited for the opportunity to throw the bomb, which finally came toward the end of the parade.[5]

No doubt such a clearly presented and precise account of the events leading up to the bombing lent credibility to the government's case against the anarchists. What was not mentioned in this version, however, was that the details had been obtained by means of torture, and that there was no corroborating evidence presented at the trials which could substantiate the conspiracy theory. In view of this, it is not surprising that all of the above named anarchists were indicted for and then convicted of the crime.

THE REPRESSION AND TRIALS

The *attentat* itself unleashed a wave of reprisals which quickly spread throughout the city and its environs. The general public and authorities alike instinctively blamed the anarchists, although their wrath was so intense that even groups remotely associated with the anarchism fell victim to the police dragnet. Within days, hundreds of anarchists, free-thinkers, republicans, and anyone else suspected of being sympathetic to the anarchist cause were rounded up by the authorities and thrown into all the available jails in Barcelona. Altogether approximately 300 anarchists were arrested, most of whom were eventually deported to Africa without trial, while eighty-seven were tried. Hardest hit were workers' clubs and presses—such as *Ciencia Social*—which were summarily closed and, in some cases, ransacked.

This campaign of persecution was greatly facilitated by antiterrorist legislation promulgated by the the Cortes in September 1896. Among other things, the act gave the military sweeping powers in cases involving explosives. A particularly controversial aspect of the new law was that it retroactively applied to the Corpus Christi bombing. Led by General Despuyols, the commander of the Seventh Army Corps who was presumably one of the principal targets of the bombing, this campaign of repression was perhaps the harshest one waged against the anarchist movement during the nineteenth century. The formidable and somewhat forbidding Montjuich fortress, which towers over the Mediterranean and the harbor in Barcelona, became the focus of the government's efforts to extirpate the anarchist elements of the region. Although at one time used for military purposes, during the late nineteenth century Montjuich served as a prison, especially for political dissidents. Over the years, the prison had become notorious as a center for unspeakable acts of punishment administered to its inhabitants, many of whom were anarchists. This ominous image was especially reinforced during the trials of Pallás and Santiago Salvador, when rumors freely circulated that all the confessions made by the anarchists imprisoned there had been extorted through torture.[6]

Beginning on 11 December 1896, a military tribunal began trying eighty-seven of the prisoners—including Ascheri, Molas, and Nogues. As the mass court-martial itself progressed, it became increasingly apparent that none of the prisoners was receiving due process of the law, and that in a number of cases, the defendants had been tortured in order to extort confessions from them. Since the court proceedings were conducted behind closed doors, news of what was occurring at the trials was derived partly from the letters of prisoners who succeeded in transmitting their eyewitness accounts to friends on the outside and partly from the numerous foreign correspondents who had gathered in Barcelona to cover the controversial event. The prisoners' letters were published in newspapers of all political inclinations: international anarchist papers such as *Liberty* (Boston), *El Esclavo* (Tampa), *Freedom* (London), *Le Père Peinard* (Paris), as well as the liberal and conservative press, including the *Times* (London), *Frankfurter Zeitung* (Frankfurt), *El País* (Madrid), *El Imparcial* (Madrid), and *La Publicidad* (Barcelona).

One of the unforeseen consequences of the wholesale arrests made by the police was that the jails contained a signficant number of lawyers, writers, and other professionals who could ably record both their own and the collective experiences of the prisoners. This obviously gave the prisoners a potentially powerful weapon: a means of communicating their plight to the outside world. The fact is that most of the letters and articles issuing from Montjuich were written by some of the outstanding anarchist intellectuals of the day: Pedro Corominas, Teresa Claramunt, Anselmo Lorenzo, Tarrida del Mármol, and Federico Urales. In his autobiography, Urales refers to the camaraderie that existed among the many prisoners packed into the tiny cubicles of each cell block. Each block appears to have been well organized by the prisoners, and this made it possible for them to choose representatives to act as spokesmen for the others. Their chief task was to write letters describing prison conditions and, above all, prisoner abuse. To this end, they were well served by a network of sympathetic "informants" who fed the appointed reporters with plenty of details of the rituals of torture being conducted in the lower chambers of the fortress.

While in the prison, the accused were, unlike other, nonpolitical prisoners, deprived of any civil liberties. "Having been incarcerated for the last seven months," recorded one victim of the repression, ". . . we are without newspapers, tables, chairs, benches, or beds; our correspondence passes through the hands of a most exacting censor; and during the whole period we have not been able to see or speak to our children, parents, wives, friends, or relatives."[7]

Another notable example of the atrocious way in which the prisoners were treated is found in the testimony of a Frenchman named Joseph Thioulouse. In a letter smuggled out of Montjuich and published in the London anarchist paper *Freedom* (February 1897), Thioulouse claimed that the judge refused to provide him with an interpreter even though the accused neither spoke nor understood either Castilian or Catalan. Later, when he had returned to his cell, Thioulouse described what he was forced to endure:

> I am ordered to undress, or rather I am undressed . . . all these [clothes] were placed in one corner and myself in another, my hands tied by the wrists and the arms taken backward by a strong cord to the height of the biceps, afterward bound tightly round so that the cord penetrates the flesh. The civil guard, with a stout whip in his hand, says to me "You do not want to speak Spanish? I will make you speak before you leave this place!" And, by heaven! he showers a quantity of lashes upon me, on the calves, on the knuckles—everywhere.

Other letters recounted far more terrifying experiences than this one: while waiting for the trial to begin, Antonio Nogues spent eight days without sleeping and eating, had his fingernails and toenails torn out, was beaten repeatedly with a rod, and had his genitals tied with guitar string. Perhaps even less fortunate was Luis Mas, who was actually driven insane by his tormentors. Corroborating evidence of such draconian treatment came from one of the jailers at Montjuich, whose stricken conscience apparently impelled him to write to the Paris paper *L'Intransigeant* the following account of how confessions were extracted from the prisoners:

> [T]hey were flogged, their nails torn off, their genital parts compressed until the agony of suffering led these three [Tomas Ascheri, Antonio Nogues, and Luis Mas] to sign whatever the inquiring judge wanted them to say.[8]

Some of those who were lucky enough to be liberated fled abroad, where they appeared at public demonstrations—such as the huge meeting held in Trafalgar Square in the summer of 1897. Some of the bolder ones even publicly displayed the scars left by the bestial and cruel punishments that had been inflicted upon them.

Fernando Tarrida del Mármol was one of the more celebrated victims of the Montjuich repression. His book *Les Inquisiteurs d'Espagne* (Paris, 1897) documented the enormity of the Spanish government's policies not only in Montjuich but in Cuba and in the Philippines as well. Tarrida himself narrowly escaped prosecution and the whip of the torturers. Despite the fact that he held a respectable job teaching mathematics at the Barcelona Polytechnic and despite the fact that he was a well-known opponent of terrorism, Tarrida was arrested shortly after the Corpus Christi day bombing. Apparently the police believed an unidentified witness, who falsely accused the professor of having written to him instigating bomb outrages. In any case, Tarrida was herded along with scores of republicans, anarchists, and anarchist sympathizers into the Montjuich dungeons. Chained to his close friend and fellow anarchist Anselmo Lorenzo, Tarrida had the good fortune to be recognized by a warder who had studied mathematics under him at the Polytechnic. Feigning illness, the young lieutenant went into the city in order to telegraph friends and relatives of Tarrida, and tell them of his plight. Thanks to the intervention of several notable Spaniards, including the writer Santiago Rusiñol and the marquis of Mont Roig, a Conservative senator who also happened to be Tarrida's cousin, Tarrida was soon released from prison and then banished from Spain. Taking refuge in France, he immediately set about organizing a campaign to expose the infamies he had witnessed at Montjuich. The fruit of his efforts was *Les Inquisiteurs d'Espagne*. This book, along with Tarrida's articles that appeared in such journals as *La Revue Blanche, L'Intransigeant,* and the London *Daily Chronicle,* challenged the Spanish government to refute his indictments before an impartial international tribunal. These writings roused such a storm of protest throughout Europe and America that the Spanish government was obliged to relent in its witch-hunt of anarchists.

Meanwhile, a protest movement inside Spain was gaining momentum. Centered in Madrid, this campaign was largely conducted through the press. Papers such as *El País* and *La Justicia* printed emotionally charged letters and articles condemning the excesses of the authorities.[9] In the end, the impact of the clamoring voices of domestic and international protestors tempered the government's indubitable intention to use the trial as a vehicle for harassing the anarchist movement. The chief government prosecutor, who had demanded the death penalty for twenty-eight of those on trial, had to settle for just eight—although only five of them were ever executed. Of the remaining eighty-seven prosecuted only twelve were absolved, while the rest received long prison sentences, ranging from eight to twenty years of hard labor.

Notwithstanding the numerous confessions the courts obtained during the legal proceedings, no conclusive evidence was ever produced which could clearly identify the assailant, and just who the bomb thrower (or throwers) was remains a mystery.[10] Given the atmosphere of public hysteria in which the trials were conducted, and given the court's flagrant disregard of the rights of the accused, it is almost certain that the five anarchists executed for the bombing conspiracy and the hundreds of others victimized by it were innocent.

THE ASSASSINATION OF CÁNOVAS DEL CASTILLO

Following the massive publicity campaign reporting the Montjuich trials and persecutions, no reasonable observer at the time could help but conclude that the Spanish government had "shut its eyes to reason" and that the Montjuich trials had been a monumental miscarriage of justice. The mood among the anarchists and their supporters was one of despair mingled with anger and frustration. A strongly felt yearning for vengeance also overcame many, especially the devotees of propaganda by the deed. One such anarchist, an Italian named Michele Angiolillo, who had been living in Barcelona since 1895, decided to do something to avenge the victims of Montjuich. On 8 August 1897 he walked up to the Spanish prime minister, Antonio Cánovas del Castillo, and shot him dead.

In view of all the publicity surrounding the Montjuich affair, the assassination of Cánovas hardly shocked anyone. For though his death came suddenly and unexpectedly, there was also a certain feeling of inevitability about what had come to pass. As news began coming in about the murder, it was learned that the assassin was not a Spaniard but rather was an Italian anarchist. Michele Angiolillo was born in Foggia, Italy, in 1871. As a youth he attended a technical institute and then served in the military, where it appears he first became attracted to anarchism. He next worked as a printer until forced to flee Italy in 1895 for having published an antigovernment manifesto. He lived for a while in Marseilles, and moved to Barcelona about a year before the Corpus Christi day bombing. It is curious that Angiolillo seems to have left Spain just days before the incident. From then until the assassination of Cánovas, he wandered about Europe, living briefly in France, Belgium, and England.

Throughout his travels, Angiolillo never lost interest in the Montjuich affair. In fact, after reading Tarrida's *Les Inquisiteurs*, Angiolillo began brooding more and more about the fate of the Montjuich prisoners. The highly emotionally charged campaign waged in England,

France, and elsewhere against the excesses of Montjuich only reinforced his hatred for all forms of government and strengthened his resolve to seek retribution for his libertarian comrades.

Sometime in April 1897, he moved to Belgium, where he remained until after the executions of the five condemned anarchists on May fourth. It was most likely early July when he arrived in Madrid.[11] What we know of his movements from then until the assassination can be partially reconstructed from the recollections of José Nakens, a pro-anarchist writer who was editor of the popular anticlerical and republican Madrid weekly *El Motín*.[12] Nakens recalls meeting Angiolillo two times in the latter part of July, although it is not entirely clear why he wanted to meet with Nakens. In assuming the name Emilio Rinaldini and posing as a bookseller and part-time correspondent for the Italian paper *Il Popolo*, Angiolillo's ostensible aim was to interview the author as well as to discuss with him the Montjuich trials and executions. During one of their meetings, Nakens was struck by how eloquently the Italian visitor spoke of anarchist principles and ideals. Yet Angiolillo, Nakens goes on to say, grew visibly aroused whenever mention was made of Tarrida's book and whenever he attempted to defend the anarchists' need for using propaganda by the deed against the oppressors in society. Unable to convince Nakens of the justice of such tactics, Angiolillo decided to cut short the interview. Nevertheless, the two departed on friendly terms. He left Madrid a few days later.

Angiolillo resurfaced in Barcelona at the beginning of August. There he prepared for his journey to Santa Agueda, a small town in the Basque region known for its mineral baths where it was rumored that Señor Cánovas was staying. He reached his destination on Sunday, 8 August. Still posing as a journalist, Angiolillo managed to gain access to the hotel where Cánovas was vacationing with his wife. With complete sangfroid and without any hesitation, he walked up to the prime minister and shot him three times with a revolver. Cánovas was killed instantly. According to one newspaper account, Madame Cánovas, although stunned by the lightning speed of the shooting, went up to Angiolillo as if to challenge him. Calling him "murderer" and "assassin," she struck him in face with her fan. Angiolillo replied by bowing politely and saying: "I am not an assassin. I have avenged my Anarchist brethren, and have nothing to say to you, madam."[13]

Cánovas was buried in Madrid a few days later, and Angiollio was tried and executed less than two weeks after he had committed the crime. Grief over the nation's tragedy, though, was short-lived. By now, thanks largely to the publicity surrounding the Montjuich affair, public opinion had turned against the government. Not long after Angiollio's execution, for example, a young writer and anarchist sympathizer named Ramón Sempau attempted to assassinate Lieutenant Portas, one of the commanding officers who presided over the tortures at Montjuich, and whose infamous reputation for cruelty had prompted some to brand him the "Spanish Trepov." Portas was so unpopular that Sempau's defiant deed was generally regarded as a heroic act; and consequently no court would convict him of the crime.[14]

MONTJUICH AND AFTER

As far as the anarchist movement was concerned, the Montjuich repression had a number of significant and lasting repercussions. The most apparent one was that it abruptly halted terrorism in Barcelona as well as in Spain generally. Terrorism was, of course, not dead, for it was an aspect of the movement which was to persist well into the twentieth century. But, significantly, the Montjuich affair forced the bomb-throwing elements to suspend their activities at least until after the turn of the century.[15]

The persecutions also profoundly affected the anarchists' organizational activities. The Pacto de Unión y Solidaridad, for example, was permanently dissolved, which event effectively severed the anarchists' ties with the unions. An equally powerful blow to the movement came with the widespread disruption of anarchist associational life. This badly fragmented a movement that was already suffering from the deleterious effects of its commitment to an extreme form of decentralization. Apart from the closing of *centros obreros* and other working-class institutions, much of the anarchist press was forced to shut down permanently. And those papers that were spared, such as *La Idea Libre* (Madrid), at best faced a precarious existence. Although the workers eventually returned to their clubs, it took several years before the anarchist press recovered from the crippling blow the authorities had dealt it.

Another serious repercussion of the affair was that it drove underground or into exile a number of anarchist leaders. Among the notable anarchists obliged to retire or temporarily retreat from the Spanish movement were Teresa Claramunt, Anselmo Lorenzo, Federico Urales, Soledad Gustavo, and José Prat.

It is worth mentioning that while in exile these figures continued their political activism. Tarrida, for instance, devoted much of his time to writing and speaking in behalf of the Spanish working classes. Having been expelled from France for his vitriolic attack on the Spanish government, Tarrida lived briefly in Belgium before moving to London, where he resided until his untimely death in March 1915. There he divided his time working as an engineer and as a free-lance correspondent for several European journals and two Spanish papers, the republican *El Progreso* (Barcelona) and *El Heraldo de Madrid*. Through his close association with the anarchist émigré community then active in London, Tarrida frequently presented lectures in the East End among the Jewish anarchists or at the libertarian clubs—such as the Charlotte Street Anarchist Club, which was a popular gathering spot for foreign anarchists. Though he never repudiated his libertarian beliefs, Tarrida, like so many of his fellow political exiles living in England, gradually drifted away from anarchism and toward the "gas and water" or nonrevolutionary socialism common to the English tradition. In fact, just prior to his death, he joined the Fabian Party. Tarrida's detailed and personal knowledge of the Spanish workers made him a resource of inestimable value for English writers and politicians interested in Spanish affairs. His influence in this regard can be readily seen in at least two important books about Spain written at the turn of century: William Archer's biography of the famous libertarian pedagogue Francisco Ferrer y Guardia (1911) and G. H. B. Ward's *The Truth About Spain* (1911).

Other anarchist émigrés continued agitating for the Spanish anarchist cause in foreign lands. José Prat was particularly active following the Corpus Christi day bombing. At the height of the persecutions he had sought refuge in La Coruña at the home of his good friend Ricardo Mella. In the short time he was in hiding, he collaborated with Mella in writing an exposé of the Montjuich incident, *La barbarie gubermental en España* (1897). Gathering together all the available Spanish (and some foreign) newspaper accounts of the Corpus Christi day bombing and subsequent trials, Mella and Prat (who are identified only by their initials, R.M. and P., on the title page) wrote a devastating critique of the Spanish government. From Mella's home, Prat made his way to England so that he could represent the Spanish anarchists at the International Workers' Congress held July–August 1896 in London. Later that year he moved to Buenos Aires, where he joined the large and ever-expanding community of Italian and Spanish anarchist immigrants. During his brief sojourn there he worked alongside Antonio Pellicer on the anarchist paper *La Protesta Humana*.[16] It is interesting to note that as a contributor to the latter, Prat (who used the pen name "Urania") wrote articles in which he roundly condemned isolated acts of terrorism. He returned to Spain sometime in 1898, and once again played a leading role in anarchist affairs.

Perhaps the largest and most significant exile community was centered in Paris. For a number of years Spanish exiles of all political stripes had congregated in the French capital. A pivotal figure for the Spanish anarchists residing there was Luis Bonafoux. Born in France and raised in Puerto Rico, Bonafoux was a keen student of Spanish affairs. He not only directed and edited *La Campaña* and *Heraldo de Paris*—two important Spanish libertarian papers in which articles by Mella and Tarrida del Mármol appeared—but also maintained an extensive network of political contacts both inside and outside of Spain. At different times in the period 1898–1904 there were grouped around Bonafoux such anarchist luminaries as Tarrida del Mármol, Federico Urales, and Anselmo Lorenzo.[17]

During the hardest times of repression, the propagandizing efforts of these exiles contributed greatly to keeping alive the movement in Spain. All the international libertarian papers with which the Spanish exiles were associated—Bonafoux's *La Campaña,* for example—printed news about conditions in Spain, and those issues smuggled into the country were used as substitutes for the temporarily paralyzed indigenous anarchist press.

As there are virtually no statistical data available on the size of the anarchist community in these years, it is extremely difficult to measure numerically the impact that the Montjuich affair had on the libertarian movement. Perhaps the only reliable estimate we have is to be found in an article by Ricardo Mella, "Le socialisme en Espagne," which was published in the French journal *L'Humanité Nouvelle* (Paris) in 1897. There are several reasons why his figures can be relied on. Over the years, Mella had justly earned a reputation as a fair-minded and intellectually honest writer. His publications *Los sucesos de Jerez* (1893) and *La barbarie gubermental* were—albeit colored by a pro-anarchist slant— models of investigative reporting in that both attempted to present all the available facts of the Jerez and Montjuich affairs, respectively. In the 1897 article, which was probably written about a year after the Cambios Nuevos bombing incident, Mella provides a concise history of Spanish socialism. According to his calculations, which are presumably based on the minutes of the International Workers' Congress (London, 1896), as well as on information he obtained from the anarchist and socialist press,

Mella broke down the national membership of the libertarian movement as follows:

Regions and Provinces	Active Members	Sympathizers and Passive Members
(1) Catalonia (Barcelona, Tarragona, and Gerona)	6,100	15,000
(2) Valencia (Valencia and Alicante)	4,000	10,000
(3) Andalusia (Cádiz, Seville, Málaga, Grenada, Córdoba, and Huelva)	12,400	23,100
(4) New and Old Castille (Madrid, Valladolid, and Toledo)	1,500	2,000
(4) Basque Provinces (Bilbao)	500	500
(5) Aragón (Zaragoza)	500	1,000
(6) Galicia (La Coruña and Pontevedra)	500	1,100
(7) Estremadura (Badajoz)	200	400
(8) Murcia (Cartagena)	100	300
TOTAL	25,800	53,400

Considering the tense political atmosphere at the time, and considering that the anarchists were still being persecuted throughout Spain, these figures suggest a much more robust movement than one would have expected. Mella's article, in fact, does sound a note of optimism about the future prospects of Spanish anarchism, predicting that it would soon reassert itself as a powerful moral and social force.[18]

THE DISASTER OF 1898 AND THE REBIRTH OF ANARCHISM

Indeed, only two years after the Corpus Christi day bombing, the anarchists as a whole began slowly to recover their footing. This was partly due to the fact that some of the exiled anarchists began quietly returning to Spain. At first, the reemerging anarchist movement largely existed on an intellectual plane. For it was only as writers that the anarchists were allowed to operate without fear of harassment. In 1898, Federico Urales and Soledad Gustavo, who, it will be remembered, had also fled abroad following the Montjuich persecutions, and lived in England and France until late 1897, founded *La Revista Blanca* (Madrid). The journal, which was destined to become the longest-running and perhaps most influential anarchist periodical in Spanish history, was consciously patterned after the celebrated French monthly *La Revue Blanche* (Paris). To circumvent the censors as well as to shield the journal from government persecution, the words "anarchism" and "anarchist" were omitted from the title. In this way, *La Revista Blanca* was able to serve for a number of years as a forum for discussing an assortment of modern artistic, literary, and sociological theories, including anarchism.[19]

The revival of anarchism at this time owed much to the national crisis that shook the country in 1898: the Spanish-American War. The war was so humilatingly quick (less than eight months) that the public had little time to absorb fully the implications of an event that had caused Spain to lose the last remnants of its colonial empire: Cuba, Puerto Rico, and the Philippines. Following as it did on the heels of the Montjuich affair, the "Disaster of 1898," as this short war and its consequences came to be known, almost completely discredited the government, which had proved to be incapable of asserting itself authoritatively and effectively when faced with a national crisis.

The widespread disillusionment of the nation was most evident among the literati and political opponents of the regime. Not surprisingly, then, the reanimation of anarchism at this time was given impetus by the support it received from certain elements of this disaffected group of intellectuals and politicians. For a brief while, such accomplished writers as Azorín, Ramiro Maetzu, Miguel de Unamuno, and Pío Baroja—some of the leading figures in the so-called Generation of 1898—flirted with anarchist ideas, infusing the movement with an intellectual dynamism it had not had before. More important, this mostly young and middle-class group of intellectuals introduced to the movement new and controversial themes, although few of these were ever formally incorporated into anarchist doctrine. It is not our intention here to discuss the rich and rather complex anarchist attitude held by this generation of thinkers. We can only mention in passing some of the salient aspects of their thinking.

One was the theme of anti-industrialism, a subject which was of prevailing interest at the turn of the century, not only in Spain but in all European artistic circles. In Spain this sentiment found expression in some of the fictional works of writers like Pío Baroja, Miguel de Unamuno, and Azorín. A common theme running through these was the rejection of the technological achievements of the modern age. Their intense distaste for the cultural and ethical system found in contemporary industrial society—that is, the "ugly face" of industrial capitalism—led them to develop a backward-looking aesthetic, one that attempted to recapture the values of a distant and largely imagined past.[20]

Also popular among this generation of intellectuals was an extreme form of philosophical individualism. Friedrich Nietzsche, Max Stirner, and Henrik Ibsen were, if not always read, at least frequently talked about in the anarchist café society composed of middle-class intellectuals. Topics like Nietzche's notion of the *Übermensch* (translated as *superhombre* in Spanish) or Stirner's radical individualism were frequently debated in the pages of *Natura, La Revista Blanca,* and other libertarian theoretical organs. Significantly, these new ideas never found echo among the rank and file of the movement, primarily because of the persistence of *ouvrièrisme* among the Spanish anarchists. As a result, most were inveterately opposed to the intellectual trends popular among the middle classes.

The Spanish anarchists generally have been accused of uncritically embracing the decadent literary and philosophical trends of *fin de siècle* Europe, despite the fact that only a tiny portion of the movement—namely, middle-class intellectuals who were only briefly attracted to anarchism—ever seriously entertained such ideas.[21] The truth is that the majority of philosophical anarchists were not at all interested in the practice of anarchism, and they especially abhorred the militancy and violence associated with the movement itself. It was the aesthetic appeal of the abstract idea of anarchism which captured their attention, not the concrete objectives of a revolutionary program.

The truly representative anarchist theorists—notably, Ricardo Mella, José Prat, and Anselmo Lorenzo—regarded the individualist strain of anarchism that was inspired by the works of Stirner, Nietzsche, and Ibsen as an illegitimate deviation from their revolutionary creed. Unlike the parlor anarchists who were chiefly interested in boldly challenging the aesthetic theories of their day, this group sought to formulate a workable strategy for direct action.

Through their writings and translations of key theoretical works, Lorenzo and Prat became the leading Spanish interpreters of a brand of revolutionary syndicalism that came to be known in Spain as anarcho-syndicalism. This current of thinking was introduced to Spain around the turn of the century, when the works of such prominent European syndicalists as Fernand Pelloutier, Émile Pouget, and Arturo Labriola began appearing in Spanish translation.[22] Although strong parallels existed between the revolutionary syndicalist ideas being developed in France and Italy and the syndicalist notions common to the Spanish anarchist tradition, it took about ten years of gestation before anarcho-syndicalism fully crystallized.[23]

Epilogue

For three decades, the Spanish anarchists demonstrated a remarkable resiliency and determination that enabled them to survive in the most unpropitious circumstances. Thus, despite a troubled history marked by bitter factional quarreling and cycles of economic depression and political persecution, they managed to keep the flame of revolution from being completely extinguished. Even the ferocity of the official repression following the Montjuich affair, which had dealt a nearly fatal blow to the libertarian movement, was not enough to prevent the anarchists from regenerating their strength and influence by the turn of the century. The next two decades saw anarchism blossom into one of the largest left-wing movements in Europe: membership of the predominantly anarchosyndicalist Confederación Nacional del Trabajo (CNT) mushroomed from a mere 15,000 in 1915 to a staggering 700,000 by the end of 1919. While the details of the spectacular expansion of anarchism at this time must be left to another study, a few general observations about this phenomenon can be made here.

The prevailing economic and political trends in Spain during the early part of the twentieth century produced a set of circumstances that proved to be favorable to the growth of anarchism. Continuing a pattern that had begun in the mid–nineteenth century, the overall tendency of the labor force was toward urban areas and toward industry. Although Spain remained a predominantly agricultural economy well into this century, its industrial base rapidly expanded between 1900 and 1918. The meteoric growth in this economic sector was accompanied by a dramatic increase in the number of people employed in nonagricultural enterprises (that is, workers engaged in manufacturing, mining, chemical, building, and transportation industries). Between 1887 and 1900, for example, the industrial labor force almost quadrupled, from approximately 244,000 to around 995,000.[1] An obvious consequence of the prodigious growth of the proletariat in regions like Aragón, Valencia, and Catalonia was that it created a huge reservoir of potential recruits for the anarchosyndicalists. This was dramatically illustrated during World War I, when rocketing prices and falling wages provided a fertile soil for the propagation of anarchism. As the nationally based CNT had been created in 1910 it was now possible, as never before, for the libertarian movement to absorb the soaring numbers of militant urban workers.

It is interesting to note that the demographic shift in the Spanish working population signaled a permanent shift in the locus of anarchist popular support. Whereas during the 1880s and 1890s, the libertarian movement drew most of its strength from the rural districts of the south, after 1910 the majority of its adherents were centered in urban areas. In fact, anarchists increasingly lost their hold over the agricultural work force. During the 1930s, for example, the socialist Federación Nacional de Trabajadores de la Tierra (FNTT) made great strides in recruiting landless laborers. From a membership of around 27,000 at its founding in 1930, the FNTT mushroomed to an astonishing 392,953 in just two years.[2] The anarchists never wholly recovered their rural territory, and this created profound problems for them during the Civil War and Revolution (1936–1939).

In the political sphere, the anarchist movement profited from the liberalizing moods of the Spanish government. We saw earlier that the "Disaster of 1898" had caused the government to lose much of its prestige and credibility. Partly because of this, and partly because the anarchists themselves no longer posed a serious threat to public order, the authorities occasionally eased up on their aggressive stance toward the anarchists. One indication of this was the government's response to the domestic and international campaigns on behalf of Andalusian anarchist political prisoners: in 1901 workers incarcerated as a result of the Jerez rising were released, and two years later, anarchists who had been imprisoned ever since the Mano Negra scare were finally liberated. No matter how brief they may have been, respites such as these were the kind of opportunities the anarchists seized upon in order to expand their activities throughout the spectrum of working-class society. Libertarian publications (*La Huelga General,* for example) began appearing around this time, with some twenty-seven different anarchist papers coming out between 1900 and 1910. In addition to their publishing efforts, the anarchists exploited the government's benevolent attitude by creating new associations, like the Federación de Sociedades Obreras de la Región Española (FSORE), established in 1900.

In this connection it should be remembered that, throughout the history of Spanish anarchism, its survival depended in large measure on the anarchists' ability to maintain direct links with the workers. Since the 1870s, the libertarians' involvement in *ateneos, circulos,* cafés, and *centros obreros* had become one of the major means by which they managed to establish their presence in the daily lives of the working classes. The fact is that anarchists thrived best when they were free to publish their periodicals, operate their own educational centers, and attend public meetings at which they could openly debate their ideas. This was amply demonstrated both in the early 1880s, when the FTRE prospered under Sagasta's liberal reforms, and again during the first biennium of the Second Republic (1931–1933), when the CNT's membership climbed to over one million.

The shortcomings of the Restoration Settlement also nourished the development of anarchism. Despite the reformist aspirations of such able politicians as the conservative Antonio Maura, who sought to regenerate politics between 1900 and 1910 with his so-called "revolution from above," the democratic potential of the Spanish political system did not significantly change from 1876 until the establishment of the Second Republic in 1931. The degree to which the system was flawed can be measured by the impact that the Universal Suffrage Act of 1890 had on the workers. Although in theory the measure appeared to open the door for working-class political representation, it failed to do so—not least because the major parties in the Cortes chose to ignore this increasingly important segment of society. As a rule, politicians strove to absorb working-class discontent rather than incorporate workers into the political process. This was particularly true after 1900, when the ruling parties concentrated more and more on clinging to power rather than pursuing democratic reforms.

Apart from the socialists, only the Republican Party seriously attempted to develop a working-class constituency. Under the leadership of the charismatic demagogue, Alejandro Lerroux, the Radical Republican Party in Catalonia briefly attracted a significant number of workers to the polls. In the 1901 and 1903 elections, for instance, an estimated

20,000 workers voted for the Republican Party.[3] But this electoral partnership never amounted to anything more than a circumstantial political alliance, and for this reason, it disintegrated almost as quickly as it
had materialized. This was most evident in the wake of the notorious
"Semana Trágica" (Tragic Week) of 1909. This began as a general
strike in protest of the Moroccan war but resulted in a week of violent
social and economic upheaval. The uprising ended disastrously for the
organized labor movement, ushering in yet another harsh period of
government repression. In succeeding years, workers became so thoroughly disillusioned with politics that they converted in ever greater
numbers to the antipolitical CNT.

ANARCHOSYNDICALISM AND THE
LEGACY OF THE NINETEENTH CENTURY

Within the libertarian community itself, a gradual metamorphosis of
anarchist theory and practice between 1900 and 1910 gave rise to
anarchosyndicalism. While the emergence of the new doctrine represented another stage in the history of Spanish anarchism, its theoretical
and practical links to the nineteenth century are readily apparent. In
some cases, traits of the early years of the libertarian movement did not
fully manifest themselves until after 1900. Anticlericalism, for example,
played a much more important role in anarchist affairs in this century
that it had ever done up till this point. This is not to deny that anarchists
exhibited anticlerical behavior during the nineteenth century. For them,
the Church was not just a corrupt institution that grew ever more
powerful and influential at the expense of the people; it was also a
major obstacle in the path of social development as they envisioned it.
The Church was a favorite target of the anarchist press—notably, *La
Anarquía* (Madrid), *Los Desheredados* (Sabadell), and *La Tramontana*
(Barcelona)—which never tired of blaspheming religion and caricatur-
ing the clergy. For their part, the devotees of propaganda by the deed
would sometimes register their contempt for organized religion by discharging small bombs outside of churches. But while there can be no
question that anticlerical feelings ran deep among the anarchists of this
period, seldom were these sentiments translated into serious confrontations with the Church itself. It is well known, however, that in the
twentieth century the anarchists unleashed their hostilities toward the
Church with tremendous vehemence. In the first decades of this century
and on a much larger scale during the Civil War and Revolution, anar-

chists sometimes engaged in a form of open warfare with the Church and its representatives. During the early weeks of the Civil War and Revolution, for example, anarchists played a leading role in committing such antireligious outrages as the widespread destruction of Church property and the immolation of clergymen.[4]

Another characteristic that the twentieth-century anarchists inherited from their predecessors was a compelling vision of a just and harmonious society. The moralism and idealism of the older generation of anarchists were retained as central themes in much of the libertarian literature published between 1900 and 1939. Furthermore, it was the utopian elements found in the writings of Anselmo Lorenzo, Ricardo Mella, Federica Montseny (the daughter of Juan Montseny), and Isaac Puente which helped to sustain the belief among the peasantry and industrial workers that it was both possible and desirable to build a society based on anarchist values.[5]

Syndicalism also had deep roots in the Spanish libertarian tradition. It can be traced to Bakunin's revolutionary collectivism, which, as we have already seen, found expression first through the FRE and then through the FTRE. While the rise of anarchist communism and the acceptance of propaganda by the deed as the revolutionaries' principal weapon had forced the syndicalist elements to retire to the background during the 1890s, they had never completely abandoned the movement. Then, at the close of the nineteenth century, several factors contributed to the revival of the syndicalist current.

There can be no doubt that the importation of syndicalist theories, particularly those of Hubert Lagardelle, Fernand Pelloutier, Émile Pouget, Victor Griffuelhes, and Arturo Labriola, considerably broadened the anarchists' conception of the general strike. Among other things, this infusion of new ideas helped to restore faith in the efficacy of the strike tactic. The extent to which these as well as other foreign influences generated a philosophy of violence that was linked to the myth of the revolutionary potential of the general strike is exceedingly difficult to determine. For some anarchists, the general strike was understood in apocalyptic terms: it was to be a catastrophic event that would inaugurate sweeping and permanent changes in the present system. Still others held a more pragmatic view of the tactic, regarding it as the most powerful weapon in the workers' arsenal. Yet neither viewpoint can be said to have been derived from the writings of any one author.[6]

The anarchists' receptivity to syndicalism was also bound up with the emergence of a new pattern of working-class protest. After 1900, insurrections of the Jerez variety were generally condemned by revolutionaries on the ground that they were easily suppressed by the authorities, who clearly possessed superior fire power. Popular uprisings were instead inextricably linked to strike action, such as the Casas Viejas incident of 1933 and other celebrated anarchist-inspired revolts during the 1930s. Terrorism was also increasingly recognized as a bankrupt tactic, especially in the light of the Montjuich repression and again following a recrudescence of bombings between 1904 and 1907. In the latter case, random violence led to what Ricardo Mella and like-minded libertarians had predicted: it isolated the anarchists from the workers. Although terrorism remained a permanent feature of the libertarian movement, the principal forms of direct action changed with the advent of anarcho-syndicalism. According to the new theory, violence was to be retained in the revolutionary strategy, but instead of bombings and attempts at "tyrannicide," it was to be conducted primarily through the trade unions, particularly in the form of the general strike.

The multifaceted nature of Spanish anarchism, which had produced a dialectical interplay between the different elements within the nineteenth-century movement, persisted into the twentieth century. Until the Civil War (1936–1939), two principal groups dominated libertarian affairs. The first can be broadly classified as the syndicalist wing, which was responsible for reestablishing the anarchists' foothold in the trade union movement. The second group was composed entirely of anarchist militants, who, although also committed to trade unions, gave primacy to violent practices. The best-known representatives of this faction were the members of the Federación Anarquista Ibérica (FAI), a semiclandestine organization that emerged during Miguel Primo de Rivera's dictatorship (1923–1930) and rose to national prominence during the Second Republic and Civil War period (1931–1939).

In the first decade of this century, the syndicalists were in the vanguard of the general movement toward the creation of labor federations on a national scale. The first step in this direction was realized with the formation of the Federación de Sociedades Obreras de la Región Española (FSORE) in 1900, the successor to the Pacto de Unión y Solidaridad (or FRC). The FSORE was followed by the creation of Solidaridad Obrera in 1907, and was ultimately succeeded by the Confederación Nacional del Trabajo (CNT), an organization that has since become synonymous with Spanish anarchism and that has survived in one form or another up to the present.

While the establishment of the CNT in 1910 marked the true beginning of the anarchosyndicalist movement, it must be borne in mind that
the CNT itself was not originally meant to be an exclusively anarchist
body. At the outset, the CNT served as an umbrella organization, en-
compassing socialists, republicans, syndicalists, and anarchist purists—
all of whom were present at the initial meeting held in September–
October 1910. Much like the Pacto, which was formed in 1887, the
CNT was viewed by its founders as an ideologically neutral apparatus
that could effectively promote the interests of all the different unions.
Nevertheless, in the following years, the CNT developed into a predominantly anarchist organization. This was largely because the CNT, like
its nineteenth-century precursor the FRE, came into existence and then
developed during a period of chronic political and economic upheavals.
The latent revolutionism of the CNT was stimulated early on by bitter
industrial conflicts (the *Canadiense* Strike of 1919, for instance) and
government repression, and it was later reinforced by events like the
Bolshevik Revolution of 1917 and the worldwide economic depression
of the 1930s. As a result, not only did the overwhelming majority of its
members remain antipolitical, but they became increasingly radicalized
until the outbreak of the Civil War in 1936.

Between 1910 and 1930, the syndicalists constituted the largest section of the anarchosyndicalist movement. With few exceptions, they
were a homogeneous group of anarchists whose views closely paralleled
those of the collectivists of the 1870s and 1880s. Like their nineteenth-
century counterparts, the syndicalists viewed working-class associations
as the nuclei from which a new society would emerge. Through trade
unions, *círculos, ateneos,* and similar organizations, the syndicalists
strove to exercise a hegemony over the social and economic life of the
worker. On another level, the trade union was seen as the only effective
vehicle for conducting class warfare. Strikes, sabotage, and other trade
union weapons were to be employed in the daily struggle to improve the
lot of the worker, whereas the general strike was to be reserved for those
occasions when the conditions for a social revolution seemed ripe. Once
the anarchosyndicalists had established a network of organizations
throughout Spain and were capable of sustaining their own society, the
belief was that it remained only to call a general strike. Because they
wielded considerable economic power through their unions, it was assumed that bourgeois society could be brought to its knees: workers
would seize complete control of key industries and thereby cause irrevo-

cable losses. The consequent rupture in the economy was supposed to be so catastrophic that it would inevitably bring about the collapse of capitalism and the state.

When the CNT was forced underground during the Primo de Rivera dictatorship, the anarchist movement experienced further substantive changes. Because of its illegal status, the CNT rapidly lost ground both to the right-wing *sindicatos libres* and the socialist unions. As a result, syndicalist leaders like Ángel Pestaña began promoting a policy that favored closer cooperation between the CNT and the government. For example, Pestaña believed that it was necessary for the anarcho-syndicalists to play a role in the government-controlled arbitration bodies, *comités paritarios*, which the socialists were successfully exploiting in their efforts to strengthen the UGT. The fear that the anarchist movement might once and for all jettison its antistatist principles drove a small but significant group of anarchists to form the FAI in 1927.

Composed largely of militants who had fled abroad during the repression and a handful of Portuguese émigrés, the FAI was in some respects the reincarnation of Bakunin's Alliance: its primary purpose was to give the CNT a revolutionary orientation by ensuring that anarchist doctrine was not contaminated by antirevolutionary beliefs or practices. Where the FAI differed most significantly from the Alliance was in the special relationship it cultivated with the unions. During the 1930s, the age of massive syndical structures like the *sindicato único* (the practice of uniting all workers of an industry into one union), it was mandatory for any serious revolutionary organization to maintain a trade union base. Thus the FAI sought to forge what its members referred to as an organic bond ("trabazón") with the CNT. In practice, this amounted to gaining control of the trade union apparatus. By exercising a dominating influence over the activities of the *sindicatos* and other associations connected to the CNT, the FAI placed itself in a position to direct the course of this large federation of unions.

Shortly after the foundation of the Second Republic in April 1931, the FAI achieved notoriety by relentlessly pursuing ultrarevolutionary tactics—a policy that stood in bold contrast to the pragmatic trade union agenda being advocated by the syndicalists. After they announced their intention of controlling the CNT, the FAI exploited every opportunity to undermine the influence of its syndicalist rivals. Strike movements were heralded as examples of what the workers needed to build their revolutionary strength in preparation for the final struggle with the bourgeoise, and in *ateneos* and *centros obreros* everywhere *faístas* (i.e., members of FAI) energetically worked to win the minds of the workers through an intensive propaganda program. By 1933 the *faístas* had emerged as the predominant force in the CNT, and from then until the end of the Civil War in 1939, they were to play a decisive role in the fate of the anarchosyndicalist movement.[7]

ANARCHISM AND THE FAILURE OF SOCIALISM

During the heyday of "propaganda by the deed," the socialists' cautious methods helped to shield them from government repression. Even so, before 1905 socialist growth was exceedingly slow and uneven. This was especially evident in Catalonia, where UGT membership had steadily declined since its founding in 1888, so that the socialists were forced to transfer its headquarters to Madrid in 1899. The relative failure of the socialists to capture the hearts and minds of the workers before the mid-1920s helps to explain why anarchism enjoyed so much success among the industrial proletariat. While space limitations do not permit a proper discussion of why socialism fared so poorly, a few general observations about this curious fact deserve mention.[8]

One has to do with the lack of effective leadership. With few exceptions, like the popular Basque Facundo Pérezagua, the socialists failed to produce the kind of political and trade union leaders that were apparently required for them successfully to combat anarchist influence. The stolid and unimaginative Pablo Iglesias, the so-called father of Spanish socialism who lorded over the movement until the early decades of the twentieth century, steered the socialists down a solitary path, one that departed both from the revolutionary orbit of the anarchists and the antirevolutionary agenda set by the ruling middle-class parties. The policies unwaveringly pursued by Iglesias and other socialist leaders had only limited success: they attracted small but ever-growing numbers of devoted followers, especially in Asturias, the Basque country, and Madrid. Though the UGT grew from an insignificant 15,000 in 1899 to over 57,000 by 1905 (membership dropped to around 35,000 in the following year), it never rivaled the size and significance of the CNT until the early 1930s.[9]

The socialists' official position in strikes was probably another factor that isolated them from the mainstream of the working-class movement. Despite the repeated failure of strikes, and despite the fact that they often caused the militants to lose standing among the unions, most workers in Andalusia, Valencia, Aragón, and Catalonia remained sympathetic to strike action. This was probably because, at least in Spain during this period, strikes tended to foster a strong and binding sense of solidarity among the masses. Regardless of their respective ideological orientations, workers' groups usually rallied around such popular issues as anticlericalism, antimilitarism, and above all, better working conditions. The history of the Spanish working-class movement of the twentieth century abounds with extraordinary examples of solidarity shown during general strikes. The General Strike of 1902 is a case in point.

The week-long General Strike of 1902 (7–14 February) engaged an estimated 80,000 of Barcelona's working population of 144,000.[10] The strike had its origins in an industrial conflict that had begun some months earlier. The metallurgical workers of Barcelona struck in December 1901 for an eight-hour day. From the beginning, it was apparent that the workers were up against enormous obstacles: acute unemployment in the region and the absence of strike funds considerably weakened their position vis-à-vis their employers. But in the face of these circumstances, some 10,000 workers managed to stay out for the next eight weeks.

On 17 February, the Barcelona branches of the anarchist FSORE called a general strike in solidarity with the metallurgical unions. Within a few days, city life in Barcelona was at a standstill: no newspapers appeared; public transportation came to a grinding halt; and banks, cafés, and most shops were closed. The strike movement quickly spread to neighboring cities, and it even elicited scattered support from unions outside of Catalonia. It therefore came as no surprise when the military authorities declared martial law at the end of the week. Militant strikers and their leaders were rounded up and thrown into the city's jails, and though some unions attempted to defy the military's aggressive actions, they were no match for the troops of the infantry and calvary.[11]

The strike ended disastrously for the organized trade union movement in the region: worker associations were suppressed and the anarchists were driven underground. This is precisely what the socialists had expected. In Madrid, Valladolid, San Sebastian, and other socialist strongholds, the idea of joining the Barcelona strike movement was strongly discouraged by the socialist leadership, and consequently, very few workers in these cities ceased work. Speaking for the socialist hierarchy, Pablo Iglesias later publicly lambasted the anarchists for having dragged the Barcelona working classes into a headless movement that gained nothing at all for the metal workers.

Nevertheless, the 1902 strike was an impressive demonstration of working-class initiative and solidarity that was to leave its mark on the Spanish labor movement. By generally opposing strike action, the socialists may have preserved their trade union organizations, but, in doing so, they effectively lost the opportunity to exploit the moral force of the working-class community. While the symbolic significance of the 1902 strike may have eluded the socialists, it did not escape the notice of the anarchists. Far from discouraging them, the disastrous consequences of the 1902 strike stimulated them to reformulate their revolutionary strategy. This was primarily because strikes were increasingly viewed by them as a way not only of strengthening the workers' revolutionary élan but also of solidifying the organizational network of their unions. In the coming years, they successfully linked strike activity with the growth of their own strength and influence.

From the time it was introduced in 1868 until the birth of the Confederación Nacional del Trabajo (CNT) in 1910, anarchism had never sustained a mass following among working-class organizations. After the founding of the CNT, though, the possibilities for forging permanent links with the trade union movement were finally realized. Above all, the anarchosyndicalist formula enabled the anarchists to combine successfully trade unionism with the general strike tactic as well as other forms of industrial action. This fact alone made anarchism a formidable social and economic force in a rapidly modernizing Spanish society. During the Second Republic (1931–1936), anarchosyndicalism started another period of expansion which did not peak until the Civil War. At its zenith, anarchosyndicalism counted over one and a half million adherents—an impressive achievement for a movement that had endured over seventy years of state persecution.

Notes

Note: Unless otherwise indicated, all translations are mine.

INTRODUCTION

1. Several studies on nineteenth-century Spanish anarchism can be recommended: Diego Abad de Santillán, *Contribución a la historia del movimiento obrero español: Desde sus orígenes hasta 1905,* vol. 1 (Puebla, Mexico, 1962); José Alvarez Junco, *La ideología política del anarquismo español, 1868–1910* (Madrid, 1976); Murray Bookchin, *The Spanish Anarchists* (New York, 1977); Manuel Buenacasa, *El movimiento obrero español, 1886–1926* (Barcelona, 1928); Juan Gómez Casas, *Historia del anarcosindicalismo español* (Madrid, 1977); Clara E. Lida, *Anarquismo y revolución en la España del siglo XIX* (Madrid, 1972); *Antecedentes y desarrollo del movimiento obrero español (1835–1888): Textos y documentos,* ed. Clara E. Lida (Madrid, 1973); Lily Litvak, *La musa libertaria* (Barcelona, 1981); Casimiro Martí, *Orígenes del anarquismo en Barcelona,* prologue by J. Vicens Vives (Barcelona, 1959); and Josep Termes Ardevol, *Anarquismo y sindicalismo en España: La Primera Internacional (1864–1881)* (Barcelona, 1972 and 1977).

2. Eric J. Hobsbawm, *Primitive Rebels* (New York, 1965), pp. 82–83. For more on Hobsbawm's thesis see below, chap. 10.

3. It is ever more difficult to find any study on Spanish anarchism that does not in some way challenge the millenarian explanation. See, for example, Jerome Mintz, *The Anarchists of Casas Viejas* (Chicago, 1982); Joaquín Romero Maura, "The Spanish Case," in *Anarchism Today,* ed. David Apter and James Joll (London, 1971); and Michael R. Weisser, *Peasants of the Montes* (Chicago, 1976).

4. Apart from the works by Brenan, Díaz del Moral, and Eric Hobsbawm already cited, there are several studies on the Spanish left that reflect the millen-

arian interpretation of anarchism: Robert Kern, *Red Years/Black Years: A Political History of Spanish Anarchism* (Philadelphia, 1978); Edward Malefakis, *Agrarian Reform and Peasant Revolution in Spain* (New Haven, Conn., 1970); and Stanley G. Payne, *The Spanish Revolution* (London, 1970).

5. Gerald Brenan, *The Spanish Labyrinth* (Cambridge, 1971), p. 162.

6. This is not to deny that regional differences played a role in determining the praxis of anarchism.

7. See, for example, Eric J. Hobsbawm, *Revolutionaries* (London 1973).

8. The history of Spanish socialism in this period has also been ill served. With the exception of Pablo Iglesias Posse, for example, little is known about leading socialist figures. On socialism generally, see the following: Javier Aisa, with V. M. Arbeloa, *Historia de la Unión General de Trabajadores* (Madrid, 1975); V. M. Arbeloa, *Orígenes del partido socialista obrero español* (Madrid, 1972); *Estudios de historia social* (a double issue commemorating the centenary of Spanish socialism), Jan. 1979; Juan Pablo Fusi, *Política obrera en el país vasco* (Madrid, 1975); Paul Heywood, "De las dificultades para ser marxista: El PSOE, 1879–1921," *Sistema* (Madrid), Sept. 1986; Antoni Jutglar, "Notas para la historia del socialismo en España," *Revista de Trabajo* (Madrid), no. 3 (1964); Francisco Mora, *Historia del socialismo obrero español* (Madrid, 1902); Juan José Morato, *El partido socialista obrero* (Madrid, 1918 and 1976); and Manuel Tuñón de Lara, *El movimiento obrero en la historia de España* (Madrid, 1972).

1: THE ORIGINS OF THE FIRST INTERNATIONAL IN SPAIN

1. Termes, *Anarquismo*, p. 28.

2. C. A. M. Hennessy, *The Federal Republic in Spain: 1868–1874* (Oxford, 1962), pp. 28–49, where there is a discussion of the ideological contributions made by theorists such as Emilio Castelar and Pi y Margall in the preparation of the Revolution.

3. The League—known as the Liga de Paz y Libertad in Spain—assembled between 21 and 25 Sept.

4. Influenced by his experiences with the "carbonaria" in Italy, Bakunin formed his first "secret society," the Fraternité, in 1864. It appeárs as though his experience in Italy had led him to believe that it was necessary to construct a small, well-organized society in order to bring about a successful revolution, especially in countries where there was a high rate of illiteracy among the masses: "Spontaneous movements of the masses of people . . . never found any sympathy, or very little of it, among this revolutionary youth of Italy. If the latter movement had been well organised and directed by intelligent people, it might have produced a formidable revolution. Lacking organisation and leadership, it ended in a fiasco" (Michael Bakunin, *The Political Philosophy of Bakunin*, ed. G. P. Maximoff [New York, 1953], p. 378). See also Martí, *Orígenes*, pp. 77–78, and T. R. Ravindranathan, *Bakunin and the Italians* (Canada, 1988).

5. *La Federación* was founded in Aug. 1869. See Termes, *Anarquismo,* p. 31.

6. Ibid., p. 85.

7. On Garrido's relation to Bakunin's society see Arthur Lehning, "Bakunin's Conceptions of Revolutionary Organisations and Their Role: A Study of His 'Secret Societies,' " in *Essays in Honour of E. H. Carr,* ed. Chemin Abramsky (London, 1974).

8. See G. D. H. Cole, *A History of Socialist Thought,* vol. 2, *Marxism and Anarchism* (London, 1954), chap. 6.

9. David Stafford, *From Anarchism to Reformism, A Study of the Political Activities of Paul Brousse* (London, 1971), p. 8.

10. Max Nettlau gives an account of the cooperative debate within the International in his *Anarquía a través de los tiempos* (Barcelona, 1935), pp. 138–148.

11. See appendix 8a in Termes, *Anarquismo,* p. 399, for the contents of Marsal's message entitled "Informe de las asociaciones obreras de Cataluña." Whether or not he was in fact the first official Spanish representative from the labor movement to make direct contact with the International is still a mystery. Casimiro Martí points out that the minutes of the General Council record a message from a Citizen Mollard of Barcelona—whose project was to broadcast information about the IWMA in Catalonia and the United States—on 25 Sept. 1866. See Martí, *Orígenes,* p. 80, and International Working Men's Association, *General Council of the First International: Minutes, 1864–1866,* vol. 1 (Moscow, 1964), p. 37. Clara Lida, however, suggests that "Citizen Mollard" may have been an error for Joaquin Molart, who was a member of the Commission of Catalonian Workers during the strike of 1855 in Barcelona. See Lida, *Anarquismo,* p. 137.

12. Excerpts from the speech Bakunin delivered at the Second Congress of the League are reproduced in Palmiro Marba, *Origen, desarrollo y transcendencia del movimiento sindicalista obrero* (Mexico [1945?]), p. 478.

13. See Max Nettlau, *Miguel Bakunin, la Internacional y la Alianza en España (1868–1873)* (Buenos Aires, 1925).

14. See Elie Reclus's report of his trip in "Impressiones de un viaje por España en días de Revolución," *La Revista Blanca* (Barcelona), 1 Mar. 1933, p. 67; also cited in Lida, *Anarquismo,* p. 139. (This article appeared in English in *Putnam's Magazine,* Jan.–June 1869.)

15. Anselmo Lorenzo provides a colorful account of Fanelli's influence on the group in Madrid in his autobiography, *El proletariado militante* (Madrid, 1974). It is difficult, though, to assess the extent to which Fanelli was able to "radicalize" the people he had encountered in Spain. Gerald Brenan, for example, tells us that the Spanish conversion to radical ideas was instantaneous (*Labyrinth,* p. 140). This is probably an exaggeration. Casimiro Martí argues that neither the language barrier nor Fanelli's uninspiring personality could have produced the dramatic effects that Lorenzo and Brenan emphasize in their respective studies.

16. See Juan Gómez Casas, *Historia de la FAI* (Madrid, 1977), chap. 1.

17. Lorenzo, *El proletariado militante* (Madrid, 1974), p. 41.

18. Marba, *Origen,* p. 475.

19. Lida, *Anarquismo,* p. 143.

20. See appendix 5d in Termes, *Anarquismo,* p. 327, for a reproduction of Farga Pellicer's letter to Bakunin, 1 Aug. 1869.

21. See, for example, nos. 2, 3, and 4 of *La Federación* (Barcelona).

22. On 15 Aug. 1869, *La Federación* (Barcelona) argued that the true emancipation of the worker would be realized "through the long but secure road" of cooperativism. Yet it is significant that in the Nov. 7 issue, an article stressed the failure of the methods of the German cooperativist Schulze-Delitzsch.

23. Juan José Morato, *Líderes del movimiento obrero español (1868–1921)* (Madrid, 1972), pp. 79–94. This is a compendium of Morato's articles that appeared in *La Libertad* (Madrid).

24. This quote was taken from Bakunin's *The Policy of the International,* Spurs Series no. 6 (London: Bakuninist Press, 1919). The tract first appeared in the French journal *Egalité* in 1869. Also cited in Termes, *Anarquismo,* pp. 335–347.

25. Their dictum read: "Considering that the participation of the working classes in the politics of a middle-class government will inevitably result in the consolidation of the status quo, it will paralyse the revolutionary socialist actions of the proletariat."

26. According to Bakunin, the emancipation of the worker necessarily involved an organized struggle against the bourgeoisie, who were regarded by him as the class that gave rise not only to capitalism but to its organized force: the State.

27. Francisco Mora, quoted in Termes, *Anarquismo,* p. 89. The quoted passage is from a speech delivered by Mora, who later became a prominent figure in the Spanish Socialist Party (PSOE).

2: THE STRUGGLE FOR AN IDEOLOGY

1. Before the elections in Jan. 1869, Federal Republicans and workers expressed a considerable degree of enthusiasm for their political alliance at the polls. Their optimism was further reinforced when their candidates were elected—including the first working-class representative to be sent to the Cortes, Pablo Alsina. See Termes, *Anarquismo,* pp. 33–34. For a brief biographical sketch of Alsina see Morato, *Líderes,* pp. 154–158.

2. See Manuel Espades Burgos, "La primera Internacional y la historiografía español," *Hispania,* (Madrid), no. 30 (Jan.–Apr. 1970), pp. 183–196. In one sense the impact of the International at this time can be regarded as the threat it posed to Federal control over the working classes. This is clearly brought out in the debate between Fernando Garrido and the editors of *La Solidaridad* (Seville)—Anselmo Lorenzo, Francisco Mora, and others—in 1870. In brief, the central question raised in the controversy concerned the direction the workers' movement should take; that is, whether or not they should abandon politics as a method of action. See *Antecedentes,* ed. Lida, pp. 167–171.

3. Because Federal ideology was aimed at a transverse section of society, the force of its appeal to a specific group like the working class was substantially

diffused. Hennessy details the multifaceted qualities of this ideology in his study, *The Federal Republic,* pp. 73–102. For further discussion about the relation of Federal ideology to the working classes see the works by Antonio Jutglar, *Ideologías y clases en la España contemporanea (1808–1874),* vol. 1 (Madrid, 1973), pp. 245–249, 270–275; Francisco Pi y Margall, *Federalismo y revolución. Las ideas sociales de Pi y Margall* (Barcelona, 1966); and Gumersindo Trujillo, *Introducción al federalismo español* (Madrid, 1967).

4. Hennessy, *The Federal Republic,* p. 73.

5. Ibid., pp. 97–100.

6. Ibid., p. 73.

7. No accurate statistics are available as to the number and social composition of the members of the working class who could read. Judging by the accounts by or about the leading figures of this group it would appear as though most of them had received their education at home or at workers' educational clubs. Cf. Morato, *Líderes;* Juan José Morato, *Pablo Iglesias Posse: Educator de muchedumbres* (Barcelona, 1968), pp. 1–24; and Anselmo Lorenzo, *El proletariado militante* (Mexico [1945?]), vol. 1.

8. Lorenzo relates the activities of the Fomento de las Artes in *El proletariado militante.* On the origins of the *ateneos* see Pere Solà, *El Ateneus obrers i la cultura popular a Cataluñya (1900–1939)* (Barcelona, 1978).

9. Although Federal juntas throughout Spain during the September Revolution set forth similar types of reform programs—the abolition of the *quintas,* unity of the *fueros,* and educational and penal reform, for example, were all common features—the interpretation of federalism varied according to the sociopolitical and economic differences among the provinces. See Hennessy, *The Federal Republic,* pp. 50–72.

10. Quoted ibid., p. 107 (trans. Hennessy).

11. Juan Díaz del Moral points out that, during the early period of the republican movement, *reparto* was synonymous with socialism or the communalization of land. See his *Historia las agitaciones campesinas andaluzas* (Madrid, 1973), pp. 71–72. For an account of what *reparto* meant to the agricultural worker also see Juan Martínez-Alier, *La estabilidad del latifundismo* (Ruedo Iberico, 1968), chap. 1, pp. 52–86. Cf. Jutglar's view: "... los campesinos de Andalucía, se limitaban a creer que la tierra era de los que la trabajaban y que, con la República, llegaba la hora del esperado reparto social" (*Ideologías,* p. 249).

12. For examples of the role of the *Partido de la Porra* in local politics in Andalusia see Brenan, *Labyrinth,* pp. 167–168 note d, and Nuñez de Arenas and Manuel Tuñón de Lara, *Historia del movimiento obrero español* (Barcelona, 1970), pp. 107–108 n. 10, which is an account of the *Partido's* reaction to the Paris Commune of 1871.

13. The workers' Catalanist feelings were reflected at their local meetings, where they often chose to hold discussions in their native language. Nonetheless, they did not go so far as to censure the use of Castilian, which was predominantly used in their written propaganda. See Termes, *Anarquismo,* p. 113.

14. An article entitled "A las urnas, republicanos" appeared in *La Alianza*

de los Pueblos in December 1868, declaring that "las pacificas y florecientes republicas modernas se han apoyado en el proteccionismo y no en el librecambio . . . ! No temais, pues, operarios barceloneses, la republica no es el librecambio, votad sin recelo la candidatura del comité republicano Federal!" (quoted in Termes, *Anarquismo,* p. 37).

15. This is according to the Dirección Central de las Sociedades Obreras (see Termes, *Anarquismo,* p. 37).

16. Termes gives an account of the *anti-quinta* campaign, ibid., pp. 42–56.

17. Hennessy, *The Federal Republic,* pp. 110–111.

18. Ibid., p. 107.

19. Ibid.

20. Hennessy defines *abajo-arriba* in the following way: "The two words mean 'under' and 'above', hence the use of this form to refer to a federation created from below with provinces taking the initiative in declaring a federal republic" (*ibid.,* p. 266). Francisco Pi y Margall, in formulating his own theory about the restructuring of society in his *La reacción y la revolución* (Madrid, 1854) and *Las nacionalidades* (Madrid, 1876), relied heavily upon the social theory of Pierre-Joseph Proudhon. See below, chap. 6; see also P.-J. Proudhon, *Du principe fédératif* (Paris, 1863), which was translated into Castilian as *El principio federativo* by Pi in 1868, and *De la justice dans la revolution et dans l'Eglise,* 3 vols. (Paris, 1858).

21. Pi briefly highlights the general strategy for the transition to a Federal Republic in *La república de 1873* (Madrid, 1874). See especially pp. 7–16.

22. For a description of Pi's rise in the Federal party during the revolts of 1869 see Hennessy, *The Federal Republic,* pp. 120–124.

23. Cf., for example Juan Paul y Angulo, *Las verdades revolucionarios* (Madrid, 1871).

24. In fact, the Bakuninist educational program bore striking similarities to that of Charles Fourier—who advocated the creation of *écoles-ateliers* for the workers, in which apprentice skills and intellectual discipline would be combined. For the educational ideas of Proudhon, see *Selected Writings of Pierre-Joseph Proudhon,* ed. Stuart Edwards and trans. Elizabeth Fraser (London, 1970), pp. 80–83. For an account of anarchist education in Spain during the last quarter of the nineteenth century, see Carolyn Boyd, "The Anarchists and Education in Spain, 1868–1909," *Journal of Modern History* 48, no. 4 (December 1976); Clara Lida, "Educación anarquista en la España del ochocientos," *Revista de Occidente* (Madrid), no. 97 (Apr. 1971), pp. 33–47; and Yvonne Turin's *L'education et l'école en Espagne* (Paris, 1957), chap. 3, pp. 312–320.

25. Bakunin, quoted in Lida, "Educación anarquista," p. 38.

26. Hennessy, *The Federal Republic,* p. 97.

27. See Termes, *Anarquismo,* Appendix I, pp. 265ff., and Renée Lamberet, *Mouvements ouvriers et socialistes: Chronologie et bibliographie. L'Espagne (1750–1936)* (Paris, 1953).

28. See Termes, *Anarquismo;* and, for an account of the history of *la huelga* in Spain, see Alfonso Colodsón's article "La idea de la huelga general hasta 1902: Intento de encuadramiento histórico," *Revista de Trabajo* (Madrid), no. 33 (1971), pp. 69–119.

29. On the development of working-class consciousness in Spain see José Maria Jover Zamora, *La conciencia burguesía y la conciencia obrera en la España contemporanea*, 2d. ed. (Madrid, 1956), and Carlos Seco Serrano, "La toma de conciencia de la clase obrera y los partidos políticos de la era Isabelina," in *La revolución de 1868: Historia, pensamiento, literatura*, ed. Clara Lida and Iris Zavala (New York, 1971), pp. 25–48.

30. Quoted in Termes, *Anarquismo*, p. 126.

31. Letter dated 29 May 1872, in Friedrich Engels, *Correspondence with Paul and Laura Lafargue*, vol. 3, 1891–1895, trans. Yvonne Kapp (Moscow, 1966), p. 448.

32. *El Imparcial* (Madrid), 25 May 1871.

33. See A. H. Layard dispatch to Earl Granville, 23 May 1871, Madrid, F.O. 72/1274–1276, no. 133, in the Layard Papers, British Museum, B.M. Add/ mss. 39121–4.

34. Circular signed by Anselmo Lorenzo, Francisco Mora, and Tomás González Morago, enclosed in Layard's dispatch of 5 June 1871, F.O. 72/1274–76, no. 149, in British Foreign Office Records, Public Record Office, London.

35. The fear that revolutionary communism might spread throughout Europe as a result of the Commune was by no means confined to Spain. In May 1871, Layard advised the British Foreign Office, "[W]hat we have to fear is that when the Communists are put down in France they may try their game again in Spain or Italy." For the reactions of other countries see also Jeronimo Becker, *Historia de las relaciónes exteriores de España durante el siglo xix* (Madrid, 1926), chap. 105.

36. See Mora, *Historia del socialismo obrero español, pp. 149–150.*

3: THE INTERNATIONAL AND THE COLLAPSE OF THE REPUBLIC

1. Edward H. Carr, *Michael Bakunin* (New York, 1975), p. 436.

2. See Max Nettlau's articles on the Alliance in Spain, *La Revista Blanca* (Barcelona), May–July 1926.

3. The members of the Alliance were based in Madrid and Barcelona, although individuals—such as Viñas, who was a medical student from Málaga— came from other regions.

4. F. Mora, *Historia del socialismo obrero español*, pp. 52–53.

5. *Ibid.* See also Lorenzo, *El proletariado militante* (Madrid, 1974), p. 42.

6. See the important extracts of letters that Bakunin sent to Morago and that Nettlau later published under the title "Cartas de Miguel Bakunin," *La Revista Blanca* (Barcelona), 1 July 1927.

7. Carr, *Bakunin*, pp. 438–440.

8. Bert Andreas and Miklós Molnár, "L'Alliance de la Democratie Socialiste. Proces-verbaux de la section de Geneve," in *Études et documents sur la Première Internationale in Suisse*, ed. Jacques Freymond (Geneva, 1964), pp. 250–251. See also Miklós Molnár, *Le declin de la Première Internationale*, (Geneva, 1963), pp. 208–212.

9. On Lafargue's activities in Spain see especially Engels, *Correspondence*

with Paul and Laura Lafargue, vol. 3; Morato, *Líderes,* pp. 123ff; and Nettlau, *Bakunin, la Internacional.*

10. International Working Men's Association, *The First International: Minutes of the Hague Congress of 1872, with Related Documents,* ed. and trans. Hans Gerth (Madison, Wis. 1958), p. 262.

11. Ibid., p. 190.

12. Ibid., p. 225.

13. Quoted in Nettlau, *Bakunin, la Internacional,* p. 100. For a discussion of Bakunin's ideas on secret societies see Michael Bakunin, *Oeuvres complètes de Bakounine,* vol. 1, introduced and annotated by Arthur Lehning (Paris, 1974); and Lehning, "Bakunin's Conceptions," pp. 57–81. Aileen Kelly offers a relentlessly cynical assessment of Bakunin's ideas in *Michael Bakunin* (Oxford, 1982).

14. For example, during the era of the First Republic there was the quasi-republican El Tiro Nacional, whose operations Lafargue described in detail to Engels. On secret societies in Spain see the following: V. M. Arbeloa, "Los socialistas españoles y la Masoneria," *Historia* (Madrid) vol. 16 (May 1979), pp. 37–48; Hennessy, *The Federal Republic;* Conrado Roure, *Recuerdos de mi larga vida,* vols. 1–3 (Barcelona, 1925); and Iris M. Zavala, *Masones, comuneros y carbonarios* (Madrid, 1971). It is also worth noting that nearly every revolutionary movement in Spain and Europe up till then had been directed by members of secret societies, and such well-known radicals as Proudhon, Bakunin, and Garibaldi had been Freemasons.

15. The claim that Bakunin's organization scheme was not the product of a "hard-headed realism" cannot be supported in the light of the experiences of the Spanish Alliancists. It is beyond doubt that their adherence to Bakunin's program contributed greatly to the FRE's ability to flourish during the early part of the 1870s and to survive the harsh circumstances of repression in the period 1874–1881. Cf. Kelly, *Bakunin,* p. 245.

16. Bakunin, *Oeuvres complètes,* vol. 4, *Étatisme et anarchie, 1873* (Paris, 1976), p. 225.

17. The question of whether or not the Alliance did exist after 1871 as a network of secret societies scattered throughout Europe which was being used by Bakunin to wreck the International has been the source of considerable debate ever since The Hague. At the time, Bakunin and his followers asserted that his "brotherhood" was nothing more than an informal grouping of revolutionaries which was maintained through the epistolary relations of its members. As we have seen, the Marxists forcefully challenged this view, although, in the end, doubts remained among the delegates. I tend to agree with E. H. Carr that the question cannot be answered with an unqualified yes or no. In order to determine what the Alliance was objectively and what it was supposed to be according to Bakunin or the Marxists would require a detailed examination of a large body of evidence, and thus it is not our intention to resolve this controversy. The best defense of the Bakuninist position has come from the scholars Max Nettlau and Arthur Lehning. Lehning's thoroughly documented introductions to Bakunin's *Oeuvres complètes* contain valuable information on this subject. For contrasting interpretations see especially

Kelly, *Bakunin*, and Arthur Mendel, *Michael Bakunin: Roots of Apocalypse* (New York, 1981).

18. Lorenzo, *El proletariado militante* (Madrid, 1974), p. 171.

19. Abad de Santillán, *Contribución*, pp. 293–294.

20. Bakunin quoted Ibid., pp. 269–272.

21. Abad de Santillán, *Contribución*, pp. 238–239.

22. Manuel Cerda, *Lucha de clases e industrialización* (Valencia, 1980), p. 112.

23. On the Alcoy rising see the following: Cerda, ibid.; Rafael Coloma, *La Revolución Internacionalista Alcoyana de 1873* (Alicante, 1959); Lorenzo, *El proletariado;* and Antonio Revert Corbes, *Agustín Albors, entre la libertad y el orden* (Alcoy, 1975).

24. Circular quoted in Friedrich Engels, "The Bakuninists at Work," written in Sept.–Oct. 1873, full text translated from the German and published in *Marx, Engels, and Lenin, Anarchism and Anarcho-Syndicalism* (Moscow, 1972), p. 133. Engels's analysis of the cantonalist revolts in Spain was intended primarily as a diatribe against Bakuninism. Above all, Engels indicted them for having failed to play an *active political role* at this crucial juncture. Notwithstanding its biased political content, the article contains some interesting insights into the cantonalist movement.

25. Ibid.

26. See David Hannay, "The Iberian Peninsula," in *The Cambridge Modern History* (Cambridge, 1910). Hannay was particularly knowledgeable about events in Spain in that he had served as a British consul to Spain during the 1870s.

27. Termes, *Anarquismo*, p. 253.

28. Report found in International Working Men's Association, Spanish Section, *Actas de los Consejos y Comisión Federal de la Región Española, (1870–1874)*, ed. Carlos Seco Serrano (Barcelona, 1969), vol. 2, p. 209; also cited in Antonio M.Calero Amor, *Movimientos sociales en Andalucía (1820–1936)* (Madrid, 1976), p. 116.

4: THE SPANISH FEDERATION IN THE PERIOD OF REPRESSION

1. Perhaps because of the rapidly growing notoriety of the International, some foreign observers, like the British ambassador in Madrid, A. H. Layard, tended to exaggerate the FRE's role in strike activity. He reported that the Internationalists were responsible for instigating strikes in districts throughout Spain and especially in the industrial regions of Catalonia and in Andalusia. (See Layard's dispatch to Earl Granville, 21 May 1873, Madrid, in the Layard Papers, British Museum Add. mss. 39123.) There are no accurate statistics on strikes during the last quarter of the nineteenth century. Beginning in 1905, the Institute for Social Reforms (IRS)—founded in 1903—began keeping a detailed record of strike activity. For statistics on strikes during the 1870s, see Rafael Flaquer Montequi's important study, *La clase obrera madrileña y la Primera Internacional 1868–1874* (Madrid, 1977). Flaquer, who has made a thorough

analysis of the International press in Madrid between 1868 and 1873, derived these figures from the following papers: *La Solidaridad, La Emancipación,* and *El Condenado.* See also the following: Lorenzo, *El proletariado militante* (Madrid, 1974), pp. 20–24, 276–79; Abad de Santillán, *Contribución,* pp. 234–256; Manuel R. Alarcón Caracuel, *El derecho de asociación obrera en España, (1839–1900)* (Madrid, 1975), pp. 241–244; Calero Amor, *Movimientos sociales,* pp. 8–80; Temma Kaplan, *The Anarchists of Andalusia, 1868–1903* (Princeton, 1977), pp. 80–85; and Tuñón de Lara, *El movimiento obrero,* pp. 178–235. Whether or not the increased number of strikes during this period can be directly attributed to Internationalist propaganda is subject to debate. Studies by historians like Peter Stearns, *Revolutionary Syndicalism and French Labor* (Rutgers, 1971), and by sociologists like Edward Shorter and Charles Tilly, *Strikes in France, 1930–1968* (Cambridge, 1974), assert that, at best, we can only guess as to the precise relationship between the two. Lacking any method of accurately surveying the workers who were actually involved in these strikes, and lacking any systematic studies of the pattern of strike activity (frequency, duration, and size), this group would argue that there is no reliable way to determine whether or not strikes in Spain at this time were either simply opportunistic or Internationalist inspired. On this question see also F. F. Ridley, "Syndicalism, Strikes and Revolutionary Action in France," in *Social Protest, Violence and Terror in Nineteenth- and Twentieth-Century Europe,* ed. Wolfgang J. Mommsen and Gerhard Hirschfeld (London, 1982), pp. 241–242.

2. Report of the Spanish Federal Commission to the London Congress (1871), quoted in Molnár, *Le declin,* pp. 211–212 (translator not identified).

3. Kaplan, *Anarchists,* p. 83

4. Proudhon's views on strikes are discussed in the following: Arnold Noland, "History and Humanity: The Proudhonian Vision," in *The Uses of History,* comp. and ed. Hayden V. White (Detroit, 1968); Proudhon, *Selected Writings*; and George Woodcock, *Pierre-Joseph Proudhon* (New York, 1972).

5. International Working Men's Association *The General Council of the First International: Minutes, 1865–1872* (Moscow, 1974), p. 292. Also see the study by the liberal economist Émile de Laveleye, *Socialism of To-Day* (London, 1884), p. 161, and the study by Marba, *Origen,* pp. 474–475. According to Laveleye, the International did not want the workers to take strikes lightly because "it would be bound to aid them, which would be often impossible; and secondly, because, if they should fail, its prestige would be seriously affected" (*Socialism,* p. 161).

6. Karl Marx, *On the First International,* ed. and trans. Saul K. Padover (New York, 1973), p. 547.

7. Both the syndicalist and militant strands of the International stemmed from the Bakuninist tradition. Guillaume, who represented the syndicalists, was opposed by the Italians over the issue of unionism at the Hague Congress of 1872. On the differences between the Bakuninists and syndicalists see Iurii M. Stekloff, *History of the First International* (London, 1928), pp. 306–308: "The Bakuninists are likewise akin to the syndicalists in their fondness for their idea of the general strike, but the two schools are sharply differentiated by their respective attitudes towards partial strikes. Whereas the syndicalists look upon every

strike, however small, as a revolutionary act, the anarchists, at the date we are now considering, were definitely opposed to partial strikes, or at best tolerated them as casual happenings that were impossible to prevent." The best documentary source of these debates as well as for the history of the Antiauthoritarian International (which I will discuss presently) is found in James Guillaume, *L'Internationale: Documents et souvenirs*, 4 vols. (Paris, 1905–1910).

8. Bakunin, quoted in Eugene Pyziur, *The Doctrine of Anarchism of Michael A. Bakunin* (Milwaukee, 1968), p. 68.

9. Ibid.

10. De Laveleye, *Socialism*, p. 182.

11. Viñas, quoted in Stekloff, *First International,* p. 306 (trans. Stekloff).

12. Michael Bakunin, *Bakunin on Anarchy,* ed. and trans. Sam Dolgoff (London, 1973), p. 173.

13. Tomás Morago, *El Condenado* (Madrid), 23 Sept. 1873; also cited in Alfonso Colodsón, "La idea de la huelga general hasta 1902," p. 78.

14. Kaplan, *Anarchists,* p. 83; Lorenzo, *El proletariado militante* (Madrid, 1974), pp. 299–300; and Alvarez Junco, *La ideología política,* pp. 260–262.

15. Cf. Walther Bernecker, "The Strategies of 'Direct Action' and Violence in Spanish Anarchism," in Mommsen and Hirschfeld, *Social Protest,* p. 92.

16. Quoted in Lorenzo, *El proletariado militante* (Madrid, 1974), pp. 338–339.

17. Max Nettlau, *Anarchy Through the Times* (New York, 1979), p. 220.

18. Peter Kropotkin, *Memoirs of a Revolutionist* (New York, 1971), p. 398.

19. Ibid., pp. 399–400. Nettlau credits Kropotkin for having been the first anarchist to employ the term; see *Anarchy,* p. 219.

20. Malatesta and Cafiero, quoted in Richard Hostetter, *The Italian Socialist Movement, I. Origins (1860–1882)* (Princeton, 1958), p. 368. See also Nunzio Pernicone, "Italian American Radicalism: Old World Origins and New World Developments," paper delivered to the Fifth Annual Conference of the American Italian Historical Association, November 1972.

21. See Stafford, *From Anarchism*. Stafford provides an excellent study of the evolution of the term "propaganda by the deed." See also *L'Avant-Garde* (Berne, La Chaux-de-Fonds), 2 June 1877 and 1 July 1877; Guillaume, *L'Internationale,* vol. 4, pp. 223–224; Marie Fleming, *The Anarchist Way to Socialism: Elisée Reclus and Nineteenth-Century European Anarchism* (London, 1979); and Ulrich Linse, " 'Propaganda by Deed' and 'Direct Action': Two Concepts of Anarchist Violence," in Mommsen and Hirschfeld, *Social Protest.*

22. On the Benevento episode, see the following: Pier Carlo Masini, *Storia degli anarchici italiani* (Milano, 1969); Luigi Fabbri, *Vida y pensamiento de Malatesta,* trans. and prologue by D. Abad de Santillán (Barcelona, 1938), pp. 35ff; and Hostetter, *Italian Socialist Movement, I. Origins.*

23. Accounts of the Trepov affair appear in Vera Broido, *Apostles into Terrorists* (New York, 1977), and Franco Venturi, *Roots of Revolution* (New York, 1966), pp. 596–599. For an account of the German shootings see Andrew R. Carlson, *Anarchism in Germany,* vol. 1 (New Jersey, 1972).

24. Stafford, *From Anarchism,* pp. 122ff.

25. Among other things, Albarracín (who used the pseudonym G. Albáges)

also served as correspondence secretary for the Jura Federation. See Marc Vuilleumier, "L'Internationale en Espagne (1877)," *International Review of Social History* (Amsterdam), vol. 9 (1964). On Kropotkin's relationship with Spaniards, see his *Memoirs,* and George Woodcock, with Ivan Avakumović, *The Anarchist Prince: Peter Kropotkin* (New York, 1971). Correspondence between Brousse and Viñas are reproduced in Stafford, *From Anarchism.*

26. Max Nettlau, *La Première Internationale en Espagne, (1868–1888)* (Dordrecht, 1969), p. 297.

27. At the *comarcal* conference held in 1877, the statutes adopted at the Verviers Congress were endorsed by the FRE. Also, within the FRE itself special departments were created that were dedicated to matters of propaganda and to conducting class war.

28. According to Nettlau there are no extant copies of these clandestine publications. Reprints of circulars, manifestos, and other documents of the period can be found in the following: IWMA, Spanish Section, *Actas,* vols. 1–2; *Antecedentes,* ed. Lida; Nettlau, *La Première Internationale*; and Termes, *Anarquismo.*

29. After the Moncasi incident, another attempt on Alfonso XII's life was made by the Galician Francisco Otero González in Dec. 1879.

30. James Russell Lowell, *Impressions of Spain* (Boston, 1899), pp. 87–92. According to the anarchist thinker Ricardo Mella, none of the attempts on the life of Alfonso XII was "an act of anarchism or inspired by anarchism"; see his article in *Natura* (Barcelona), no. 9 (1 Feb. 1904).

31. As reported by the London *Times,* 5 Dec. 1878.

32. Abad de Santillán, *Contribución,* vol. 1, p. 295.

33. Cited in Clara E. Lida, "Agrarian Anarchism in Andalusia: Documents on the Mano Negra," *International Review of Social History* (Amsterdam), no. 14 (1969), p. 327. See also *Le Révolté* (Geneva), 23 Aug. 1879.

34. Members of the Federal Commission included J. García Viñas, T. Soriano, Miguel Nacher, Anselmo Lorenzo, and Rafael Farga Pellicer.

35. Bakunin, *Bakunin on Anarchy,* p. 255 (trans. Sam Dolgoff). Thus, according to Bakunin, trade unions were "creating not only the ideas but also the facts of the future itself." It should also be noted that Bakunin considered trade unions on the whole as insufficient in themselves to be a tool for social transformation.

36. Temma Kaplan, *Anarchists,* p. 114. Additional information on Viñas can be found in Soledad Gustavo, "El doctor José García Viñas," *La Revista Blanca* (Barcelona), 1 Oct. 1931, and Morato, *Líderes,* p. 102.

37. Paul Lafargue, in Engels, *Correspondence with Paul and Laura Lafargue,* vol. 3, pp. 413, 430.

38. Lorenzo, *El proletariado militante* (Madrid, 1974), p. 350.

39. Bakunin, *Bakunin on Anarchy,* p. 167 (trans. Sam Dolgoff). He went on to say: "The preamble of the statutes of the International states: 'The emancipation of the workers is the task of the workers themselves.' It is absolutely right. This is the fundamental principle of our great association. But the workers know little about theory and are unable to grasp the implications of this principle. The only way for the workers to learn theory is through practice: *emancipa-*

tion through practical action. It requires the full solidarity of the workers in their struggle against their bosses, through the *trade unions* and the building up of resistance (strike funds)" (ibid.).

40. Biographical information on the Internationalists discussed in this section was obtained from a variety of sources. Apart from the anarchist press (1872–1896), the following were consulted: Abad de Santillán, *Contribución*; Lorenzo, *El proletariado militante*; Morato, *Líderes*; Vladimiro Muñoz, *Antología acrata español* (Barcelona, 1974); Nettlau, *La Première Internationale en Espagne*; the journals *Reconstruir* (Buenos Aires), 1960–1977, and *La Revista Blanca* (Barcelona), segunda época, 1923–1936; and Termes, *Anarquismo*.

41. J. Termes, *Anarquismo*, pp. 232–233.

42. See Max Nettlau, "La Internacional en España, 1874–1888: Impressiones sobre el socialismo en España," a series of articles which first appeared in *La Revista Blanca* (Barcelona) in Oct. 1928.

43. Nettlau to José García Viñas, 16 Jan. 1929, in the Max Nettlau Papers, International Institute for Social History, Amsterdam.

5: ANARCHISM AND THE RESTORATION

1. The Fusionist Liberal party, as Sagasta and his supporters were called, comprised groups that had descended from the old Progressives. See Raymond Carr, *Spain, 1808–1939* (Oxford, 1970), pp. 356–358.

2. On the Restoration period see especially Melchor Fernández Almagro, *Historia política de la España contemporanea*, vols. 1–2 (Madrid, 1969); Joan Connelly Ullman, *The Tragic Week* (Harvard, 1968); and G. H. B. Ward, *The Truth About Spain* (London, 1911).

3. Raymond Carr, *Modern Spain* (Oxford, 1980), p. 8.

4. Alarcón Caracuel, *Derecho de asociación obrera*, pp. 257–258.

5. Lorenzo, *El proletariado militante* (Mexico [1945?]), pp. 421–422.

6. Circulation figures for *La Revista Social* were obtained from Abad de Santillán, *Contribución*, vol. 1, p. 341, and Nettlau, *La Première Internationale en Espagne*. *La Anarquía* (Madrid), 28 Nov. 1890, gives a higher circulation figure of 24,000, whereas José Cascales y Muñoz gives the much more conservative estimate of 10,000 in his *El apostolado moderno. Estudio histórico-crítico del socialismo y el anarquismo hasta terminar el siglo XIX* (Barcelona, 1913).

7. See Abad de Santillán, *Contribución*, vol. 1.

8. On congresses held in this period see *Crónica de los Trabajadores de le Región Española* (Barcelona) 1882–1884.

9. These statistics are taken from the official publication of the FTRE that appeared between Dec. 1882 and 1885, *Crónica de los Trabajadores de la Región Española* (Barcelona), libro primero (n.d.), p. 3. Lorenzo, *El proletariado militante* (Madrid, 1974), p. 425, puts the total membership of the Regional Federation in 1882 at 49,000 of whom 30,047 were from Andalusia, 13,181 from Catalonia, 2,355 from Valencia, 1,550 from Castile, 847 from Galicia, 689 from Aragon and 710 from the Basque region. Figures used by Juan Díaz del Moral differ significantly from Lorenzo's because he includes sections in Andalusia which were affiliated with the Federation but which were not

represented at Seville: 218 federations, 663 sections, and 57,934 members. See his *Historia de las agitaciones,* p. 129. The statistics on the FRE in 1881 also vary according to the source. The ones used here were given to the anti-authoritarian Congress of London in July 1881 by the Federal Commission. See also Abad de Santillán, *Contribución,* pp. 301–302.

10. See *La Federación Igualadina* (Igualada), 30 Mar. 1883 (this periodical was published between Feb. 1883 and July 1885), and *La Propaganda* (Vigo), 25 Feb. 1883.

11. The literature on the *Mano Negra* affair is extensive. For contemporary accounts see especially *El Imparcial* (Madrid) and *La Revista Social* (Madrid). The ethnographic study made by Bernaldo de Quiros y Pérez, *Bandolerismo y delincuencia subversiva en Andalucía,* was published in Madrid in 1913. The debates surrounding the affair were rekindled several times. For those at the turn of the century, see *La Mano Negra* (Paris, 1902) and *La Mano Negra et l'opinion française* (Paris, 1903). The debates were again renewed during the twenties, when Soledad Gustavo (*La Revista Blanca* [Barcelona], 15 Oct 1927) challenged the interpretation given by Conrado Roure in his autobiography, *Recuerdos* (originally published serially in *El Diluvio* [Barcelona]). The debates were rekindled in recent years with the publication of several books and articles on the subject; see Demetrio Castro Alfín, *Hambre en Andalucía: Antecedentes y circunstancias de la Mano Negra* (Córdoba, 1986); Lida, "Agrarian Anarchism"; Jacques Maurice, "Conflicto agrario y represión preventiva: Los grandes procesos de Jerez en 1883," *Estudios de Historia Social* (Madrid), nos. 22–23, (1982); and Glen A. Waggoner, "The Black Hand Mystery: Rural Unrest and Social Violence in Southern Spain, 1881–1883," in *Modern European Social History,* ed. Robert J. Bezucha (Lexington, Mass., 1972).

12. Reprinted in Lida, "Agrarian Anarchism," pp. 337ff.

13. *Crónica de los Trabajadores de la Región Española* (Barcelona), libro primero (1883), p. 25.

14. Ibid., pp. 51–52.

15. Cited in Waggoner, "The Black Hand," p. 183.

16. See Lida, "Agrarian Anarchism," p. 336.

17. For examples of such fabrications see Brenan, *Labyrinth,* p. 69, and Termes, *Anarquismo.*

18. Waggoner, "The Black Hand," p. 181.

19. *La Revolución Social* (clandestine), April 1885.

20. Statutes reproduced in Lida, "Agrarian Anarchism," p. 341–344.

21. *La Revolución Social* (clandestine), the mouthpiece of Los Desheredados, declared itself the organ of anarchist collectivist principles.

22. Kaplan, *Anarchists,* p. 148.

23. According to Eudaldo Canibell, the Federal Commission received death threats from a group calling itself *La Mano Negra.* Max Nettlau, who believed that the group never existed, claimed that Canibell had erred in the letter by calling it "La Mano Negra" and that he had probably meant to say "Los Desheredados." However, there is no hard evidence linking the *Los Desheredados* with death threats of any kind. It is likely that Canibell was referring to

the mysterious letters—presumably faked by the authorities—sent to the Federal Commission just before the Mano Negra scandal erupted. See Nettlau, *La Première Internationale*, p. 430.

24. *La Revolución Social* (clandestine), Apr. 1885. See also Nettlau, *La Première Internationale*, p. 430.

25. For the Valencia Congress, see *La Autonomía* (Seville), 1883, and *Crónica de los Trabajadores de la Región Española* (Barcelona), 1883. Decline in actual membership of FTRE is quoted in Federación de Trabajadores de la Región Española, *Memoria de los Trabajos realizados por la C.F. en la desempeño de su cargo, 1887 a 1889* (Valencia, 1889).

26. Nettlau, "La Internacional en España," *La Revista Blanca* (Barcelona), Oct. 1928, p. 518.

27. Francisco Tomás's articles, entitled "Del Nacimiento de las ideas anarco-colectivistas en España," *La Revista Social* (Madrid), were serialized between 1883 and 1884.

28. On the activities of José Llunas and Rafael Farga Pellicer, see Morato, *Líderes*, pp. 169–175 and 79–94, respectively. On Francisco Tomás, see the necrology published in *La Revista Blanca* (Barcelona), 1 Jan. 1929, pp. 436–438.

29. In its new location (Sans), *La Revista Social* survived for several months, 15 Jan. 1885 until Nov. of that year. Throughout this time, Serrano seems to have retained his dominating influence on the paper.

30. Nettlau, "La Internacional en España," pp. 547–548.

6: THE DEVELOPMENT OF A SCHISM

1. There are in fact differing interpretations of the collectivist/communist debate, most of which contrast significantly with the one offered here. Gerald Brenan tells us that the real meaning of this dispute lay in the issue whether or not the anarchists should open up their organization to the masses or close their ranks to a core of devoted revolutionaries. Temma Kaplan argues that the debate involved much more than this. She sees it as a conflict between, on one hand, the so-called reformist elements within the anarchist movement—i.e., the collectivists/syndicalists—and, on the other hand, the genuinely revolutionary elements of the "communalist" tendency. The former, according to her, were concerned primarily with winning rights and reforms for workers within individual labor organizations, whereas the latter sought to achieve unity among all the different kinds of workers within the anarchist movement, including the *braceros*, the unemployed, and women. For further information on the collectivist/communist debate see the following sources: Alvarez Junco, *La ideología política*; Cascales y Muñoz, *El apostolado moderno*; and Juan Montseny y Carret (Federico Urales), *La evolución de la filosofía en España*, ed. and intro. Rafael Pérez de la Dehesa (Madrid, 1968).

2. Palmiro de Lidia, "Evocando el pasado," *La Revista Blanca* (Barcelona), July 1927, p. 211.

3. Pi y Margall, *La reacción y la revolución*, pp. 180ff. See also the appendix in Hennessy, *The Federal Republic*, pp. 258–265, for a concise exegesis of Pi's political theory. On Pi's legacy to the anarchists, see *Huelga General* (Barce-

lona), 5 Dec. 1901; Ricardo Mella, *Ideario,* vol. 1 of *Obras completas* (Toulouse, 1975), pp. 247–249; and Urales, *La evolución.*

4. For a discussion of the impact of positivism on the Spanish socialists, see especially E. Fernández García, *Marxismo y positivismo en el socialismo español* (Madrid, 1981). On Darwinism in Spain, see the essay by Thomas Glick in *The Comparative Reception of Darwinism,* ed. Thomas Glick (Austin, Tex., 1972).

5. See the biographical sketches found in Serrano's posthumously published study, *La moral del progreso o la religion natural* (Madrid: Sabadell, 1888), and in *La Anarquía* (Madrid), 22 Nov. 1890.

6. Lorenzo, *El proletariado militante* (Madrid, 1974), p. 32.

7. *La Revista Social,* which was until Feb. 1874, published as the organ of the Union of Manufacturers, maintained an apolitical but nonrevolutionary line during the repression, and as such it was not forced into clandestinity. With the reemergence of the working-class movement in 1881, it resumed its role as an anarchist organ.

8. Juan Serrano y Oteiza, *La Revista Social* (Madrid), June 1881.

9. Ibid.

10. See, for example, the underground newspaper *El Municipio Libre* (1879–1880) and "Asociacion Internacional de los Trabajadores: Programa de realización práctica inmediata aprobado por las conferencias," in which one of the stated goals of the International movement was to establish a "Municipio libre, junta revoluciónaria que empezará a funcionar cuando la Federación local lo determine" (document reproduced in *Antecedentes,* ed. Lida, pp. 416–418.

11. Serrano, *La Revista Social* (Madrid), 10 Jan. 1882. See also, Nettlau, *Anarchy,* p. 282.

12. For ideas of José Llunas y Pujols, see his "Organización y aspiraciónes de la Federación de Trabajadores de la Región España," in *Certámen socialista. Primer* (Catalonia, 1885), and Nettlau, *Anarchy* pp. 284–287.

13. Max Nettlau discusses the origins of anarchist communism in "La idea anarquista: Su pasado, su provenir," *La Revista Blanca* (Barcelona), 1925, and in his biography *Errico Malatesta. La vida de un anarquista* (Buenos Aires, 1923), chap. 10.

14. For further information on the differences between collectivism and communism see: Fleming, *Anarchist Way;* Martin A. Miller, *Kropotkin* (Chicago, 1976), esp. chap. 9; and Stafford, *From Anarchism,* chap. 3.

15. A good summary of anarchist communism can also be found in Carlo Cafiero, *Anarchie et communisme* (Foix, 1899), extracted from Cafiero's contributions to *Le Révolté* (Geneva), 1880.

16. James Guillaume, "On Building the New Social Order," full text reprinted in Bakunin, *Bakunin on Anarchy,* pp. 361–362 (trans. Sam Dolgoff). Guillaume's pamphlet was translated into Spanish in 1876.

17. On the congress held in La Chaux-de-Fonds, see *Le Révolté* (Geneva), 4 and 18 Oct. 1879.

18. See Nettlau, *Anarchy,* p. 291.

19. Lida, "Evocando el pasado," pp. 138–139.

20. Francisco Pagés (?), in *La Justicia Humana* (Gracia), 18 Apr. 1886.

21. This characterization of the divisions in the FTRE appeared in *Los Desheredados* (Sabadell), 26 Dec. 1884.

22. Serrano, *La Revista Social* (Sans), 2 Apr. 1885.

23. Ibid.

24. Serrano, *La Revista Social* (Sans), 23 Apr. 1885.

25. *Certámen socialista. Primer* (Catalonia, 1885).

7: THE DEMISE OF THE FTRE

1. Accounts of the Madrid Congress appear in Abad de Santillán, *Contribución;* FTRE, *Memoria;* and Max Nettlau, *Die Erste Bluetezeit der Anarchie, 1886–1894* (Liechtenstein, 1981), and his *La Première Internationale en Espagne.*

2. See *El Productor* (Barcelona), 8 and 22 Feb. 1889.

3. Ibid.

4. *La Solidaridad* (Seville), 19 Aug. 1888.

5. Mella, *La Solidaridad* (Seville), 6 Jan. 1889.

6. *El Proletario* (San Feliu de Guixols), 17 Oct. 1890.

7. On the formation of the OARE, see FTRE, *Memoria.*

8. Mella, *La Solidaridad* (Seville), 6 Jan. 1889.

9. Tony Judt, *Socialism in Provence* (Cambridge, 1981), p. 59. Cf. the example of working-class associational life found in Standish Meacham, *A Life Apart: The English Working Class, 1890–1914* (London, 1977).

10. *Acracia* (Barcelona), Jan. 1886, p. 2.

11. An excellent survey of anarchist literature of the period 1880–1913 is Litvak, *La musa libertaria.* See also Lily Litvak, ed., *El cuento anarquista, (1880–1911)* (Madrid, 1982); Clara E. Lida, "Literatura anarquista y anarquismo litertario," *Nueva Revista de Filología Hispánica* (Mexico City), vol. 19 (1970), no. 2; and José Carlos Mainer, "Notas sobre la lectura obrera en España (1890–1930)," in *Teoría y práctica del movimiento obrero en España (1900–1936),* ed. Albert Balcells (Valencia, 1977).

12. The behavior Mella is referring to is an example of the influence of a puritanical strain in anarchist thought. Puritanism is one of several strands of anarchist ideology that can be traced from the beginnings of the movement in 1868 up to the Civil War. This tendency, which sprang from the recognition of a moral dichotomy between the proletariat and the middle classes, promoted a life-style unfettered by materialistic values. Thus, excessive drinking, smoking, and other practices that were perceived as middle-class attributes were nearly always censured. Some anarchists even went so far as to claim that alcoholism was encouraged by the state since the government—which controlled the production and sale of alcohol—grew richer as the number of alcoholics climbed. For examples of this tendency, see *El Productor* (Barcelona), 1887–1893, *El Socialismo* (Cádiz), 1886–1891, and *La Solidaridad* (Seville), 1888–1889. Later, puritanism was promoted in such prestigious and influential journals as *La Revista Blanca* (Madrid), 1898–1905, and (Barcelona) 1923–1936. A vivid portrait of the self-abnegating revolutionary type is found in Vicente Blasco Ibáñez, *La bodega* (Madrid, 1904; English trans., New York, 1919), in which

the character Fermín Salvatierra is modeled on the the legendary anarchist Fermín Salvochea.

13. See Jover Zamora, *Conciencia burguesía.*

14. There are no accurate statistics on the number of women employed during the 1880s and 1890s. According to one source—Great Britain, Royal Commission on Labour, *Foreign Reports,* vol. 9, *Report on the Labour Question in Spain and Portugal (1893–1894)* (London, 1894)—women were to be found engaged in all sorts of work. Among other occupations, they were employed in mining, the textile trades, dynamite works, laundry work, dressmaking, and home industries such as weaving and lacemaking. See also Temma Kaplan, "Women and Spanish Anarchism," in *Becoming Visible,* ed. Renate Bridenthal and Claudia Koonz (Boston, 1977).

15. On anarchist cafés see Pedro Esteve, *A los anarquistas de España y Cuba* (Chicago, 1893), pp. 53–55.

16. See, for example, *La Alarma* (Seville), 22 Nov. 1889.

17. De Lidia, "Evocando el pasado," p. 117. Another contemporary account of anarchist associational life can be found in Juan Montseny y Carret (Federico Urales), "Mi paso por las sociedades obreras españoles," *La Revista Blanca* (Barcelona), 1 Sept. 1928.

18. *Tierra y Libertad* (Barcelona), 1 Nov. 1888.

19. Brenan, *Labyrinth,* p. 163.

20. Gil Maestre, "El anarquismo en España. Y el especial en Cataluña," *Revista Contemporanea* (Barcelona), 30 Aug. 1897, p. 371. A different estimate is given by Stoddard Dewey, who cites a private investigation completed in 1893 which was conducted in workingmen's clubs, cafés, and other haunts of anarchists in Barcelona. According to this there were some 200 *anarquistas de acción* in the city. See Dewey, "The Anarchist Movement in Spain," *The Contemporary Review* (London), 1902.

8: ANARQUISMO SIN ADJETIVOS

1. *Tierra y Libertad* (Barcelona), 16 June 1888.

2. Max Nettlau, *La anarquía a través de los tiempos* (Madrid, 1978), p. 157–159. See J. Vives Terradas's correspondence with Nettlau in the Max Nettlau Papers.

3. See, for example, Paul Avrich, *An American Anarchist: The Life of Voltairine de Cleyre* (Princeton, 1978); Muñoz, *Antología;* Nettlau, "La idea anarquista," and his "Ricardo Mella y el anarquismo sin adjetivos (1900)," *La Protesta Humana* (Buenos Aires), suplemento semenal, 1926; and Urales, *La evolución.*

4. Two other distinguished representatives of *anarquismo sin adjetivos* were Juan Montseny y Carret (Federico Urales), e.g., *Las preocupaciones de los despreocupados* (1891), and Anselmo Lorenzo.

5. There is very little biographical material on Tarrida. I found the following quite useful: P. Friedberg, "Tarrida del Mármol," *The Socialist Review* (London), 1915; Nettlau's correspondence with Tarrida del Mármol in the Max Nettlau Papers; Pedro Vallina, *Mis memorias,* vol. 1 (Caracas, Venezuela,

1967); and Juan Montseny y Carret's (Federico Urales) prologue to Tarrida's posthumously published *Problemas trancendentales* (Barcelona, 1930). Tarrida himself wrote that of all the anarchists of the period Anselmo Lorenzo was most responsible for "planting in my mind seeds of love for libertarian ideas." See his preface to Anselmo Lorenzo, *Justo Vives* (Barcelona, 1893).

6. Friedberg, "Tarrida," p. 688.

7. Ibid., p. 683.

8. Fernando Tarrida del Mármol, "Anarquismo sin adjetivos," quoted in Muñoz, *Antología*, pp. 31–32.

9. Ricardo Mella, in *La Solidaridad* (Seville), 13 Jan. 1889. Nettlau (as well as those who follow him) errs when he cites the date of this article as 12 Jan. 1889.

10. The best biographical studies on Mella are Diego Abad de Santillán, "Septiembre de 1861: Nacimiento de Ricardo Mella," *Reconstruir* (Buenos Aires), no. 14 (Sept.–Oct. 1961); J. A. Durán, "Ricardo Mella. Nacimiento y muerte de un anarquista (1861–1925)," *Tiempo de Historia* (Madrid), Feb. 1976; Morato, *Líderes*, pp. 247–253; Muñoz, *Antología*, pp. 83–147; José Prat's prologue to Mella's *Ideario*; and Eleuterio Quintanilla's prologue to Mella's *Ensayos y conferencias*, vol. 2 of *Obras completas* (Gijon, 1934). On his political philosophy, see Agustí Segarra, *Federico Urales y Ricardo Mella, teóricos anarquismo español* (Barcelona, 1977).

11. Juan Montseny y Carret (Federico Urales), *Mi vida*, vol. 3 (Barcelona, 1932), p. 26.

12. Collections of Mella's writings have appeared regularly since the turn of the century, especially during the Second Republic and Civil War era. I have consulted the following anthologies of his works: *Los anarquistas* (Madrid, 1977), which is a reprint of his 1896 study of Cesare Lombroso's theory of anarchism's connection to criminality; *Breves apuntes sobre las pasiones humanas* (Barcelona, 1976), a reprint of various essays, many of which appeared in an earlier collection entitled *Cuestiones sociales* (Valencia, 1912); *Cuestiones de enseñanza libertaria* (Madrid, 1979); *Forjando un mundo libre* (Madrid, 1978), which reprints most of Mella's major essays, including his valuable study on the Jerez rising; *Ideario*; and *El pensamiento de Ricardo Mella*, ed. B. Cano Ruiz (Mexico D.F., 1979).

13. Ricardo Mella, in *La Propaganda* (Vigo), 25 Aug. 1882; also cited in J. A. Durán, *Entre el anarquismo y el librepensamiento* (Madrid, 1977), p. 78.

14. Abad de Santillán makes the point that, in his early writings on communism, Mella was probably unfamiliar with the works of Kropotkin and Reclus. Yet we know that Mella knew French, so he could easily have read their writings in *La Révolte*. In addition, Mella never lost his distrust of communism, even years after he had read the leading anarchist communists.

15. Ricardo Mella, "Evolución y revolución," *La Solidaridad* (Seville), 20 Jan. 1889.

16. Ricardo Mella, "Diferencias entre el comunismo y el colectivismo," in *Certámen Socialista. Primer*, p. 219.

17. Mella's "La reacción y la revolución" appeared serially in *Acracia* (Barcelona) between June 1887 and Apr. 1888.

18. Ricardo Mella, *La Nueva Utopía*, in *Certámen Socialista. Segundo* (Barcelona, 1889), p. 212.

19. Ibid., p. 210.

20. Mella has been unfairly criticized by historians like Nettlau and Temma Kaplan for ignoring the plight of the old, the infirm, and others who could not produce in future society. This is based on a misunderstanding of one of Mella's articles, which appeared in *La Solidaridad* (Seville), 12 September 1888. In this, he makes the point that in an anarchist society there will be no need for *state-organized* relief for the poor and sick because the solidarity of the spontaneous associations of free people will provide for such needs. Cf. Kaplan, *Anarchist,* p. 141.

21. *Certámen Socialista. Segundo,* p. 210.

22. Cf. Herbert Spencer's view of social evolution in *Social Statics* (New York, 1870). On the relationship between science and Spanish anarchism, see Floreal Castilla, "Ciencia y anarquismo," *Ideas* (Barcelona), November–December 1980.

23. Another example of an anarchist utopia is by M. Burgués, *El siglo de oro* (Barcelona, 1890), which was also written for the Segundo Certámen Socialista.

24. *La Controversia* (Valencia), 17 June 1893.

25. Paul Avrich, *An American Anarchist,* chap. 6.

9: THE HAYMARKET TRAGEDY AND THE
ORIGINS OF MAY DAY

1. The best secondary works on the subject of May Day, the Haymarket affair, and Spanish anarchism are Abad de Santillán, *Contribución,* vol. 1; Alvarez Junco, *La ideología política*; Juan Hernández Les, "En los inicios del primero de mayo. La cuestión de las ocho horas," *Tiempo de Historia* (Madrid), May 1977; Temma Kaplan, "Civic Rituals and Patterns of Resistance in Barcelona, 1890–1930," in *The Power of the Past,* ed. Pat Thane, Geoffrey Crossick, and Roderick Floud (Cambridge, 1984); Litvak, *Musa libertaria*; Nettlau, *La Première Internationale en Espagne*; Rafael Núñez Florencio, *El terrorismo anarquista, 1888–1909* (Madrid, 1983); and Lucia Rivas, *Historia del primero de Mayo en España: Desde 1900 hasta la segunda república* (Madrid, 1987).

2. *Acracia* (Barcelona), Oct. 1886, p. 110.

3. *Tierra y Libertad* (Barcelona), 1 Nov. 1888.

4. *Víctima del Trabajo* (Valencia), no. 11, 10 Jan. 1891.

5. *Acracia* (Barcelona), Nov. 1887, p. 377.

6. Mella's statement appeared in his pamphlet entitled "La tragedia de Chicago" (1889). This edition was later reprinted in *Cuestiones sociales,* with the quote appearing on p. 269. See also *La Solidaridad,* 9 Dec. 1888. It should be pointed out that the "Martyrs" included not only those who had died—four were hanged and Louis Lingg committed suicide while awaiting execution—but also Samuel Fielden, Oscar Neebe, and Michael Schwab, all of whom were later pardoned.

7. See Peter Kropotkin's statement to this effect in *Freedom* (London), Dec. 1888; cited in Henry David, *History of the Haymarket Affair* (New York,

1958), p. 534, and in Paul Avrich, *The Haymarket Tragedy* (Princeton, 1984), p. 412.

8. *Freedom* (London), Jan. 1890.

9. *La Alarma* (Seville), 22 Nov. 1889; *Tierra y Libertad* (Barcelona), 1 Nov. 1888.

10. Mella, "La tragedia de Chicago," in his *Cuestiónes sociales*, p. 271. See also *El Productor* (Barcelona), issues for May and June 1890.

11. Pablo Iglesias, quoted in Maurice Dommanget, *Histoire du Premier Mai* (Paris, 1972), p. 415.

12. See James Joll, *The Second International* (New York, 1966), pp. 48–65.

13. Quoted in G. D. H. Cole, *History of Socialist Thought*, vol. 3, pt. 1, *The Second International, 1889–1914* (London, 1956), p. 9.

14. Pablo Iglesias, in *El Socialista* (Madrid), 1 May 1910.

15. Phil H. Goodstein, *The Theory of the General Strike from the French Revolution to Poland* (New York, 1984), pp. 110–114. Although at the Paris Congress (1889) it was decided to hold May Day manifestations on the first, in Great Britain and in parts of Spain demonstrations were held on the fourth (Sunday). In Great Britain this practice reflected the trade unions' desire to avoid both violent confrontations with the authorities and any stoppage of work.

16. For a description of May Day festivities in Madrid, see *El Socialista* (Madrid), 16 May 1890, and *El Socialista* (Toulouse), 1 May 1950.

17. Among other things, they asked for the eight-hour day, the abolishment of night work for women and workers less than eighteen years of age, and the prohibition of labor for children under fourteen years old. Detailed accounts of the 1890 May Day celebrations can be found in *El Socialista* (Madrid) and the anarchist paper *El Productor* (Barcelona). On the socialists generally, see Aisa, with Arbeloa, *Historia*; José Andrés Gallego, "La UGT no nació socialista," *Historia* (Madrid), vol. 16 (May 1979); Fusi, *Política obrera*; Miguel Izard, *Revolució industrial i obrerisme: Les "Tres Clases de Vapor" a Cataluñya (1869–1913)* (Barcelona, 1970); Morato, *El partido*; Manuel Pérez Ledesma, "El Primero de Mayo de 1890. Los orígenes de una celebración," *Tiempo de Historia* (Madrid), May 1976; also his "La Unión General de Trabajadores: Socialismo y reformismo," *Estudios de Historia Social* (Madrid), January–June 1979; Manuel Tuñon de Lara, "Días de infancia," *Historia* (Madrid), vol. 16, (May 1979); and chap. 7 of his *El movimiento obrero*.

18. On the Bilbao strike see Great Britain, Royal Commission on Labour, *Foreign Reports*, vol. 9, *Report (1893–1894)*; and Eugenio Lasa Ayestaran, "Socialismo en Viscaya: La huelga general de Mayo de 1890," *Tiempo de Historia* (Madrid), June 1975.

10: TERRORISM AND THE ANARCHIST
MOVEMENT

1. *The New Review*, Jan. 1894, cited in Nhat Hong, *The Anarchist Beast: The Anti-Anarchist Crusade in Periodical Literature (1884–1906)* (Minneapolis, n.d.), p. 16.

2. *El Eco de Rebelde* (Zaragoza), 6 June 1895.

3. Dynamite, which was invented by Alfred Nobel in 1866, was manufactured widely in Europe for its industrial applications. It was not until the 1880s and 1890s that it was commonly used as a weapon by the anarchists.

4. Robert Hunter, *Violence and the Labor Movement* (New York, 1914), p. 69.

5. *El Eco de Ravachol* (Sabadell), 21 Jan. 1893.

6. In July 1889, the anarchists had sent representatives to the two socialist congresses (Possibilist and Marxist) held in Paris. The anarchist meeting was held six weeks after these; see *La Revolución Social* (Barcelona), 2 Sept. and 12 Oct. 1889.

7. Ward, *Truth About Spain*, p. 138.

8. Ricardo Mella, *Natura* (Barcelona), no. 9 (1 Feb. 1904) p. 135.

9. *Times* (London), 14 Jan. 1889.

10. *New York Times*, 3 Apr. 1892. The police eventually named some dozen conspirators in the bombing plot.

11. Brenan, *Labyrinth*, pp. 156–157.

12. Ricardo Mella, *Los sucesos de Xeres* (Barcelona, 1893).

13. The standard work from the millenarian perspective is Hobsbawm's, *Primitive Rebels*. More recently, this explanation of the Jerez rising has been advanced by José Aguilar Villagran, *El asalto campesino a Jerez de la Frontera en 1892* (Jerez de la Frontera, 1984). For a contrasting view, see, Gérard Brey, "Crisis económica, anarquismo y sucesos de Jerez, 1886–1892," in *Seis estudios sobre el proletariado Andaluz (1868–1939)* (Córdoba, 1984).

14. On the life of Fermín Salvochea see the following: *Un anarchiste entre la legende et l'histoire: Fermín Salvochea*, by Gerard Brey et al. (Paris, 1987); Ignacio Moreno Aparicio, *Aproximación histórica a Fermín Salvochea* (Cádiz, 1982); Vladimiro Muñoz, "Una cronólogia de Fermín Salvochea," *Reconstruir;* (Buenos Aires), no. 63.; *El Porvenir Social* (Barcelona), 21 Mar. 1896, p. 1; Rudolf Rocker, *Fermín Salvochea* (Toulouse, France, 1945); Pedro Vallina, *Crónica de un revolucionario. Trazos de la vida de Salvochea* (Paris, 1958).

15. Díaz del Moral, *Historia de las agitaciones*, p. 138.

16. Vallina, *Crónica*, p. 34.

17. Max Nettlau, *Errico Malatesta* (Barcelona, 1933), p. 28. See also Fabbri, *Errico Malatesta*.

18. For Spanish press reports on the Jerez incident, see especially *El Heraldo de Madrid* and *El Imparcial* (Madrid), Jan.–Feb. 1892. The anarchist version of events appeared in *La Anarquía* (Madrid) and *El Productor* (Barcelona).

19. Mella, *Los sucesos*, pp. 41–44.

20. Kaplan, *Anarchists*, p. 172.

21. See Mella, *Los sucesos*, and Vallina, *Crónica*.

22. *La Anarquía* (Madrid), 1892. This tactic was used the next year by Belgian miners during a general strike. See Arnold Roller, *The Social General Strike* (Chicago, 1905), pp. 9–10.

23. Quoted in José Acosta Sánchez, *Andalucía* (Barcelona, 1978), pp. 167–168.

24. Vicente Blasco Ibáñez, *La bodega,* trans. Isaac Goldberg (New York, 1919), pp. 292–293.

25. *El Heraldo* article quoted in *El perseguido* (Buenos Aires), 14 Feb. 1892.

26. Hobsbawm, *Primitive Rebels,* p. 89. For further discussions on the primitive rebel thesis see especially, Jon Amsden, "Spanish Anarchism and the Stages Theory of History," *Radical History Review,* fall 1978; James Casey, "The Spanish Anarchist Peasant: How Primitive a Rebel?," *Journal of European Studies* 8 (1978); and the feature articles of the *Slavic Review* 41, no. 3 (Fall 1982).

27. On Pallás, see Joaquín Romero Maura, "Terrorism in Barcelona and Its Impact on Spanish Politics, 1904–1909," *Past and Present* (Oxford), no. 41 (1968); Juan Montseny y Carret (Federico Urales), *El proceso de un gran crimen* (La Coruña, 1895); *The Spectator* (London), 30 Sept. 1893; *El Perseguido* (Buenos Aires), 22 Oct. 1893; *El Imparcial* (Madrid), Sept.–Oct. 1893; Enric Jardí, *La ciutat de les bombes: El terrorisme anarquista a Barcelona* (Barcelona, 1964); and Núñez Florencio, *El terrorismo anarquista.*

28. *La Controversia* (Valencia), 7 Oct. 1893, p. 1.

29. Santiago Salvador French, quoted in M. Gil Maestre, "El anarquismo en España," *Revista Contemporanea* (Madrid), vol. 107 (Aug. 1897), p. 256.

30. On Santiago Salvador French, see Núñez Florencio, *El terrorismo anarquista.*

11: AFTERMATH OF REPRESSION

1. The procession itself was an example of the "public rituals" that were so common to Spanish cultural life during the nineteenth century. The celebration of Corpus Christi was an important date on the religious calendar, and as such it usually attracted key figures both from the church hierarchy and from the military. Thus it was significant that a bomb was thrown on this particular occasion, as it offered the best opportunity to attack these symbols of ruling-class power and authority.

2. Details of the bombing incident can be found in the following: *Times* (London), Aug. 1897; *The Spectator* (London), Aug.–Sept. 1897; Joseph McCabe, *The Martyrdom of Ferrer* (London, 1909), pp. 57–61; *Freedom* (London), Sept. 1897; Ricardo Mella and José Prat (R. M. y J. P.) *La barbarie gubermental en españa, Documentos sobre las torturas de Montjuich* ("Brooklyn," i.e., La Coruña, 1897); Fernando Tarrida del Mármol, *Les Inquisiteurs d'Espagne* (Paris, 1897); *El Imparcial* (Madrid), June–Aug. 1896 and Aug. 1897; *El Despertar* (New York), Aug. 1896; *El Socialista* (Madrid), June 1896; Ernest A. Vizetelly, *The Anarchists* (London, 1911; New York, 1972).

3. See Mella and Prat, *La barbarie.* Mella and Prat also warned the anarchists that they should no longer use terrorism as a way of demonstrating anarchist practices.

4. On Bonafoux's statement see Joaquín Romero Maura, "Terrorism in Barcelona."

5. Mella and Prat, *La barbarie,* pp. 11–12.

6. For an account of Montjuich tortures during the Pallás case, see Montseny (Urales), *El proceso*.

7. Quoted in *Liberty* (Boston), 7 Feb. 1897. This quote is taken from a letter sent by a "Brodjaga," the pseudonymn of a physician (German by birth) who was then living in Spain. While serving as an occasional correspondent for the Milwaukee paper *Der Freidenker*, he was arrested following the Corpus Christi day bombing incident.

8. Quoted in *Spanish Atrocities: The Barcelona Anarchists* (London, 1897), p. 3.

9. The Montjuich affair cut across class lines, and thus many middle-class politicians and intellectuals intervened on behalf of the prisoners. The case of pro-anarchist lawyer Pedro (Pere) Corominas, who had been accused of being one of the chief instigators of the bombing, became a *cause célèbre* during the trials. Thanks to the intervention of such notables as Joaquín Costa and Miguel de Unamuno, Corominas was spared his life. See G. J. G. Cheyne, "La intervención de Costa en el proceso de Montjuich," *Bulletin Hispanique* (Bordeaux), vol. 68, nos. 1–2 (Jan.–June 1966).

10. After examining all the available police records, Joaquín Romero Maura also reached the conclusion that there is no way of knowing the true identity of the bomb thrower. See his "Terrorism in Barcelona," p. 131.

11. The fact that Angiolillo was passionately moved by the Montjuich repressions gave rise to the mistaken view that he had personally witnessed the exhibition of former Montjuich prisoners in Trafalgar Square. According to the American anarchist Emma Goldman, for example, Angiolillo's crime was triggered by this dramatic expression of government cruelty and oppressiveness. See her *Anarchism and Other Essays* (New York, 1969), p. 102. The historian Hermia Oliver points out in her carefully researched study on anarchists in late Victorian England that the demonstration at Trafalgar took place after Angiolillo had killed Cánovas. See her *The International Anarchist Movement in Late Victorian London* (London, 1983).

12. On Angiolillo's meeting with Nakens, see Rafael Salillas, "Una página histórica fotografiada: La ejecución de Angiolillo," *Revue Hispanique* (Paris), vol. 19 (1908). Another version of Angiolillo's plot to kill Cánovas was advanced by Constant Leroy, the pseudonym of a former anarchist named José Sánchez González, who was at one time close to such Spanish libertarian figures as Pedro Esteve and Tarrida del Mármol. According to him, several foreign anarchist exiles living in Paris conspired to assassinate the prime minister. Francisco Ferrer, Charles Malato, Lorenzo Portet, Tarrida del Mármol, and the French journalist Henry Rochefort were the brains behind the conspiracy. They supposedly selected Angiolillo, who was known for his violent leanings, to carry out the deed. While residing in Marseilles, Angilollio was approached by Portet, who had been nominated by the Paris group to enlist his services as an assassin. Portet then accompanied Angiolillo to Spain, both posing as journalists. Although full of details, Leroy's theory rings false for several reasons. Given the prevailing state of repression in Spain, it is highly unlikely that anarchists like Tarrida—who not only was in principle opposed to regicide but who also knew first-hand the devasting effects of the Montjuich persecutions—would have participated in a

scheme that would most probably have invited further government action against the anarchists. Moreover Leroy was considered by some anarchists to be a police informant. And, finally, he wrote this exposé in the light of two widely publicized events: the Ferrer trial and execution of 1909 and the assassination of Canelejas in 1912. See Constant Leroy (José Sánchez Gonzáles), *Los secretos del anarquismo: Asesinato de Canalejas y el caso Ferrer* (Mexico, 1913). Yet another version of the plot to assassinate Cánovas suggested that Angiolillo was financed by Cuban rebels. See Fernández Almagro, *Historia política*.

13. *Times* (London), 9 Aug. 1897.

14. Ramón Sempau later wrote a novel about the Montjuich affair and his assassination attempt, *Los victimarios* (Barcelona, 1900).

15. On the resurgence of terrorism at the turn of the century see especially Romero Maura, "Terrorism in Barcelona," and Núñez Florencio, *El terrorismo anarquista*.

16. On José Prat's activities at this time, see the following: Iaacov Oved, *El anarquismo y el movimiento obrero en Argentina* (Mexico, 1978), pp. 67ff; José Prat's letters to Nettlau in the Max Nettlau Papers; and Prat's obituaries in *Cultura Libertaria* (Barcelona), 4 Aug. 1932, and *La Revista Blanca* (Barcelona), Aug. 1932.

17. A brief review of Bonafoux's anarchist associations in Paris is found in E. Inman Fox, "Two Anarchist Newspapers of 1898," *Bulletin of Hispanic Studies* (Liverpool), no. 41 (1964).

18. Ricardo Mella, "Le socialisme en Espagne," *L'Humanité Nouvelle* (Paris), vol. 1 (1897), no. 1. Mella gives the following totals for the socialist movement: 7,300 active members and 17,400 sympathizers. Mella's figures approximate those published in A. Hamon, *El socialismo y el Congreso de Londres. Estudio histórico* (La Coruña, 1896). In this report, which was derived from the minutes of 1896 International Workers' Congress (July and Aug.), the Spanish socialist movement was estimated to be 7,000 strong, with around 17,000 sympathizers. Anarchist membership was reported as 26,000, with 54,000 sympathetic to their cause.

19. *La Revista Blanca* survived in Madrid until 1905; a new series began in Barcelona in 1923 and continued until 1936. On the founding of the journal see Montseny (Urales), *Mi vida*, vol. 3.

20. For further discussion of the social views of the Generation of 1898 and their relationship to anarchism see the following: Carlos Blanco Aguinaga, *Juventud del 98* (Madrid, 1970); E. Inman Fox, "José Martínez Ruiz; Sobre el anarquismo del futuro Azorín," *Revista de Occidente* (Madrid), Feb. 1966; Lily Litvak, *A Dream of Arcadia. Anti-Industrialism in Spanish Literature 1895–1905* (Austin, Tex., 1975); Rafael Pérez de la Dehesa, "Estudio preliminar," in Montseny (Urales), *La evolución;* Donald L. Shaw, *The Generation of 1898 in Spain* (London, 1975); and Michael R. Weisser, *The Peasants of the Montes* (Chicago, 1976), chap. 6.

21. See Hobsbawm, *Revolutionaries*. Specifically, Hobsbawm asserts that Spanish anarchism had an irrational dimension that was given a philosophical basis by such thinkers as Friedrich Nietzsche, Georges Sorel, and Max Stirner. As we have already said, though, this current of thinking was confined to a tiny

group of middle-class anarchists and never informed the actions of the deeply committed members of the movement.

22. Fernand Pelloutier's early syndicalist writings were first translated into Spanish around the time of the Montjuich affair. See, for example, his "La anarquía Burguesía," *La Ciencia Social* (Barcelona), December 1895. Spanish translations of both Émile Pouget and Arturo Labriola first appeared in 1904: Arturo Labriola, *Reforma y revolución social* (Valencia), trans. by Soledad Gustavo; and Émile Pouget, *Las bases del sindicalismo* (Madrid), trans. Anselmo Lorenzo. This does not mean that their syndicalist ideas were unknown to the Spaniards, especially among those who could read French and Italian.

23. The following studies on early twentieth-century anarchism are indispensable: Antonio Bar, *La CNT en los años rojos: Del sindicalismo revolucionario al anarcosindicalismo (1910–1926)* (Barcelona, 1981); Xavier Cuadrat, *Socialismo y anarquismo en Cataluña: Los orígenes de la CNT (1899–1911)* (Madrid, 1976); Joaquín Romero Maura, *La rosa de fuego: Repúblicanos y anarquistas* (Barcelona, 1975, c. 1974); and Ullman, *The Tragic Week.*

EPILOGUE

1. These approximations were based on figures taken from the censuses of 1887 and 1900; cited in Tuñón de Lara, *El movimiento obrero,* pp. 305–307.

2. Paul Preston, "The Agrarian War in the South," in *Revolution and War in Spain, 1931–1939,* ed. Paul Preston (London, 1984), pp. 165–166.

3. Romero Maura, "Terrorism in Barcelona," p. 134.

4. On anarchism and anticlericalism see José M. Sánchez, *The Spanish Civil War as a Religious Tragedy* (Notre Dame, 1987), and Ullman, *The Tragic Week,* translated into Spanish as *La semana trágica* (Barcelona, 1972).

5. See, for example, Anselmo Lorenzo's imaginative *El banquete de la vida* (Barcelona, 1905) and Isaac Puente's succinct treatment of anarchist aims, *Finalidad de la CNT: El comunismo libertario* (1936).

6. A distinct philosophy of industrial violence was developed by Georges Sorel in the early 1900s. His widely circulated *Reflexiones sur violence* appeared as a series of articles in *Mouvement Socialiste* (Paris) from Jan. to June 1906, and was later translated into several languages, including Spanish. In Spain, though, it appears as though the Sorelian vision of revolution found little echo among the rank and file of the CNT. During the 1920s, a small but influential group of communist syndicalists in the CNT embraced Sorel's views. Led by Joaquín Maurín, one of the most distinguished Marxist intellectuals in Spanish history, this faction thought that they had found in Sorel's works a way of combining revolutionary syndicalism with Marxism. Although this group briefly held a leadership role in the CNT, their efforts to convert the membership to their revolutionary strategy were to no avail.

7. Several studies on the anarchist movement during the 1920s and 1930s can be recommended: John S. Brademas, *Anarcosyndicalismo y revolución en España* (Barcelona, 1974); Bookchin, *Spanish Anarchists*; Gómez Casas, *Historia de la FAI*; and José Peirats, *La CNT en la revolución Española,* vols. 1–3 (Paris, 1951–1953).

8. See Juan Pablo Fusi, "El movimiento obrero en España, 1876–1914," *Revista de Occidente* (Madrid) no. 131 (Feb. 1974), pp. 204–237.

9. On the socialists during the Second Republic, see Malefakis, *Agrarian Reform;* Paul Preston, *The Coming of the Spanish Civil War* (London, 1977), and the collection of essays issued by the Fundación Pablo Iglesias entitled *El socialismo en España* (Madrid, 1986).

10. W. H. Cook, *The General Strike* (Chapel Hill, N.C., 1927), p. 179.

11. For the General Strike of 1902, see Xavier Cuadrat, *Socialismo y anarquismo en Cataluña: Los orígenes de la CNT (1899–1911)* (Madrid, 1976), and Romero Maura, *La rosa de fuego.*

Bibliography

Entries are arranged in the following sections:
- I. Bibliographies
- II. Primary Sources
  - (A) Unpublished Sources: Private and Public Papers, Correspondence, and Manuscripts
  - (B) Minutes of Congresses and Meetings
  - (C) Circulars, Newspapers, and Periodicals
  - (D) Articles, Books, and Pamphlets
- III. Secondary Sources: Articles, Books, and Pamphlets

I. BIBLIOGRAPHIES

Bibliografía dels moviments sociales. Edited by E. Giralt i Raventos et al. Barcelona: Lavínia, 1972.

French Institute for Social History (Paris). *L'anarchisme: Catalogue de livres et brochures.* Paris and New York: K. G. Saur, 1982.

Fundación Pablo Iglesias. *Catálogo de publicaciones periódicas.* Madrid: Editorial Pablo Iglesias, 1978.

—————. *100 (i.e., Cien) años de socialismo en España. Bibliografía.* Madrid: Editorial Pablo Iglesias, 1979.

Lamberet, Renée. *Mouvements ouvriers et socialistes: Chronologie et bibliographie. L'Espagne (1750–1936).* Paris: Editions Sociales, 1953.

Mintz, Frank. *La collectivisation en Espagne, 1936–1939 / Esquisse bibliographie.* Archives Internationales de Sociologie de la cooperation et du developpment, no. 22. Paris, 1967.

Nettlau, Max. *Bibliographie de l'anarchie.* Paris, 1897. Reprint, New York: Burt Franklin, 1968.

Ribas, Pedro. *La introducción del marxismo en España, 1869–1939*. Madrid: Ediciones de la Torre, 1981.

Sierra, Pedro. "Bibliografía de Ricardo Mella." *Tiempos Nuevos* (Barcelona), July–August 1937.

Silvin, Edwin. *Index to Periodical Literature on Socialism*. Santa Barbara, 1909.

Université de Toulouse-Le Mirail. *30 années d'edition: Catalogue des livres, brochures, periodiques*. Edited by Organisations Libertaires Espagnoles Reconstituées en France. Toulouse, 1945–1975.

II. PRIMARY SOURCES

(A) UNPUBLISHED SOURCES: PRIVATE AND PUBLIC PAPERS, CORRESPONDENCE, AND MANUSCRIPTS.

British Foreign Office Records Public Record Office, London:
Series F.O. 72. Vols. 1207–1211. 1869. Crampton, Ffrench, Layard dispatches.
Series F.O. 72. Vols. 1274–1282. 1871. Layard and Ffrench's dispatches and consuls' reports.
Series F.O. 72. Vol. 1365. 1874. Layard's dispatches.

Layard Papers, British Museum:
British Museum Add/MSS. 38932–3. Vols. 2–3. Layard's memoirs, "The Story of My Mission to Spain."
British Museum Add/MSS. 39121–4. Four volumes of letterbooks, including dispatches from A. H. Layard to Lord Granville covering the period 1870–1877.

Joaquín Maurín Papers. Hoover Institution, Stanford, Calif.

Max Nettlau Papers. International Institute for Social History, Amsterdam:
Correspondence with Manuel Buenacasa.
Correspondence with José García Viñas.
Correspondence with José Prat.
Correspondence with Fernando Tarrida del Mármol
Correspondence with Jaime Vives Terrades.
"Die erste Bluetezeit der Anarchie (1886–1894)." A continuation of Nettlau's monumental history of anarchism, which was begun in 1925. The MS was published as vol. 4 in this series by the IISH in 1981 (Verlag, Lichtenstein).

(B) MINUTES OF CONGRESSES AND MEETINGS

Anarchist International. *Congrès de London, Bulletin. 1881.*
———. *International Anarchist Congress, 1907*. Amsterdam, 1907.
Certámen socialista. Primer. Catalonia: Centro de Amigos de Reus, 1885.
Certámen socialista. Segundo. Barcelona, 1889.
Certámen socialista. Tercer. La Plata, 1898.
Congreso Revolucionario Internacional de Paris, 1900. Buenos Aires, 1902.

Congresos Anarcosindicalistas en España, 1870–1936. Toulouse, 1977.
Études et documents sur le Première Internationale. No. 44. Edited by Jacques
  Freymond. Geneva: Institut Universitaire de Hautes Études Internacionales,
  1964.
Federación de Trabajadores de la Región Española (FTRE). *Circular no. 13.*
  1882.
———. *Memoria de los trabajos realizados por la C.F. en el desempeño de su
  cargo, 1887 a 1889.* Valencia, 1889.
International Working Men's Association. *The First International: Minutes of
  the Hague Congress of 1872, with Related Documents.* Edited by Hans
  Gerth. Madison, Wis., 1958.
———. *The General Council of the First International: Minutes, 1865–1872.* 5
  vols. Moscow: Progress, 1974.
———. *Illustrated Report of the Workers' Congress held in London, July,
  1896.* London, 1896.
———. *Resolutions of the Conference of Delegates of the IWMA.* 1871.
International Working Men's Association, Spanish Section. *Actas de los Con-
  sejos y Comisión Federal de la Región Española (1870–1874).* Transcription
  and preliminary study by Carlos Seco Serrano. 2 vols. Barcelona, 1969.
———. *Primer Congreso Obrero Español.* Preliminary study and notes by V.
  M. Arbeloa. Madrid, 1972.
Rosal, Amaro del. *Los congresos obreros internacionales en el siglo XIX.* Barce-
  lona: Grijalbo, 1975.
Unión General de Trabajadores de España (UGT). *Actas de la Unión General de
  Trabajadores de España.* Prologue and notes by Amaro del Rosal. Barcelona:
  Grijalbo, 1977–.

(C) CIRCULARS, NEWSPAPERS, AND
     PERIODICALS

Note: Dates given are those actually consulted.
Acción Libertaria. Vigo, 1910–1911.
Acracia. Barcelona, 1886–1888.
La Alarma. Seville, 1889–1890.
Almanaque de Tierra y Libertad. Barcelona, 1915.
American Review of Reviews. New York, 1897.
The Anarchist Labour Leaf. London, 1890.
*Anarchist Newspapers: A Collection of Anarchist Newspapers in the British
  Museum.* 1885–1894.
La Anarquía. Madrid, 1890–1893.
Ariete Anarquista. Barcelona, 1896.
La Autonomía. Seville, 1883–1884.
L'Avant-Garde. Berne, La Chaux-de-Fonds 1877–1878.
La Bandera Roja. Madrid, 1888.
La Bandera Social. Madrid, 1885–1887.
Cenit. Toulouse, 1985–1986.

La Ciencia Social. Barcelona, 1895–1896.
El Combate. Bilbao, 1891.
El Condenado. Madrid, 1872–1873.
La Conquista del Pan. Barcelona, 1893.
La Controversia. Valencia, 1893.
El Corsario. La Coruña, 1891–1896.
El Cosmopolite. Valladolid, 1901.
Cuadernos para el Dialogo. Madrid, 1973–1976.
La Cuestión Social. Valencia, 1892.
Cuestiones de la Alianza. Barcelona, 1872.
Cultura Obrera. New York, 1912–1927.
Los Desheredados. Sabadell, 1884.
El Despertar. New York, 1893, 1896.
El Eco de Ravachol. Sabadell, 1893.
El Eco de Rebelde. Zaragoza, 1895.
Edinburgh Review. 1892–1897.
La Emancipación. Madrid, 1871–1873.
La España Moderna. 1896–1897.
Espoir. Toulouse, 1964–.
Estudios de Historia Social. Madrid, 1977–.
La Federación Igualadina. Igualada, 1883–1885.
The Fortnightly Review. London, 1883–1900.
Free Society. San Francisco, 1897–1903.
Freedom. London, 1886–1900.
Huelga General. Barcelona, 1901.
La Idea Libre. Madrid, 1894–1898.
El Imparcial. Madrid, 1883–1896.
Internationale Anarchiste. 1908–1910).
El Invencible. Zaragoza, 1895.
La Justicia Humana. Gracia, 1886.
Liberty. Boston, 1882–1897.
The Nation. New York, 1882–1896.
Natura. Barcelona, 1903–1905.
New York Times. 1883, 1892, 1896.
The Nineteenth Century and After. London, 1886–1915.
La Nueva Idea. Gracia, 1885.
El Obrero. Barcelona, 1880–1881.
El Oprimido. Algeciras, 1893.
Otero (formerly *Ideas*). Barcelona, 1980–.
El País. Madrid, 1896–1897.
El Perseguido. Buenos Aires, 1892–1893.
El Porvenir Social. Barcelona, 1895–1896.
El Productor. Barcelona, 1887–1893.
El Proletario. San Feliu de Guixols, 1890.
La Propaganda. Vigo, 1882.
La Protesta. Cádiz, 1902.
La Protesta. Valladolid-Sabadell, 1899–1902.

La Protesta. Suplemento quincenal. Buenos Aires, 1926–1930.
La Protesta Humana. Buenos Aires, 1900.
Ravachol. Sabadell, 1892.
El Rebelde. Buenos Aires, 1901.
El Rebelde. Zaragoza, 1893.
Reconstruir. Buenos Aires, 1961–1977.
La Revancha. Reus, 1893.
La Revista Blanca. Madrid, primera época, 1898–1905; Barcelona, segunda época, 1923–1936.
Revista Catalana. Barcelona, 1889–1892.
Revista Contemporanea. Barcelona, 1885–1898.
Revista de Trabajo. Madrid, 1968–1976.
La Révolte. Paris, 1885–1887.
Le Révolté. Geneva, 1879–1882.
La Revolución Social. Barcelona, 1889–1890.
La Revolución Social. Clandestine, 1884–1885.
Serra d'Or. Barcelona, 1974–.
El Socialista. Madrid, 1886–1890.
El Socialista. Toulouse, 1950.
La Solidaridad. Madrid, 1870.
La Solidaridad. Seville, 1888–1889.
Suplemento de La Protesta. Buenos Aires, 1926–1927.
Tierra y Libertad. Barcelona, 1888–1889.
Times. London, 1883–1896.
La Tramontana. Barcelona, 1881–1893.
La Tribuna Libre. Seville, 1891–1892.
Umbral. Paris, 1966.
La Víctima del Trabajo. Valencia, 1889–1890.

(D) ARTICLES, BOOKS, AND PAMPHLETS

Adrian del Valle (Palmiro de Lidia). "Evocando el pasado, 1886–1892." *Revista Blanca* (Madrid), 15 July–15 September 1927.
Antecedentes y desarrollo del movimiento obrero español (1835–1888): Textos y documentos. Edited by Clara E. Lida. Madrid: Siglo Vientiuno, 1973.
Arrow, Charles. *Rogues and Others.* London: Duckworth, 1926.
Bakunin, Michael. *Bakunin on Anarchy.* Edited, translated, and introduced by Sam Dolgoff. London: Allen and Unwin, 1973.
———. *Oeuvres complètes de Bakounine.* Introduced and annotated by Arthur Lehning. Vol. 1, pts. 1–2, *Michel Bakounine et Italie, 1871–1872.* Vol. 4, *Étatisme et anarchie, 1873.* Vol. 7, *Bakounine sur la guerre franco-allemande et la revolution sociale en France, 1870–1871.* Paris: Editions Champ Libre, 1973–1979.
———. *The Policy of the International.* London, 1919.
———. *The Political Philosophy of Bakunin.* Compiled and edited by G. P. Maximoff. New York, 1964.
———. *Selected Writings of Michael Bakunin.* Edited and introduced by Arthur

Lehning. Translated from the French by Steven Cox and from the Russian by Olive Stevens. London: Cape, 1973.

Blasco Ibáñez, Vicente. *La bodega*. Madrid, 1904. English translation by Isaac Goldberg, New York: Dutton, 1919.

Cafiero, Carlo. *Anarchie et communisme*. Paris: Temps Nouveaux, 1899.

Cherkezov, V. *Páginas de historia socialista*. Translated by José Prat. La Coruña: "El Progreso," 1896.

Constituciones, cortes y elecciones españolas (1810–1936). Edited by Miguel Angel González Muñiz. Madrid: Ediciones Júcar, 1978.

Darnaud, Émile. *Notes sur le mouvement*. Foix, 1891.

——. *La Révolte*. Edited extracts from the anarchist paper. Paris, 1889.

Engels, Friedrich. *Correspondence with Paul and Laura Lafargue*, Vols. 1–3. Translated by Yvonne Kapp. Moscow: Progress Publishers, 1966.

Esteve, Pedro. *A los anarquistas de España y Cuba*. Paterson, N.J.: "El Despertar," 1900.

——. *Socialismo anarquista*. New York, 1927.

García Ruiz, Eugenio. *Historia de la Internacional y del federalismo*. Madrid, 1872.

Garrido, Fernando. *Legalidad de la Internacional*. Madrid, 1871.

Grave, Jean. *La société future*. Paris: P. V. Stock, 1895.

Great Britain, Royal Commission on Labour. *Foreign Reports*. Vol. 9, *Report on the Labour Question in Spain and Portugal (1893–1894)*. London: Eyre and Spotiswoode, 1894.

Guillaume, James. *Idées sur l'organsation social*. La Chaux-de-Fonds: Courvoisier, 1876.

——. *L'Internationale: Documents et souvenires (1864–1878)*. 4 vols. Paris: G. Bellais, 1905–1910.

Gustavo, Soledad [pseud. of Teresa Mañé]. "El Doctor José García Viñas." *Revista Blanca* (Barcelona), 1 October 1931.

Hugas, E., and Serrano, V. *Diálogo del calabozo*. Barcelona: "La Catalana," 1890.

Ishill, Joseph. *Elisée and Elie Reclus, In Memoriam*. Berkeley Heights, N.J.: Oriole, 1927.

Kropotkin, Peter A. *Dos cartas de Kropotkin*. San Juan, Puerto Rico, 1968.

——. *Paroles d'un révolté*. Paris, 1978.

——. *Selected Writings on Anarchism and Revolution*. Edited by Martin A. Miller. Cambridge, Mass.: M.I.T. Press, 1973.

——. *Les temps nouveaux*. Paris, 1894.

Lagardelle, Hubert. *La grève générale et le socialisme*. Paris: Edouard Cornély, 1905.

La Iglesia y García, Gustavo. *Carácteres del anarquismo en la actualidad*. Madrid: Imprenta del Asilo de Huerfanos del S.C. de Jesús, 1905.

Leroy, Constant [pseud. of José Sánchez Gonzáles]. *Los secretos del anarquismo: Asesinato de Canelejas y el caso Ferrer*. Mexico: Renacimiento, 1913.

Litvak, Lily, ed. *El cuento anarquista (1880–1911)*. Madrid: Taurus, 1982.

Llunas y Pujols, José. *Estudios filosofías sociales*. Barcelona: "Biblioteca del Proletaria," 1883.

——*La ley y la clase obrera*. Barcelona: Literatura Obrerista, 1893.

——. *Organización y aspiraciónes de la FTRE*. Barcelona, 1883.

——. *Los partidos socialistas españoles*. Barcelona: Biblioteca "La Tramontana," 1892.

Lombroso, Cesare. *Los anarquistas. Estudio de sociología*. Madrid, 1894.

——. "Crime in Spain and in History." *Independent Review* (London), 9 December 1909.

——. "The Status of Anarchism Today in Europe and the United States." *Everybody's Magazine*, 1902.

Lorenzo, Anselmo. *El banquete de la vida*. Barcelona, 1905.

——. *Criterio libertario*. Barcelona: Calamus Scriptorius, 1978.

——. *Justo Vives. Episodio dramático-social*. Prologue by José Llunas. Biographical study by F. Tarrida del Mármol. Buenos Aires: B. Fueyo [191?].

——. *El proletariado militante*. 2 vols. Barcelona, 1902 and 1925; reprint, Madrid: Alianza Editorial, 1974.

——. *Vía libre. El Trabajador, su ideal emancipador*. Prologues by J. Mir y Mir and Fernando Tarrida del Mármol. Barcelona, 1905.

Lowell, James Russell. *Impressions of Spain*. Boston and New York: Houghton and Mifflin, 1899.

Lum, Dyer D. *The Economics of Anarchy*. New York: Twentieth Century Library, 1890.

Malato, Charles. *Filosofía del anarquismo*. Prologue by Carlos Díaz. Madrid: Ediciones Júcar, 1978.

Marx, Karl; Engels, Friedrich; and Lenin, V. I. *Anarchism and Anarcho-Syndicalism*. Moscow: Progress, 1972.

Mella, Ricardo. *La coacción moral*. Madrid, 1901.

——. *Cuestiónes de enseñanza*. Madrid: Acción Libetaria, 1913.

——. *Cuestiones sociales*. Valencia: F. Sempere y Cía, 1912.

——. *Doctrina y combate*. Córdoba: Renovación Proletaria, 1922.

——. *Ensayos y conferencias*. Prologue by Eleuterio Quintanilla. *Obras completas*, vol. 2. Gijón: La Industria, 1934.

——. *Evolución y revolución*. Sabadell, 1892.

——. *Forjando un mundo libre*. Madrid: La Piqueta, 1978.

——. *Ideario*. Prologue by José Prat. *Obras completas*, vol. 1. Gijón: La Victoria, 1926; reprint, Toulouse: Ediciones "CNT," 1975.

——. *La ley del numero*. Vigo: Cerdeira y Farina, 1899.

——. *Lombroso y los anarquistas*. Barcelona: Ciencia Social, 1896.

——. *Mirando hacia el futuro*. Buenos Aires: Bautista Fueyo, 1925.

——. *Plumazos*. La Coruña: La Internacional, 1912.

——. "Le socialisme en Espagne." *L'Humanité* (Paris), no. 1 (1897).

——. *Los sucesos de Jeres*. Barcelona, 1893.

——. *Táctica socialista*. Madrid: El Progreso, 1900.

Mella, Ricardo, and Prat, José. *La barbarie gubermental en España. Documentos sobre las torturas de Montjuich*. "Brooklyn" (i.e., La Coruña), 1897.

Mir y Mir, Juan. *Dinamita cerebral: Los cuentos anarquistas más famosas.* Barcelona, 1913.

Montseny y Carret, Juan [pseud. Federico Urales]. "La anarquía en el Ateneo de Madrid." *La Revista Blanca* (Madrid), 1903.

———. *Consideraciónes sobre el hecho y la muerte de Pallás.* La Coruña: La Gutenberg, 1893.

———. *Correspondencia selecta de Federico Urales.* Compiled and edited by Vladimiro Muñoz. Madrid, 1970.

———. *España 1933: La barbarie gubermantal en Barcelona.* Barcelona, 1933.

———. *La evolución de la filosofía en España.* Prologue and preliminary study by Rafael Pérez de la Dehesa. Madrid: Ediciones de Cultura Popular, 1968.

———. *Mi vida.* 3 vols. Barcelona: Revista Blanca, 1932.

———. *El proceso de un gran crimen.* La Coruña: La Gutenberg, 1895.

———. *Sociología anarquista.* La Coruña: Biblioteca "El Corsario," 1896.

Muñoz, Vladimiro. *Antología acrata español.* Barcelona: Grijalbo, 1974.

Naquet, Alfred. *La anarquía y el colectivismo.* Translated from the French by C. Rodríguez Avecilla. Valencia: Sempere, 1905.

Nieva, Teobaldo. *La quimica de la cuestión social.* Madrid: Ulpiano Gómez, 1886.

Pamphlets on Social Subjects (*in British Museum*). No. 1. 1871.

Parsons, A. R. *Anarchism: Its Philosophy and Scientific Basis.* Chicago, 1887; Westport: Greenwood, 1970.

Pellicer, Antonio. *En defensa de nuestros ideales.* Gijón, 1894.

Pi y Margall, Francisco. *Las nacionalidades.* Madrid, 1876.

———. *La reacción y la revolución. Estudias políticos y sociales.* vol. 1. Madrid, 1854.

———. *La República de 1873.* Madrid, 1874.

Prat, José. *La burquesía y el proletariado.* Valencia: Sempere, 1909.

———. *Crónicas demoledores.* Valencia, n.d.

———. *Ser o no ser.* Barcelona: Biblioteca el Productor, 1905.

———. *El sindicalismo.* Toulouse: Ediciones "CNT," 1974. Published as *Sindicalismo y socialismo.* La Coruña: Cultura Proletaria, 1909.

Proudhon, Pierre-Joseph. *De la capacidad política de las clases jornaleros.* Translated by Francisco Pi y Margall. Madrid, 1869.

———. *General Idea of the Revolution in the Nineteenth Century.* Translated by John Beverley Robinson. London, 1923.

———. *Selected Writings of Pierre-Joseph Proudhon.* Edited and introduced by Stuart Edwards. Translated by Elizabeth Fraser. London: Macmillan, 1970.

———. *What Is Property?* Translated by B. J. Tucker. 2 vols. The Bellamy Library, 1890–.

Puig y Serall, Luis. *La ciencia del trabajo.* Barcelona, 1882.

Reclus, Elisée. *A los campesinos.* Sabadell, 1887.

———. *An Anarchist on Anarchy.* London [1886?].

———. *Correspondence, (1850–1905). 3 vols.* Paris: Librairie Schleicher, 1911–1925.

———. *Evolution and Revolution.* London: International, 1885.

———. *El hombre y la tierra.* Barcelona, 1906–1909.

La República y los Repúblicanos. Madrid, 1873.

Rocker, Rudolf. *Anarchism and Anarcho-Syndicalism*. London: Freedom, 1973.

————. *La juventud de un rebelde*. Translated by D. A. de Santillán. Buenos Aires: Editorial Américalee, 1947.

————. *The London Years*. Translated by Joseph Leftwich. Kent: Robert Anscombe, 1956.

Roller, Arnold. *The Social General Strike*. Chicago: Debating Club, 1905.

Roure, Conrado. *Recuerdos de mi larga vida*. 3 vols. Barcelona: "El Diluvio," 1925.

Sanz y Escartín, E. "La filosofía del anarquismo." In *La Lectura*, vol. 2. 1902.

Sempau, Ramon. *Los victimarios*. Barcelona: Manent, 1901.

Sender, Ramon. *Mr. Witt Among the Rebels*. Translated from the Spanish by Sir Peter Chalmers Mitchell. Boston: Houghton Mifflin,

Serrano y Oteiza, Juan. *La moral del progreso*. Madrid: Sabadell, 1888.

Solano, E. G. *El sindicalismo en la teoría y en la práctica*. Barcelona: B. Bauza [1920?].

Spanish Atrocities Committee. *Revival of the Inquisition*. London, 1897.

Tarrida del Mármol, Fernando. "El anarquismo español hace ochenta y dos años." *Reconstruir* (Buenos Aires), no. 78 (May–June 1972).

————. *Anselmo Lorenzo*. Barcelona, n.d.

————. *Les Inquisiteurs d'Espagne*. Paris: P. V. Stock, 1897.

————. *Problemas transcendentales*. Barcelona, 1930.

————. "Spain To-Day and To-Morrow." *Independent Review* (London), 1903–1904.

Trigo, Felipe. *Socialismo individualista*. Madrid: Renacimiento, 1912.

Tucker, Benjamin R. *Instead of a Book*. New York, 1893.

Unamuno, Miguel de. "El socialismo en España." In his *Obras completas*, vol. 9. Madrid, n.d.

Vallina, Pedro. *Mis memorias*, vol. 1. Caracass, 1967.

Ventosa, Ricardo. *Las asociaciones de obreras*. Madrid, 1882.

————. *El comunismo, el derecho al trabajo, la libertad del trabajo*. Madrid, 1882.

————. *Las huelgas de trabajadores, los asociaciónes de obreros y las cajas de chorros*. Madrid, 1882.

Vicente, Antonio P. *Socialismo y anarquismo*. Valencia, 1893.

Zancada Ruata, Práxedes. *El obrero en España. Notas para su historia política y social*. Barcelona: Maucci, 1902.

III. SECONDARY SOURCES: ARTICLES, BOOKS, AND PAMPHLETS

Abad de Santillán, Diego. *Contribución a la historia del movimiento obrero español: Desde sus orígenes hasta 1905*. Puebla, Mexico: Ediciones Cajica, 1962.

Abad de Santillán, Diego. *Memorias, 1897–1936*. Barcelona: Planeta, 1977.

Abelló i Güell, Teresa. *Les relacions internacionals de l'anarquisme català (1881–1914)*. Barcelona: Editions 62, 1987.

Abendroth, Wolfgang. *A Short History of the European Working Class.* New York: Monthly Review Press, 1972.

Acebo y Modet, Juan. *Origen, desarrollo y transcendencia del movimiento sindical obrero.* Madrid, 1915.

Aguilar Villagran, José. *El asalto campesino a Jerez de la Frontera en 1892.* Jerez de la Frontera, 1984.

Aisa, Javier, with Arbeloa, V. M. *Historia de la Unión General de Trabajadores.* Madrid: Editorial Zero, 1975.

Aja, Eliseo. *Democracia y socialismo en el siglo XIX: El pensamiento político de Fernando Garrido.* Madrid: Cuadernos Para el Diálogo, 1976.

Alarcón Caracuel, Manuel R. *El derecho de asociación obrera en España (1839–1900).* Madrid: Ediciones de la Revista de Trabajo, 1975.

Alberola, Octavio. *El Anarquismo español y la acción revolucionaria, 1961– 1974.* Paris: Ruedo Ibérico, 1975.

Álvarez, Cirilo. *Individualistas, socialistas, y comunistas.* [Madrid?] 1873.

Álvarez, Ramón, *Eleuterio Quintanilla.* Mexico, D.F.: Editores Mexicanos Unidos, 1973.

Álvarez Junco, José. "Anselmo Lorenzo y su tiempo." *Tiempo de Historia* (Madrid), no. 6 (1975).

———. *La comuna en España.* Madrid: Siglo Vientiuno, 1971.

———. "Los dos anarquismos." *Cuadernos de Ruedo Ibérico* (Paris), January– June 1977.

———. *La ideología política del anarquismo español, 1868–1910.* Madrid: Siglo Vientiuno, 1976.

———. "Sobre el anarquismo y el movimiento obrero andaluz." *Estudios de Historia Social* (Madrid), July–December 1979.

L'anarchie espagnole. [Paris?] 1868.

Anarchici e anarchia nel mondo contemporaneo: Atti del convegno promosso dalla Fondazione Luigi Einaudi. Torino, 1971.

Anarchism. Edited by J. Roland Pennock and John W. Chapman. New York: New York University Press, 1978.

Un anarchiste entre la legende et l'histoire: Fermín Salvochea. By Gerard Brey et al. Paris: Presses Universitaires de Vincennes, 1987.

El anarquismo en Alicante (1868–1945). Alicante: Instituto de Estudios Juan Gil-Albert, 1986.

Aranco, Emilio, and Abad de Santillán, Diego. *El anarquismo en el movimiento obrero.* Barcelona, 1925.

Arbeloa, V. M. *Orígenes del Partido Socialista Obrero Español.* Madrid: Editorial Zero, 1972.

———. "Pablo Iglesias y Miguel Unamuno: Correspondencia, 1894–1918." *Tiempo de Historia* (Madrid), no. 5 (1975).

Archer, William. *The Life, Trial, and Death of Francisco Ferrer.* New York: Moffat, Yard, 1911.

Arranz, Luis, and Elorza, Antonio. " 'El Boletín de las clases trabajadores': La definición bakuninsta de la clase obrera madrileña." *Revista de Trabajo* (Madrid), 1975.

Avrich, Paul. *An American Anarchist: The Life of Voltairine de Cleyre.* Princeton, N.J.: Princeton University Press, 1978.

———. *The Haymarket Tragedy.* Princeton, N.J.: Princeton University Press, 1984.

Azcárate, Gumersindo de. *Vestiges del primitivo comunismo de España.* [Madrid?] n.d.

Balcells, Alberto. *El arraigo del anarquismo en Cataluña: Textos de 1928–1934.* Barcelona: Ediciones Júcar, 1980.

———. *Crisis económica y agitación social en Cataluña de 1930 a 1936.* Barcelona: Ediciones Ariel, 1971.

Bar, Antonio. *La CNT en los años rojos.* Madrid: Akal, 1981.

———. *Syndicalism and Revolution in Spain.* New York: Gordon, 1981.

Barrio Alonso, Angeles. *El anarquismo en Gijón.* Gijon: Silverio Cañada, 1982.

Bayo, Eliseo. *Trabajos duros de la mujer.* Barcelona: Plaza y Janés, 1970.

Beck, Earl R. *A Time of Triumph and of Sorrow: Spanish Politics During the Reign of Alfonso XII. 1874–1885.* Carbondale: University of Southern Illinois Press, 1979.

Bernaldo de Quirós y Pérez, Constancio. *Bandolerismo y delincuencia subversiva en la baja Andalucía.* Madrid, 1913.

———. *Información sobre el problema agrario.* Madrid, 1919.

———. *Modern Theories of Criminality.* Boston: Little, Brown, 1911.

Bookchin, Murray. *The Spanish Anarchists.* New York: Harper and Row, 1977.

Boyd, Carolyn P. "The Anarchists and Education in Spain, 1868–1909." *Journal of Modern History* 48, no. 4 (December 1976).

Brandt, Joseph. *Toward the New Spain.* Chicago: University of Chicago Press, 1933; Philadelphia: Porcupine, 1976.

Brenan, Gerald. *The Spanish Labyrinth.* Cambridge: Cambridge University Press, 1971.

Breve historia del movimiento anarquista en Estados Unidos de America del Norte. By Alberto Martin, Vladimiro Muñoz, and Federica Montseny. Toulouse, n.d.

Brupbacher, Fritz. "James Guillaume." *Reconstruir* (Buenos Aires), May–June 1965.

Buenacasa, Manuel. *El movimiento obrero español, 1886–1926.* Barcelona: Impresos Costa, 1928; Madrid: Ediciones Júcar, 1977.

Burgos, Manuel Espados. "La Primera Internacional y la historiografía española." *Hispania* (Madrid), no. 30 (January–April 1970).

Cabonero, F. *La cuestión social y las escuelas socialistas.* Madrid, 1903.

Cadalso, F. *El anarquismo y los medios de represión.* Madrid: Romero, 1896.

Calero Amor, Antonio M. *El movimiento obrero en Granada, 1909–1923.* Madrid: Editorial Tecnos, 1973.

———. *Movimientos sociales en Andalucía (1820–1936).* Madrid, 1976.

Cánovas del Castillo, Antonio. *Problemas contemporaneos.* vols. 1–2. Madrid, 1884.

Carlson, Andrew R. *Anarchism in Germany.* New Jersey: Scarecrow, 1972.

Carner, Antonio. *L'anarco-sindicalisme a Cataluñya*. Barcelona: Rafael Dalmau, 1971.

Carr, Edward H. *Michael Bakunin*. New York: Octagon, 1975.

————. *The Romantic Exiles*. London: Penguin, 1968.

Carr, Raymond A. *Modern Spain*. Oxford: Oxford University Press, 1980.

————. *Spain, 1808–1939*. Oxford: Oxford University Press, 1970.

Carrera Pujol, Jaime. *Historia política y económica de Cataluña en el siglo XIX*. Barcelona, 1958–1959.

Carvajal y Hue, Juan. *Los anarquistas en Madrid*. Madrid, 1894.

Cascales y Muñoz, José. *El apostolado moderno. Estudio histórico-critico del socialismo y el anarquismo hasta terminar el siglo XIX*. Barcelona: F. Granada, 1913.

————. *Los conflictos del proletariado*. Madrid: Aldrededor del Mundo, 1912.

Castellanos, J. "La escuela y la educación en los medios anarquistas de Cataluña, 1903–1909." *Nueva Revista de Filología Hispánica* (Mexico City), no. 19, pp. 37–54.

Castillejo, José. *War of Ideas in Spain: Philosophy, Politics, Education*. London: J. Murray, 1937.

Castro Alfín, Demetrio. *Hambre en Andalucía: Antecedentes y circunstancias de la Mano Negra*. Córdoba: Ayuntamiento de Córdoba, 1986.

Cerda, Manuel. *Lucha de clases e industrialización*. Valencia: Almudin, 1980.

Chueca, José. *Anarquismo y terrorismo*. Zaragoza, 1960.

Cierva, Ricardo de la. *Historia del socialismo en España, 1879–1983*. Barcelona: Planeta, 1984.

Clarke, H. B. *Modern Spain (1815–1898)*. Cambridge: Cambridge University Press, 1906.

Clemens, G. C. *Elementos de anarquía*. Barcelona, n.d.

Cole, G. D. H. *A History of Socialist Thought*. vol. 2, *Marxism and Anarchism*. London: Macmillan, 1954.

————. *A History of Socialist Thought*, vol. 3, pt. 1., *The Second International, 1889–1914*. London: Macmillan, 1956.

Colodsón, Alfonso. "La idea de la huelga general hasta 1902: Intento de encuadramiento histórico." *Revista de Trabajo* (Madrid), no. 33 (1971).

Coloma, Rafael. *La Revolución Internacionalista Alcoyana de 1873*. Alicante, 1959.

Comín Colomer, Eduardo. *Historia del anarquismo español*. Vols. 1–2. Madrid: Editorial A.H.R., 1956.

Costa, Joaquín. *Oligarquía y caciquismo, colectivismo agrario y otros escritos*. Madrid: Alianza Editorial, 1973.

La crisis de fin de siglo: Ideológica y literatura, Essays in honor of Rafael Pérez de la Dehesa. Espulgues de Lobregat: Ariel, 1975.

Cuadrat, Xavier. *Socialismo y anarquismo en Cataluña: Los orígenes de la CNT (1899–1911)*. Madrid: Ediciones de la Revista de Trabajo, 1976.

Dewey, Stoddard. "The Anarchist Movement in Spain." *The Contemporary Review* (London), 1902.

Díaz del Moral, Juan. *Historia de las agitaciones campesinas andaluzas*. Madrid: Alianza Editorial, 1973.

Díaz Plaja, Fernando. *La Historia de España en sus documentos: El siglo XIX.* Madrid: Instituto de Estudios Políticos, 1954.

Dunbar, Gary S. *Elisée Reclus: Historian of Nature.* Hamden, Conn.: Archon, 1978.

Durán, J. A. *Crónicas.* Vols. 1–3. Madrid: Akal, 1977–.

———. *Historia de caciques, bandos e ideologías en la Galicia no urbana.* Madrid: Siglo Vientiuno, 1972 and 1976.

———. "Ricardo Mella. Nacimiento y muerte de un anarquista (1861–1925)." *Tiempo de Historia* (Madrid), February 1976.

Ehrenberg, John R. "Proudhon." Ph.D. diss., Stanford University, 1975.

Elorza, Antonio. "Los orígenes del asociacionismo obrero en España." *Revista de Trabajo* (Madrid), no. 37 (1972).

———. *La Utopía anarquista bajo la Segunda República.* Madrid: Ayuso, 1973.

Eltzbacher, Paul. *Anarchism.* Tranlated by Steven T. Byington. Edited by James J. Martin. Plainview, N.Y.: Books for Libraries, 1972.

Enciclopedia anarquista: Edición castellana. Mexico: Tierra y Libertad, 1972.

España, 1898–1936: Estructuras y cambio. Edited by José García Luis Delgado. Madrid, 1983.

Fabbri, Luigi. *La vida y pensamiento de Malatesta.* Translation and prologue by D. Abad de Santillán. Barcelona: Editorial Tierra y Libertad, 1938.

Fanaticism: A Historical and Psychoanalytical Study. Edited by André Haynal, Miklós Molnár, and Gérard de Puymege. New York: Schocken, 1983.

Fernández Almagro, Melchor. *Historia política de la España contemporanea.* vols. 1–3 (covering the period 1868–1902). Madrid: Alianza Editorial, 1969.

Ferri, Enrico. *Criminal Sociology.* Edited by W. D. Morrison. New York: D. Appleton, 1895.

———. *Socialism and Positive Science: Darwin, Spencer, Marx.* London: Independent Labor Party, 1905.

Fishman, William J. *East End Jewish Radicals.* London: Duckworth, 1974.

Flaquer Montequi, Rafael. *La clase obrera madrileña y la Primera Internacional (1868–1874).* Madrid: Cuadernos para el Diálogo, 1977.

Fleming, Marie. *The Anarchist Way to Socialism: Elisée Reclus and Nineteenth-Century European Anarchism.* London: Croom Helm, 1979.

———. "Propaganda by the Deed: Terrorism and Anarchist Theory in Late Nineteenth-Century Europe." *Terrorism* 4, nos. 1–4 (1980).

Fox, Edward Inman. "José Martínez Ruiz; Sobre el anarquismo del futuro Azorín." *Revista de Occidente* (Madrid), February 1966, pp. 157–174.

———. "Two Anarchist Newspapers of 1898." *Bulletin of Hispanic Studies* (Liverpool), no. 41 (1964), pp. 160–168.

Fusi, Juan Pablo, "El movimiento obrero en España, 1876–1914." *Revista de Occidente* (Madrid), no. 131 (February 1974), pp. 204–237.

———. *Política obrera en el país vasco, 1880–1914.* Madrid: Ed. Turner, 1975.

Galván, Tierno *Leyes políticas fundamentales, 1808–1936.* Madrid: Editorial Tecnos, 1972.

García Venero, Maximiano. *Historia de las Internacionales en España.* vol. 1. Madrid: Ediciones del Movimiento, 1956.

Gil Maestre, Manuel. "El anarquismo en España y especial de Cataluña." *Revista Contemporánea* (Madrid), vol. 107 (July–September 1897).

Gilimon, Eduardo G. *Un anarquista en Buenos Aires (1890–1910).* Buenos Aires, 1910.

Giralt y Raventos, Emilio. *Los movimientos sociales en Cataluña, Valencia y Baleares* ed Emilio Giralt, Albert Balcels, Josep Termes. Barcelona: Editorial Nova Terra, 1970.

Gómez Casas, Juan. *Historia de la FAI.* Madrid: Editorial Zero, 1977.

———. *Historia del anarcosindicalismo español.* Madrid: Ed. Aguilera, 1977.

———. *La Primera Internacional en España,* Madrid: Ed. Zero, 1974.

Gómez Latorre, Matías. *Historia del socialismo en España.* Madrid, 1918.

Gómez Llorente, Luis. *Aproximación a la historia del socialismo español (hasta 1921).* Madrid: Cuadernos para el Dialogo, 1972.

González Casanova, José Antonio. *Federalismo y autonomía. Cataluña y el Estado español, 1868–1938.* Barcelona: Crítica, 1979.

González Urien, Miguel, and Gonzáles, Fidel Revilla. *La CNT a través de sus congresos.* Mexico, D. F.: Editores Mexicanos Unidos, 1981.

Guérin, Daniel. *Anarchism.* Translated by Mary Klopper. Introduction by Noam Chomsky. New York: Monthly Review Press, 1970.

Harrison, Joseph R. *An Economic History of Modern Spain.* London: Manchester University Press, 1978.

Haymarket Scrapbook. Edited by Dave Roediger and Franklin Rosemont. Chicago: Charles Kerr, 1986.

Hennessy, C. A. M. *The Federal Republic in Spain: 1868–1874.* Oxford: Oxford University Press, 1962.

Hobsbawm, Eric J. *Primitive Rebels.* New York: Norton, 1965.

———. *Revolutionaries.* New York: Pantheon, 1973.

Hoffman, Robert L. *Revolutionary Justice: The Social and Political Theory of P.-J. Proudhon.* Urbana: University of Illinois Press, 1972.

Hong, Nhat. *The Anarchist Beast: The Anti-Anarchist Crusade in Periodical Literature (1884–1906).* Minneapolis, Minn.: Haymarket Press, n.d.

Hostetter, Richard. *The Italian Socialist Movement, I. Origins (1860–1882).* Princeton, N.J.: Princeton University Press, 1958.

Hunter, Robert. *Violence and the Labor Movement.* New York: Macmillan, 1914.

Hyams, Edward. *Pierre-Joseph Proudhon.* New York: Taplinger, 1979.

Iscaro, Rubens. *Breve historia del Primero de Mayo.* Buenos Aires: Ed. Anteo, 1961.

Izard, Miguel. *Revolució industrial i obrerisme: Les "Tres Clases de Vapor" a Cataluñya (1869–1913).* Barcelona: Ediciones Ariel, 1970.

Jackson, Gabriel. "Spanish Anarchism." *South Western Social Sciences Quarterly,* no. 36 (1955).

Jardi, Enric. *La cuitat de les bombes. El terrorisme anarquista a Barcelona.* Barcelona: R. Dalmau, 1964.

Joll, James. *The Anarchists.* London: Eyre and Spottiswoode, 1964; Cambridge, Mass.: Harvard University Press, 1980.

————. *The Second International.* Weidenfeld and Nicolson, 1955, and Routledge and Kegan Paul, 1973.

Jover Zamora, José María. *La conciencia burguesía y conciencia obrera en la España contemporanea.* 2 ed. Madrid, 1956.

Jutglar, Antonio. *El constitutionalismo revolucionario de Pi y Margall.* Madrid: Taurus, 1970.

————. *Ideologías y clases en la España contemporanea.* Vols. 1–3. Madrid: Cuadernos para el Diálogo, 1968–.

————. "Notas para la historia del socialismo en España." *Revista de Trabajo* (Madrid), no. 3 (1964).

Kaplan, Temma. *The Anarchists of Andalusia, 1868–1903.* Princeton, N.J.,: Princeton University Press, 1977.

————. "Women and Spanish Anarchism." In *Becoming Visible,* edited by Renate Bridenthal and Claudia Koonz. Boston: Houghton Mifflin, 1977.

Kelly, Aileen. *Michael Bakunin.* Oxford: Oxford University Press, 1982.

Kenafick, K. J. *Michael Bakunin and Karl Marx.* Melbourne, 1948.

Kenny, Michael. *A Spanish Tapestry.* Bloomington: Indiana University Press, 1962.

Kern, Robert W. *Liberals, Reformers and Caciques in Restoration Spain.* Albuquerque: University of New Mexico Press, 1975.

Lamberet, Renée. "Soledad Gustavo et la pensée anarchiste espagnole." *Convivium* (Barcelona), 1976.

Landeira, Ricardo. *Ramiro de Maeztu.* Boston: Twayne, 1978.

Laveleye, Émile de. "The European Terror." *The Fortnightly Review* (London), vol. 33 (1883).

————. *The Socialism of To-Day.* Translated by Goddard H. Orpen. London: Field and Tuer, Leadenhall Press, 1884.

Lehning, Arthur. *From Buonarroti to Bakunin.* Leiden, Netherlands: E.J. Brill, 1970.

————. *Michel Bakounine et les autres.* Paris, 1976.

Leval, Gaston de [pseud. of Pedro Piller]. *Collectives in the Spanish Revolution.* London: Freedom, 1975.

Lida, Clara E. "Agrarian Anarchism in Andalusia: Documents of the *Mano Negra.*" *International Review of Social History* (Amsterdam), no. 14 (1969).

————. *Anarquismo y revolución en la España del siglo XIX.* Madrid: Siglo Vientiuno, 1972.

————. "Educación anarquista en la España del ochocientos." *Revista de Occidente* (Madrid), no. 97 (April 1971).

————. "Literatura anarquista y anarquismo litertario." *Nueva revista de filología hispánica* (Mexico City), vol. 19 (1970), no. 2.

Lindholm, F. *El anarquismo según las fuentes suecas y extranjeras.* Prologue by Emilio Miñana. Madrid: Editorial de Góngora, 1906.

Linse, Ulrich. " 'Propaganda by the deed' and 'Direct Action': Two Concepts of Anarchist Violence," In *Social Protest, Violence and Terror in Nineteenth- and Twentieth-Century Europe.* edited by Wolfgang J. Mommsen and Gerhand Hirschfeld. London: St. Martin's, 1982.

Litvak, Lily. *La musa libertaria: Arte, literatura y vida cultural del anarquismo español (1880–1913)*. Barcelona: Antoni Bosch, 1981.

López González, Juan Jaime, and García Lasaosa, J. *Orígenes del movimiento obrero en Aragón (1854–1890)*. Zaragoza: Institucíon "Fernando el Católico," 1982.

Lorenzo, César M. *Les anarchistes espagnoles (1868–1969)*. Paris: Editions du Seuil, 1969.

Lorwin, Val. *The French Labor Movement*. Cambridge, Mass.: Harvard University Press, 1966.

McCabe, Joseph. *The Martydom of Ferrer*. London, 1909.

McClellan, Woodford. *Revolutionary Exiles: The Russians in the First International and the Paris Commune*. London: Cass, 1979.

Maestre, Alonso J. *Orígenes, hechos y documentos del anarco-sindicalismo español*. Madrid: Castellote, 1977.

Maitron, Jean. *Le mouvement anarchiste en France*. Vols. 1–2. Paris: François Maspero, 1975.

Malefakis, Edward. *Agrarian Reform and Peasant Revolution in Spain*. New Haven, Conn.: Yale University Press, 1970.

Malon, Benoit. "Le socialisme en Espagne." *La Revue Socialiste* (Paris), Vol. 9 (1889).

La Mano Negra. Translated into French by *Les Temps Nouveaux*. Paris, 1902.

Marba, Palmiro. *Origen, desarrollo y trascendencia del movimiento sindicalista obrero*. In *El proletariado militante*, by Anselmo Lorenzo, 2 vols. in 1, pp. 447–619. Mexico: Vertice [1945?].

Martí, Casimiro. *Orígenes del anarquismo en Barcelona*. Prologue by J. Vicens Vives. Barcelona: Editorial Teide, 1959.

Martínez-Alier, Juan. *Labourers and Landowners in Southern Spain*. London: Allen and Unwin, 1971.

Marvaud, Angel. *La question sociale en Espagne*. Paris: F. Alcan, 1910.

Meaker, Gerald. *The Revolutionary Left in Spain, 1914–1923*. Stanford, Calif.: Stanford University Press, 1974.

Mena, Antonio. *Del anarquismo y su represión*. Madrid, 1906.

Mercier Vega, Luis. *Anarquismo, ayer y hoy*. Caracas, 1970.

Miller, David. *Anarchism,* London: J. M. Dent, 1984.

Mintz, Jerome R. *The Anarchists of Casas Viejas*. Chicago: University of Chicago Press, 1982.

Molnár Miklós. *Le déclin de la Première Internationale: La Conférence de Londres de 1871*. Geneva: Librairie Droz, 1963.

Molnár, Miklos, and Pekmez, Juan. "Rural Anarchism in Spain and the 1873 Cantonalist Revolution." In *Rural Protest: Peasant Movements and Social Change,* Edited by Henry A. Landsberger. New York: Barnes and Noble, 1974.

Montseny, Federica. *Anselmo Lorenzo*. Barcelona, 1938; Toulouse: Ediciones "Espoir,"1970.

Mora, Francisco. *Historia del socialismo obrero español, desde las primeras manifestaciones hasta nuestros días*. Madrid: Imprenta de J. Calleja, 1902.

Moral Sandoval, Enrique. "Estudios sobre el socialismo en España." *Sistema* (Madrid), October 1976.

Morato, Juan José. *La cuña de un gigante: Historia de la Asociación General del Arte de Imprimir.* Madrid: J. Molina, 1925, and Revista de Trabajo, 1984.

———. *Líderes del movimiento obrero español (1868–1921).* Madrid: Cuadernos para el diálogo, 1972.

———. *Pablo Iglesias Posse: Educator de muchedumbres.* Madrid: Espasa-Calpe, 1931; Espulgues de Llobregat: Ariel, 1968.

———. *El partido socialista obrero.* Madrid, 1918; Madrid: Ayuso, 1976.

Moreno Aparicio, Ignacio. *Aproximación histórica a Fermín Salvochea.* Cádiz: Diputación de Cádiz, 1982.

"Mouvements ouvriers espagnols et questions nationales, 1868–1936." *Le Mouvement Social* (Paris), July–September 1984.

Muñoz Cerisola, Nicolás. *Los anarquistas.* Malaga, 1894.

Nadal, Jordi. "The Failure of the Industrial Revolution in Spain 1830–1914." In *The Fontana Economic History of Europe: The Emergence of Industrial Societies—2,* edited by Carlo M. Cipolla. London: Fontana, 1977.

Nettlau, Max. *Anarchy Through the Times.* New York: Gordon, 1979.

———. *La anarquía a través de los tiempos.* Barcelona: Maucci, 1935. Reissued with a prologue by Carlos Díaz, Madrid: Ediciones Júcar, 1978.

———. *Documentos ineditos sobre la Internacional y la Alianza en España.* Buenos Aires: Ediciones "La Protesta," 1930.

———. *Errico Malatesta: La vida de un anarquista.* Buenos Aires: Ediciones "La Protesta," 1923.

———. *Esbozo de historia de las utopías.* Buenos Aires: Ediciones Iman, 1934.

———. *Impresiones sobre el desarrollo del socialismo en España.* Madrid: Editorial Zero, 1971.

———. *Miguel Bakunin, la Internacional y la Alianza en España (1868–1873).* Preliminary study by Clara E. Lida. New York: Iberama, 1971.

———. *La Première Internationale en Espagne, 1868–1888.* Dordrecht, Holland: D. Reidel, 1969.

Nomad, Max. "The Anarchist Tradition." In *The Revolutionary Internationals,* edited by Milorad M. Drachkovitch. Stanford, Calif.: Stanford University Press, 1966.

———. *Rebels and Renegades.* New York: Macmillan, 1932.

Núñez Florencio, Rafael. *El terrorismo anarquista, 1888–1909.* Madrid: Siglo Vientiuno, 1983.

Olive i Serret, Enric. *La pedagogía obrerista de la imagen.* Barcelona / Palma de Majorca: J. J. de Olañeta, 1978.

Oliver, Hermia. *The International Anarchist Movement in Late Victorian London.* London: Croom Helm / St. Martin's, 1983.

Oliveros, Antonio L. *Asturias en el Resurgimiento Español.* Madrid, 1934.

Oved, Iaacov, *El anarquismo y el movimiento obrero en Argentina.* Mexico: Siglo Vientiuno, 1978.

"Pablo Iglesias, El Socialismo en España." *Anthropos* (Barcelona), vols. 45–47 (1985).

Padilla Bolívar, Antonio. *El movimiento anarquista español.* Barcelona: Planeta, 1976.

———. *El movimiento socialista español.* Barcelona: Planeta, 1977.

Palacio Atard, Vicente. *La España del siglo XIX, 1808–1898*. Madrid: Espasa-Calpe, 1978).

Paniagua Fuentes, Xavier. *La sociedad libertaria: Agrarismo e industrialización en el anarquismo español (1930–1939)*. Barcelona: Editorial Crítica, 1979.

Patt, Beatrice P. *Pío Baroja*. New York: Twayne, 1971.

Payne, Stanley G. *The Spanish Revolution*. London: Weidenfeld and Nicolson, 1970.

Peirats, José, *Los anarquistas en la crisis política español*. Madrid: Júcar, 1977.

———. *Figuras del movimiento libertario Español*. Barcelona: Editorial Picazo, 1978.

La Première Internationale. Recueil de documents. Edited and introduced by Jacques Freymond. 4 vols. Geneva: E. Droz, 1962–1971.

Ramsden, H. "The Spanish Generation of 1898." *Bulletin of the John Rylands University Library* (Manchester), vol. 56 (1974).

Ravindranathan, T. R. *Bakunin and the Italians*. Kingston, Montreal, Canada: McGill-Queen's University Press, 1988.

Regla Campistol, Juan. *Aproximació a la historia del país Valencia*. Valencia 1978: Eliseu Climent.

Revert Corbes, Antonio. *Augustín Albors, entre la libertad y el orden*. Alcoy, 1975.

La revolución de 1868: Historia, pensamiento, literatura. Edited by Clara E. Lida and Iris M. Zavala. New York: Las Americas, 1971.

Richards, Vernon. *Errico Malatesta: His Life and Ideas*. London: Freedom, 1977.

Ridley, F. F. *Revolutionary Syndicalism in France*. Cambridge: Cambridge University Press, 1970.

Rivas, Lucia. *Historia del primero de Mayo en España: Desde 1900 hasta la segunda república*. Madrid: Universidad Nacional de Educación a Distancia, 1987.

Rocker, Rudolf. *Fermín Salvochea*. Toulouse, France: Tierra y Libertad, 1945.

Romero Maura, Joaquín. "Les origines de l'anarcho-syndicalisme en Catalogne: 1900–1909." In *Anarchici e Anarchia nel Mondo Contemporaneo*. Torino: Fondazione Luigi Einaudi, 1967.

———. *La rosa de feugo: Repúblicanos y anarquistas*. Barcelona: Ediciones Grijalbo, 1975, c. 1974.

———. "Terrorism in Barcelona and Its Impact on Spanish Politics, 1904–1909," *Past and Present* (Oxford), vol. 41 (1968).

Rosal, Amaro del. *Historia de la UGT de España*. Vol. 1. Barcelona: Ediciones Grijalbo, 1977.

———. *La violencia, enfermedad del anarquismo*. Barcelona: Ediciones Grijalbo, 1976.

Ruediger, Helmut [a.k.a. M. Dashar]. *The Revolutionary Movement in Spain*. New York, 1934.

Ruiz, David. *El movimiento obrero en Asturias*. Madrid: Siglo Vientiuno, 1968.

Ruiz Lagos, Manuel. *Ensayos de la revolución. Andalucía en llamas. 1868–1875*. Madrid: Ed. Nacional, 1977.

Saltman, Richard B., *The Social and Political Thought of Michael Bakunin*. Westport, Conn.: Greenwood, 1983.

Sana Alcón, Heleno. *Líderes obreros: Biografías.* Bilbao: Editorial Zero, 1974.

Sánchez Jimenez, J. *El movimiento obrero y sus orígenes en Andalucía.* Madrid: Editorial Zero, 1969.

Santamaria de Paredes, Vicente. *El movimiento obrero contemporaneo.* Vol. 6. Madrid, 1894.

Sanz Escartín, Eduardo. *Federico Nietzsche y el anarquismo intelectual.* Madrid, 1898.

Schulte, Henry F. *The Spanish Press, 1470–1966.* Urbana: University of Illinois Press, 1968.

Seco Serrano, Carlos. *Sociedad, literatura, y política Español.* Madrid: Guadiana de Publicaciones, 1973.

Segarra, Agustí. *Federico Urales y Ricardo Mella, teóricos anarquismo español.* Barcelona: Ed. Anagrama, 1977.

Seis estudios sobre el proletariado Andaluz (1868–1939). Córdoba: Ayuntamiento de Córdoba, 1984.

Shaw, Rafael. *Spain from Within.* London: T. F. Unwin, 1910.

Sobejano, González. *Nietzsche en España.* Madrid: Editorial Gredos, 1967.

El socialismo en España. Coordinated by Santas Juliá. Madrid: Editorial Pablo Iglesias, 1986.

Solà, Pere. *El ateneus obrers i la cultura popular a Cataluñya (1900–1939).* Barcelona: Edicions de la Magrana, 1978.

Stafford, David. *From Anarchism to Reformism, A Study of the Political Activities of Paul Brousse.* London: Weidenfeld and Nicolson, 1971.

Stekloff, Iurii M. *History of the First International.* Translated from the Russian by Eden and Cedar Paul. New York: International, 1928.

Tavera i García, Susanna. "La premsa anarco-sindicalista (1868–1931)." *Recerques* (Barcelona), no. 8 (1979).

Teoría y práctica del movimiento obrero en España, 1900–1936. Edited by Albert Balcells. Valencia: F. Torres, 1977.

Termes Ardevol, Josep. *Anarquismo y sindicalismo en España: La Primera Internacional (1864–1881).* Espulges de Llobregat: Ariel, 1972, and Barcelona: Crítica, 1977.

———. *Federalismo, anarcosindicalismo y catalanismo.* Barcelona: Anagrama, 1976.

———. "Il movimento operaio spagnole e l'illustrazione satirica nella stampa anarchia (1889–1893)." *Movimento Operario e Socialista* (Torino), no. 5 (1982).

Tomasi, Tina. *Ideología, libertaria y educación.* Madrid: Campo Abierto, 1978.

Trend, J. B. *The Origins of Modern Spain.* Cambridge: Cambridge University Press, 1934; New York: Russell and Russell, 1965.

Trujillo, Gumersindo. *Introducción al federalismo español.* Madrid: Cuadernos para el Diálogo, 1967.

Tuñón de Lara, Manuel. *Estudios sobre el siglo XIX español.* Barcelona: Siglo Vientiuno, 1972.

———. *El movimiento obrero en la historia de España.* Madrid: Taurus, 1972.

Turin, Yvonne, *La educación y la escuela en España, 1874–1902.* Madrid: Aguilat, 1967.

Ullman, Joan Connelly. *La semana trágica*. Espulges de Llobregat: Ariel, 1972.
———. *The Tragic Week, A Study of Anticlericalism in Spain, 1875–1912*. Cambridge, Mass.: Harvard University Press, 1968.
Una y Sarthou, Juan. *Los asociaciones obreras en España*. Madrid, 1900.
Utopias. Edited by Peter Alexander and Roger Gill. London: Duckworth, 1984.
Vallina, Pedro. *Crónica de un revolucionario. Trazos de la vida de Salvochea*. Paris: Ediciones "CNT," 1958.
Vérges Mundo, Oriol. *La Ia Internacional en las Cortes de 1871*. Barcelona: Cátedra de Historia General de España, 1964.
Vicens Vives, Jaime. *Approaches to the History of Spain*. Translated by Joan Connelly Ullman. Los Angeles, London: University of California Press, 1970.
———. *Cataluña en el siglo XIX*. Madrid: Rialp, 1961.
———. *An Economic History of Spain*. Translated by Frances López-Morillas. Princeton, N.J.: Princeton University Press, 1969.
Vincent, K. Steven. *Pierre-Joseph Proudhon and the Rise of French Republican Socialism*. Oxford: Oxford University Press, 1984.
Vizetelly, Ernest Alfred. *The Anarchists*. London: John Lane, 1911; reprint, New York: Kraus, 1972.
Waggoner, Glen A. "The Black Hand Mystery: Rural Unrest and Social Violence in Southern Spain, 1881–1883." In *Modern European Social History*, edited by Robert J. Bezucha. Lexington, Mass.: D. C. Heath, 1972.
Ward, G. H. B. *The Truth About Spain*. London, 1911.
Woodcock, George. *Anarchism*. Harmondsworth, England: Penguin, 1963.
Woodcock George, with Ivan Avakumović. *The Anarchist Prince: Peter Kropotkin*. New York: Schocken, 1971.
———. *Pierre-Joseph Proudhon*. New York: Schocken, 1972.
Zaragoza, G. "Antoni Pellicer i Paraire i l'anarquisme argenti." *Recerques* (Barcelona), no. 7 (1977–1978).
Zavala, Iris M. *Ideología y política en la novela española del siglo XIX*. Salamanca: Anaya, 1971.
———. *Masones, comuneros y carbonarios*. Madrid: Siglo Vientiuno, 1971.
———. *Romanticos y socialistas*. Madrid: Siglo Vientiuno, 1972.
Zoccoli, Ettore G. *L'anarchia. Gli agitatori, le idee, i fatti*. Milan: Fratelli Boca, 1907.
Zugasti y Saenz, Julián de. *El bandolerismo*. Vols. 1–10. Madrid: T. Fortanet, 1876–1880.
Zugazagoitia, Julián. *Una vida heroica. Pablo Iglesias*. Madrid, 1925; and Madrid: Akal Editor, 1976.

Index

Designer:	U.C. Press Staff
Compositor:	Huron Valley Graphics
Text:	10/13 Sabon
Display:	Sabon
Printer:	Bookcrafters, Inc.
Binder:	Bookcrafters, Inc.